GLOBALIZATION

Selected Titles in ABC-CLIO's
CONTEMPORARY
WORLD ISSUES
Series

For a complete list of titles in this series, please visit
www.abc-clio.com.

Books in the Contemporary World Issues series address vital issues in today's society such as genetic engineering, pollution, and biodiversity. Written by professional writers, scholars, and nonacademic experts, these books are authoritative, clearly written, up-to-date, and objective. They provide a good starting point for research by high school and college students, scholars, and general readers as well as by legislators, businesspeople, activists, and others.

Each book, carefully organized and easy to use, contains an overview of the subject, a detailed chronology, biographical sketches, facts and data and/or documents and other primary-source material, a directory of organizations and agencies, annotated lists of print and nonprint resources, and an index.

Readers of books in the Contemporary World Issues series will find the information they need in order to have a better understanding of the social, political, environmental, and economic issues facing the world today.

GLOBALIZATION

A Reference Handbook

Justin Ervin and Zachary A. Smith

CONTEMPORARY
WORLD ISSUES

ABC◆CLIO

Santa Barbara, California
Denver, Colorado
Oxford, England

Library of Congress Cataloging-in-Publication Data

Globalization : a reference handbook / Justin Ervin and
    Zachary A. Smith.
        p. cm. — (ABC-CLIO's contemporary world issues)
    Includes bibliographical references and index.
    ISBN 978-1-59884-073-5 (hard copy : alk. paper) -
    ISBN 978-1-59884-074-2 (ebook : alk. paper)
    1. Globalization—Handbooks, manuals, etc.
    I. Smith, Zachary A. (Zachary Alden), 1953–   II. Title.
JZ1318.E77 2008
303.48'2—dc22

                                              2008016627

12   11   10   09   08   1 2 3 4 5 6 7 8 9 10

This book is also available on the World Wide Web as an ebook.
Visit www.abc-clio.com for details.

ABC-CLIO, Inc.
130 Cremona Drive, P.O. Box 1911
Santa Barbara, California 93116–1911

This book is printed on acid-free paper ∞

Manufactured in the United States of America.

To Sarah, for her love,
patience, and understanding.

To my family:
none of this would be possible
without you

—J. E.

For Alden, Amy, and Genevieve

—Z. A. S.

Contents

Preface

Globalization is a controversial term referring to the concept of increased human interaction and interdependence across the globe. Some people regard globalization as a useful notion describing the evolution of human civilization. Others believe the term is merely a buzzword that is too confusing to provide meaningful understanding in our complex human world. Given the complexity of global human affairs, holders of both views have good reason to believe the way they do.

This book is designed as an introduction to the concept of globalization and offers three worldviews on its benefits and problems. The writing focuses on central issues of globalization, including the challenges and controversies associated with it.

A key factor behind globalization is the rapid development of technology, which has "shrunk" the world in ways not before possible. Increased human interaction has created problems and controversies that escape the ability of national governments to address. This book explains these problems, focusing on the global economy, issues of culture, environmental problems, and national security. These controversial areas are central to the concept of globalization. They represent difficult issues concerning all of humanity.

Several questions illustrate the importance of issues surrounding globalization: How do countries pass laws to regulate economic processes that happen beyond their borders? How do cultures deal with the impact of the global economy and the symbols, images, and norms foreign impressions have on their society? How do countries solve international environmental problems? How do countries remain secure with advanced weaponry without threatening others? These are issues that arise in the process of globalization representing complex concerns that are not easily solved.

Chapter 1 of this book introduces the concept of globalization. It begins by addressing the concept as a buzzword and then offers different definitions showing the confusion that exists in interpreting globalization. Next, it provides a history of globalization, focusing primarily on the current era. Finally, it offers an explanation of the major actors or forces that affect the globalization process.

Chapter 2 focuses on the controversies and problems associated with the globalization process, including the issues of technology, culture, the global economy, environmental problems, and national security, explaining and interpreting each issue area through the varying worldviews. In some worldviews, certain aspects of globalization are seen as serious problems. In others, the same issue is seen as beneficial. It is important to understand that when discussing globalization, certainty and agreement are not the order of the day.

Chapter 3 centers on the role the United States plays in the globalization process. This chapter focuses on the United States not because it is exceptional or special but because its importance cannot be ignored. The United States has played a pivotal role in world affairs since the end of World War II and the future course of globalization will be greatly affected by this country's decisions and actions. The chapter assesses the impact of the United States on the global economy, the environment, and global security.

Chapter 4 offers a chronology of pivotal events in the history of globalization. This timeline of major events shows that processes of globalization have existed throughout human history. Much of what we see today as globalization is the result of processes that have been unfolding for thousands of years.

Chapter 5 presents biographical profiles of individuals who play an important role in the study of globalization. These individuals are authors, journalists, scholars, investors, and activists whose work concentrates on globalization.

Chapter 6 provides facts and data presented in tables that relate their importance to the study of globalization. It also includes pertinent documents derived from sources such as the United Nations, the North Atlantic Treaty Organization, the World Trade Organization, and the European Union.

Chapter 7 provides a directory of organizations directly involved in the globalization process as well as those who study and critique it.

Chapter 8 offers an annotated list of print and nonprint resources that can help further the reader's study of globalization.

This book is intended to provide an objective overview of the globalization process, interpreting the problems and controversies associated with globalization through different worldviews. As a project designed to introduce globalization, the book encourages readers to look at the facts for themselves to conclude what worldview best describes and explains this phenomenon. The ability to make individual judgments about complex issues should be the aim of the student and the educator.

Remember that globalization is a contested concept, characterized by extreme complexity and disagreement. It has a differential impact on individuals, communities, and countries. Worldviews concerning globalization will reflect, and be affected by, these differences in experience. To gain a comprehensive picture of globalization, it is important to maintain an open mind, accepting the limitations of our understanding.

Justin Ervin and Zachary A. Smith

1

Background and History

This chapter first introduces globalization by providing multiple definitions and some ideas that are helpful in framing the concept. It then offers a history to identify themes that have led to the contemporary era of globalization. This history is a brief description of social processes in past eras that serve as the foundation for the current era, focusing on the 20th century as it gave rise to the forces of globalization. Finally, the chapter explains the major actors that operate within globalization.

So What Is Globalization?

Globalization: The "Buzzword"

Globalization is a concept that has gained much attention in the last 20 years. When we read newspapers or watch the evening news on television we are exposed to stories that are related to globalization. Nighttime broadcast news and daily newspapers regularly report stories about manufacturing jobs being shipped overseas; the financial instability in one country affects others; viruses such as SARS or bird flu threaten international pandemics through modern air travel; scientists warn that the devastation of natural disasters will increase as the climate changes; and political instability threatens to disrupt global oil markets. All of these examples are related to and affected by globalization.

These examples show that as individuals, we are no longer isolated and unaffected by the actions of distant others. Human society is increasingly interconnected and interdependent. Our actions now impact others on a global scale. Our use of technology, our consumption patterns, our relation to the natural environment, and our decisions to go to war have far-reaching consequences. These consequences reverberate across the globe. Their effects cannot be fully determined, but they can be studied. This is what makes the study of globalization important.

Globalization refers to real changes that are important to human society. These changes do not impact everyone in the same manner. The process of globalization does not imply a homogeneous process characterized by universality (Nye and Donahue 2000). The word implies a "shrinking" of the world in terms of time and space. Globalization increases the "thickness" of human interaction and the impact this interaction has on the Earth itself.

The next section provides definitions of globalization. These definitions will clarify the concept while showing that interpretations of globalization rely on the way the world is viewed.

Definitions of Globalization

There are many definitions of the concept of globalization. This section provides a few definitions to help the reader understand different uses of the term. The first, provided by the Cato Institute, represents the neoliberal, or free market view. The Cato Institute is an influential free market think tank (see chapter 7). According to Cato's definition,

> "globalization" describes the ongoing global trend toward the freer flow of trade and investment across borders and the resulting integration of the international economy. Because it expands economic freedom and spurs competition, globalization raises the productivity and living standards of people in countries that open themselves to the global marketplace (Cato Institute 2006).

The Cato definition focuses on the economic aspects of globalization. It sees globalization as a beneficial process that enables free markets to provide for individual freedom. Free markets also lead to increasing standards of living for those participating in the globalization process. This is called the "neoliberal" worldview. It will be explained in detail in chapter 2.

Similarly, the World Bank (see chapter 7) definition supports the Cato Institute's view that globalization is beneficial for it has reduced poverty. The World Bank definition, however, admits that not everyone agrees that globalization is a good thing:

> Globalization—the growing integration of economies and societies around the world—has been one of the most hotly debated topics in international economics over the past few years. Rapid growth and poverty reduction in China, India, and other countries that were poor 20 years ago has been a positive aspect of globalization. But globalization has also generated significant international opposition over concerns that it has increased inequality and environmental degradation (World Bank 2006).

The International Monetary Fund (IMF) (see chapter 7) offers an expanded scope in defining globalization. The IMF definition implies that there are many dimensions to the globalization process on which it admittedly does not focus. Globalization, to the IMF, is not limited to the global economy:

> Economic "globalization" is a historical process, the result of human innovation and technological progress. It refers to the increasing integration of economies around the world, particularly through trade and financial flows. The term sometimes also refers to the movement of people (labor) and knowledge (technology) across international borders. There are also broader cultural, political and environmental dimensions of globalization that are not covered here (IMF 2006).

Combined, these definitions expand the scope of globalization and show that there is tension within the globalization process. The IMF and World Bank support the process but note that it should be managed. This represents the liberal institutionalist worldview that will be explained later in chapter 2.

A definition that is critical of the process is offered by the political economist Edward Herman who argues that globalization supports the ideology of free markets. This ideology represents a dominant discourse that justifies a modern form of imperial domination that has existed for a very long time. Herman's definition represents the critical worldview of globalization, explained in chapter 2.

Globalization is both an active process of corporate expansion across borders and a structure of cross-border facilities and economic linkages that has been steadily growing and changing as the process gathers steam. Like its conceptual partner, "free trade," globalization is also an ideology, whose function is to reduce any resistance to the process by making it seem both highly beneficent and unstoppable (Herman 1999).

The final definition of globalization captures the essence of the term while being free from the controversies created by conflicting worldviews. This definition is offered by David Held, Anthony McGrew, David Goldblatt, and Jonathan Perraton. In their comprehensive examination of globalization, *Global Transformations. Politics, Economics, and Culture* (see chapter 8), they state that globalization is

a process (or set of processes) which embodies a transformation in the spatial organization of social relations and transactions—assessed in terms of their extensity, intensity, velocity, and impact—generating transcontinental or interregional flows and networks of activity, interaction, and the exercise of power (Held et al. 1999, 16).

This definition is deep in academic verbiage but it can be simplified. Globalization represents "shrinkage" of the world with an increase in the "thickness" of human interaction. This is characterized by an increase in the intensity, extensity, velocity, and impact that human actions have on one another. Globalization increases the distance over which these human impacts reach. The stretching of these impacts is realized in the geographical dimension. This makes the impact of globalization more extensive. Human interaction also increases in magnitude as human interactions become more entangled and interdependent. This increases the intensity of human interactions. Due to technological innovation, human interactions are also increasing in speed or velocity. Combined, these factors lead to an increase in the impact that our actions have on one another in the shrinking world of globalization (Held et al. 1999).

Globalization can now be seen as a process that "shrinks" the world as human interaction "thickens." The actions of individuals impact others on a scale never before possible. The increasing intensity, extensity, and velocity of these impacts blur national boundaries and affect national and subnational society. In this sense, globalization has made many of our assumptions regarding political governance and sovereignty problematic. Now that multiple definitions of globalization have been provided, the next sections discuss ideas that simplify the concept of globalization. These ideas, or metaphors, allow us to better conceive globalization, which increases our understanding (Morgan 1997).

Globalization as a Common Pool Issue

The concept of globalization and the issues that define it relate to the idea of the common pool. A "shrinking" globe characterized by "thick" interaction among all its parts implies that globalization exists as a global commons. This holistic notion makes consideration of the entire globe necessary when we judge our actions. Although local problems and local solutions remain important, these issues often spill over, affecting interests beyond those we perceive to be our own.

This notion is captured by Garrett Hardin's famous "Tragedy of the Commons." Hardin's metaphor takes place in a common pasture where individual farmers work to achieve their individual self-interest by raising as many cattle on the common pasture as they can. The more cattle each farmer can raise, the more profits he or she receives. This is the rational process of seeking to maximize the benefits of one's actions.

The problem, however, arises when each individual operates under this logic. The farmers soon degrade the pasture to the point that there is not enough grass to feed all the cattle. The destruction of the common pasture diminishes the benefits of all individual actors. These farmers, limited to concentrating on their individual interest, had no interest in defending the common pasture. In fact, if some farmers chose to worry about the common pasture and limit their use, their benefits would have decreased relative to those who did not! Without cooperation and mutual understanding, the common pasture would be depleted beyond use for everyone involved (Hardin 1996). Simply put, the tragedy of the commons explains to us that rationally self-interested individuals can create irrational destruction for everyone.

Globalization reflects the tragedy of the commons scenario. Globalization transcends individual actors and even the most powerful nations. In this era, individual actors concerned with self-interest affect many aspects of globalization. It is important to recognize the metaphor of the common pool in the era of globalization. Individuals who do not recognize a collective global interest will be frustrated in attempting to solve problems associated with globalization.

The Ecology of Globalization: Spaceship Earth

The science of ecology teaches us that every part within a natural system is interconnected, even if we do not readily perceive it. In such a system, such as the planet Earth, there is no "away" that does not affect our individual being. Alterations that take place in one part of the system will impact all others, even if in an imperceptible manner.

Ecological economist Kenneth Boulding (see chapter 5) describes this condition as "Spaceship Earth." In the past, humans could treat the Earth as a cowboy treated the wide open prairie. Humans could consider the Earth an open expanse, providing for all the material wants our hearts could desire. The Earth could also assimilate all the wastes that resulted from our desire to consume. In the past, we could live as freely as we wished, unconcerned with the impacts our actions had on one another and the natural environment.

However, as humans increased in population and technological ability, our relationship with the Earth changed forever. Humanity transformed itself from a species that could do as it wished to a species constrained by a limited natural environment. This situation is similar to astronauts living in a spaceship. Astronauts are reliant on the spaceship's limited resources for their survival. In a spaceship, all people and systems must operate cooperatively and efficiently for survival. Astronauts must take care not to squander their resources. Humanity, like astronauts, must learn to take great care in preserving their natural and social systems or face a threat to their very survival (Boulding 1996). Boulding argues that our social and natural systems, rather than being like the open frontier, rest on a fragile stability. We are all confined to Spaceship Earth; this is what globalization is about.

The ecological outlook of Spaceship Earth stresses the importance of understanding how our actions impact the planet and its diverse social systems. With such an understanding, we can judge whether our actions promote stability or work to destabilize the complex global system. To do this, students of globalization must grasp a basic understanding of the social, economic, political, and natural processes within which we live our lives. To assess our impact on the global system, it is necessary to build a coherent mental picture of where we come from, where we are, and where we are likely to go. This is the study of globalization.

A History of Globalization

To understand globalization, it is important to have a basic understanding of the processes and events that have led up to what we see today. This section is a short history of globalization. Chapter 4 offers a comprehensive timeline that offers a broad look into the history of globalization that has led to the current era.

The interaction between different human societies was limited for most of human history. Until very recently, humans were hindered by their inability to transverse geographical space in a short period of time, but human history is characterized by the shrinking of the time and space dimension that separated human societies. This shrinking is the result of advances in transportation and communication technology. Human interaction has expanded over the course of thousands of years. This expansion has increased the diffusion of culture and ideas.

Ancient Civilizations

Early human civilizations took the form of distinct and separate societies. Early civilizations were created without major outside influences. The Mesopotamian, Egyptian, Greek, Chinese, and Indus civilizations grew from internal mechanisms, being only slightly affected through interaction with others. Ancient civilizations were aware of each other and interacted with one another. However, they were formed around internal social dynamics, not by the interaction and influence of outside forces (Held et al. 1999).

Meso-American civilizations, such as the Incan, Mayan, and Aztec, were also distinct civilizations formed through internal social dynamics. The Mayan civilization collapsed for reasons that archaeologists have yet to conclusively discover. Some archaeologists believe the Mayan collapse was due to environmental degradation. The Aztec and Incan civilizations, on the other hand, failed due to their conquest by Spanish conquistadors in the 16th century.

Ancient Empire

As history progressed, many ancient civilizations dissolved and interaction between civilizations increased. It is at this time that human society first took the form of empires. Empires are characterized by the ability of one civilization to dominate others. This interaction altered the internal dynamics of both civilizations. Examples of such empires are the Macedonian and the Roman. Alexander the Great, a student of the Greek philosopher Aristotle, expanded the Macedonian Empire throughout the Mediterranean, Northern Africa, and India. The Macedonian Empire was followed by the Roman Empire, which existed from the first century BCE to 476 CE. The Roman Empire expanded throughout the Mediterranean, across Northern Africa, and into Europe and Asia.

Though empire became a characteristic of human civilization, empires did not last. They, like the civilizations before them, were subject to failure and dissolution. Alexander the Great's Macedonia fell when Alexander died. Alexander failed to announce a successor, causing the Macedonian Empire to split along regional lines. The Roman Empire, after a long decline, was invaded by Germanic tribes.

History shows that empires rise, expand, and consolidate their power. Eventually, however, they succumb to internal and external pressures that result in their decline and dissolution. Historically, empires have a tendency to become organizationally rigid and socially stratified. They also accumulate enemies through expansionist policies. In the long term, maintaining an empire has never been a simple or successful process. This observation is important as we explore globalization and judge what form it should take.

The Rise and Expansion of European Powers

With the fall of Rome the Western world declined into the Middle Ages. Many advances made in culture, the arts, technology, and civil society were lost. The religious doctrine of Christianity replaced philosophical disciplines developed by the Greeks. European culture became dominated by the Roman Catholic Church under a socioeconomic system of feudalism. Under feudalism, serfs worked manors owned by nobility of the warrior class. It is during the Early Middle Ages that the warrior nobility of European fiefdoms set off on multiple crusades to reclaim the Middle East for Christendom. This reclamation brutally displaced Islamic control from what was, and is, considered by many to be holy land.

The Rise of European Powers

Europe emerged from the Middle Ages with the Renaissance, which lasted from the beginning of the 14th to the end of the 16th century. Renaissance, meaning "rebirth," was Europe's return to the intellectual and cultural traditions of the classical civilizations of Greece and Rome. This rebirth began among the Italian city-states of Venice, Milan, Florence, the Papal States, and Naples (Matthews, Platt, and Dewitt 1992). Florence, the focal point of the Renaissance, formed an economic system based on international trade, which allowed the city to accumulate wealth. The economic system of Florence included a system of credit that serves as the foundation of modern finance. Florence's strategy was further pursued by the city-state of Genoa. Genoa's successful accumulation of wealth led to the consolidation of political society under a unified authority. Genoa represents a precursor to the modern nation-state (Arrighi 1994).

When Christopher Columbus landed in the Americas in 1492, European powers began to expand across the globe. Technological advances in oceangoing ships allowed these powers to search the globe for new territories whose wealth they sought to exploit to enrich their domestic economies. The 15th and 16th centuries saw the rise of the Spanish Empire. The Spanish Empire enriched itself with the gold and silver imported from its colonies in the Americas. The Spanish conquest destroyed the Aztec and Incan Empires through war and disease.

In the 16th century, European powers formed trade networks to Asia and the Americas. International trade required agreements between trading partners to form a system that defended property rights and provided rules of trade. These agreements institutionalized *lex mercatoria*, or Merchant Law, a precursor of trade agreements that became prevalent in the latter part of the 20th century (Held et al. 1999, 153). Note, however, that international trade was negligible in relation to the economic activity of European powers in the 16th century.

In the 17th century, the Netherlands became the center of the financial world. The Dutch became a financial power through fractional banking. Fractional banking is the creation of money made possible by the low probability that deposits in banks were likely to be removed at the same time. The Dutch realized that they could create money through public confidence in their financial institutions. Britain soon followed with this strategy when William Paterson created the Bank of England in 1694. Fractional banking became central in the economic planning of Britain. Britain's use of fractional banking enabled it to finance wars against Louis XIV of France in the early 18th century and Napoleon in the early 19th century. The use of fractional banking allowed Britain to conduct wars through credit. Issuing credit is a central factor in present-day economic globalization.

Politically, European fiefdoms consolidated into kingdoms controlled by a political system of absolute monarchies. In absolute monarchies, kings ruled by the divine right of God. Along with the Reformation, absolute monarchies displaced the power of the Roman Catholic Church in much of Europe. In the 17th century, the Thirty Years' War led to the modern nation-state system with the Treaty of Westphalia in 1648.

The Treaty of Westphalia established the concept of nation-state sovereignty, which established the legal rights and recognition that define modern nation-states. The signing of the Treaty of Westphalia was an understanding among European powers that their problems were not easily solved through conflict. Recognition of the sovereignty of other nation-states and the use of diplomacy became central factors in the political affairs of Europe. The nation-state system consolidated large populations and geographical areas under a single political authority. Today, nation-states are the dominant agents of political governance in the global system.

Warfare among European nation-states, however, did not end with the recognition of sovereignty and diplomacy. The 17th and 18th centuries were characterized by multipolarity (multiple powers) in Europe, which led to competition and warfare among European nation-states. At the time, European nation-states adhered to mercantilism, an economic system based on the accumulation of wealth and national power at the expense of other nation-states. Mercantilist policies included the protection of domestic merchants and trade routes against foreign competition. Mercantilism encouraged the use of military power to maintain and expand the power of the nation-state.

Piracy was an economic policy of nation-states under mercantilism. Pirate ships employed by European nation-states attacked merchant ships of rival nation-states. The goal was to pillage the wealth of others for their monarch patrons. For example, the Dutch East India Company, one of the world's first multinational corporations (MNCs), "employed 30,000 fighting men and 20,000 sailors aboard 200 ships" to conduct the economic policy of piracy (Tabb 2004, 277). Sir Francis Drake, the famous British pirate, provided Britain with pillaged wealth that helped that nation become the dominant global power by the 19th century (Chomsky 1993, 6). Under mercantilism, it is estimated that "world exports amounted to only 1–2 percent of world Gross Domestic Product (GDP)" (Held et al. 1999, 154). With the mercantilist economic policy of piracy, it is not surprising that international trade among European nation-states remained at a low level.

Though international trade among European powers was low throughout the 16th to 18th centuries, the international slave trade flourished. According to Held et al. (1999), "the African slave trade lasted from the middle of the 15th century to the middle of the 19th century" (292). It is estimated that 9–12 million African slaves were transported across the Atlantic to the New World. The slave trade provided the labor force for European powers in the Americas.

The transatlantic slave trade was first dominated by Portugal. This control was followed by Dutch, French, and British interests. The international slave trade operated in a triangular fashion across the Atlantic Ocean. European slave merchants would export slaves from Africa and trade them for commodities produced in the Americas. These commodities included precious metals, rum, and agricultural goods. Commodities produced through slave labor in the Americas were then transported across the Atlantic Ocean to Europe. In Europe, these commodities were traded for manufactured goods that included guns, gunpowder, chain restraints, and textiles. These goods were then traded in Africa to supply slave merchants with more slaves. The transatlantic slave trade was profitable at each point in the triangular relationship. The international slave trade was a major factor fueling the economic development of Europe and the American colonies.

By the mid-19th century Britain had consolidated its position as the dominant world power. Britain's rise to power resulted from its ability to exploit a worldwide network of colonies from which it could extract wealth. Britain dominated international trade with its naval supremacy, creating an empire that surpassed all those that preceded it, reaching into Africa, Asia, and North America.

The most important factor providing for British power was its transition to an industrial economy. Britain's lead in the Industrial Revolution gave it a political and economic advantage over other nation-states. The Industrial Revolution is also the catalyst that gave rise to the modern era of globalization.

Industrialization and the Modern Era

The Industrial Revolution represents the greatest alteration and advancement of human society. It began in Britain with the invention of the steam engine by James Watt. Initially, the steam engine provided power for Britain's growing textile industry. Soon, the steam engine powered a machine-based economy, replacing human and animal labor in many production processes.

In the Industrial Revolution, coal replaced wood as the primary energy source. Britain possessed a great supply of coal to power factories, to propel the locomotives of new railroad systems, and to power its fleets of merchant and naval vessels. The coal extraction industry in Britain employed millions of miners. Following coal, oil became the dominant fuel. The use of oil became widespread when Britain realized that oil was a much more efficient fuel for powering its navy during World War I.

The Industrial Revolution increased economic efficiency and productive capacity. The technological innovations of the Industrial Revolution spread quickly throughout the British Empire, Europe, the United States, and Japan. It dramatically reduced the time and space dimension between nation-states and their colonies.

The rise of the industrial factory system led to an increase in urbanization. Industrialization and urbanization produced social instability in Europe and the United States. The transformation of an agrarian society into an industrial society upset social relations that had slowly formed over hundreds of years. People who had once farmed the land flooded into cities looking for work in the new factory economy. Migration from Europe intensified as transatlantic ocean liners dispersed populations across the globe. Millions of these immigrants came to the United States. The rapid social transformation produced by the Industrial Revolution resulted in socialist challenges to capitalist governments (see "Karl Marx" in chapter 5). The rise of industrialization was an era characterized by upheaval and uncertainty. In this era relatively few people amassed great fortunes while many others experienced economic destitution and misery.

The rise of classical free trade theory (see "David Ricardo" and "Adam Smith" in chapter 5) combined with the Industrial Revolution led to an increase in international trade. The Industrial Revolution led to technological advances in transportation, cutting the costs of shipping goods to and from countries and colonies. Classical free trade theory convinced industrial countries that international trade is beneficial for all participants. The productivity gains made through industrialization spurred economic growth in industrialized countries. This growth led to increased demand for primary commodities from colonies.

International trade expanded in the late 19th and early 20th centuries. This era is often labeled the "classical gold standard," because gold served as the global monetary unit for transactions in international trade. In this era international trade grew faster (3.5 percent annually) than growth in world economic output (2.7 percent annually) (Held et al. 1999, 156). By the beginning of World War I, it is estimated that international trade accounted for 16–17 percent of total global income (Held et al. 1999, 156). The transition from mercantilism to classical free trade theory combined with industrialization and increasing international trade created the first era of globalization, which lasted from 1870 to 1914.

The 20th Century

The 20th century was characterized by dramatic technological innovation. The automobile, the airplane, the widespread use of electricity, modern computing, and satellite communications have altered social relations in ways not possible in the past. Oceanic voyages between continents that took months in the 18th century were reduced to weeks in the 19th century. By the second half of the 20th century this time was reduced to mere hours with the invention of jet-powered aviation. Information and communication, once handwritten, sealed in wax, and transported by horse-riding couriers, was replaced by the telegraph. The telegraph, in turn, was replaced by the telephone. The telephone has now been combined with Internet technology making human interaction increasingly mobile. Information can now be transferred instantaneously on a global scale. To those privileged to use these technologies, life has changed dramatically in the last century.

This section focuses on the major events of the 20th century that have led to the current era of globalization. Although the 20th century has been characterized by great advances in technology, it has also been plagued by human-caused disasters. In the current era of globalization, a repeat of such disasters could be terminal for modern civilization. This is why the study of globalization has gained such importance.

Uncertainty and Chaos: 1900–1945

From 1914 to 1945, the 20th century was characterized by instability and chaos. World War I, the Great Depression, and World War II shook Western civilization to its core. World War I, famously noted as the "war to end all wars," killed an estimated 15 million people. At the end of World War I, the Bolshevik Revolution overthrew the decaying monarchy of Nicholas II in Russia, creating the Soviet Union. The interwar period (1917–1939) saw a short-lived economic prosperity that was quickly dissolved by the Great Depression, which began with the stock market crash in the United States in 1929. The stock market crash began a series of events that would affect industrial nations around the world. International economic problems led industrial nations to pursue economic policies that further aggravated the situation. Industrial production dropped significantly, creating high unemployment and political instability.

World War I and the Great Depression diminished international trade as a global system. International trade shifted to regional systems dominated by European powers, Japan, and the United States. Economic protectionism became the norm. Every industrial country attempted to protect its own economy by shifting economic problems to others. This strategy employed "beggar thy neighbor" economic policies that included increases in tariffs, the imposition of quotas, and currency manipulations.

Together, these policies tended to support domestic economic health at the expense of others. Before the Great Depression the volume of global trade increased an average of 2.2 percent per year from 1913 to 1929. During the Great Depression the volume of global trade decreased 0.4 percent per year from 1929 to 1937 (Held et al. 1999, 157).

World War II began with the German invasion of Poland. The United States entered the conflict after the Japanese bombed its naval base at Pearl Harbor, Hawaii, on December 7, 1941. The countries of Germany, Italy, and Japan formed a security alliance called the Axis Powers. Britain, the United States, and the Soviet Union formed a security alliance called the Allied Powers. The Allied Powers defeated the Axis Powers in Europe on May 8, 1945 (V-E Day). The Japanese unconditionally surrendered on September 2, 1945, following the use of nuclear weapons by the United States on the cities of Hiroshima and Nagasaki. The estimated death toll from World War II was 65 million people.

World War II represents the greatest disaster in human history. World War II altered the relations between nation-states and changed the nature of warfare forever. The first half of the 20th century stands as a dire warning for the current era of globalization. It is still possible that economic, political, and social instability can give rise to devastating conflict. The emergence of the first era of globalization was followed by chaotic events that took nearly 30 years to subside. War, depression, the rise of fascism, and authoritarian socialism are all consequences that arose from social instability and uncertainty. With the technology of the current era of globalization, a reemergence of such chaotic forces would likely be much more destructive.

Postwar Era: 1945–1973

The United States was the lone industrial country to escape the destruction of World War II. All other industrial countries were ravaged by the war. Their economic systems virtually collapsed due to the destruction of their industrial infrastructure. The United States fought World War II on foreign soil. Its industrial infrastructure was not subject to any destructive actions of war. The destruction of all other industrial countries enabled the United States to take on the role of the sole hegemon of a new global system. The Soviet Union worked to limit United States hegemony, but it had been devastated by World

War II. A relatively undeveloped country, the Soviet Union possessed much less economic and military power than the United States.

The United States worked to rebuild and redesign the global economy with its hegemony in mind. The rebuilding of the industrial countries took place with financing from the United States in the form of the Marshall Plan. Along with the Marshall Plan, the United States worked to rebuild the global economic system that had risen in the first era of globalization. In 1944 the United States hosted an economic conference at Bretton Woods, New Hampshire. The Bretton Woods Conference established the IMF and the International Bank for Reconstruction and Development, now known as the World Bank (see chapter 7).

Along with these institutions the General Agreement on Tariffs and Trade (GATT) was created to set the rules of international trade in the post–World War II era. The GATT was negotiated at the Bretton Woods Conference to establish an international trading order. In its original form, the GATT was little more than a forum where trade ministers of nation-states could meet and discuss the rules of international trade.

The GATT operated under the assumption of nondiscrimination in international trade. This is the basis for the principle of "most favored nation status" (MFN). MFN status holds that nation-states should not discriminate against foreign businesses operating within their borders. MFN states that foreign investment and imports into a nation-state should be treated equally with domestic business and investment. GATT stressed the reduction of tariffs and promoted a transparent trading regime. It also eliminated unfair trade practices such as the dumping of goods in international markets below market prices. The intent of the GATT, the IMF, and the World Bank was to open up foreign markets to investment. In this era, international trade as a percentage of global output rose from 7 per cent in 1950 (Held et al. 1999, 168) to 12.6 per cent in 1960 (Dembinsky 2003, 86).

To provide for the security of the new global system, the United States led the formation of the North Atlantic Treaty Organization (NATO) (see chapter 7). NATO created a transatlantic security alliance between the United States and Western Europe. The Soviet Union allied itself with the Eastern European countries it occupied during World War II, forming the Warsaw Pact.

The Warsaw Pact was a security alliance of communist countries meant to deter the capitalist countries of NATO.

The Soviet Union, it can be argued, had good reason to create a security alliance and close down Eastern Europe to NATO countries. The Soviet Union was invaded twice by European countries and the United States. The first invasion, which involved the United States, followed the Bolshevik Revolution. The second invasion was undertaken by Hitler's Germany during World War II. In any event, history had not been kind to the Soviet Union. The Warsaw Pact and the Cold War between these security alliances ended with the collapse of the Soviet Union in 1991.

The 20th century also saw the emergence of anticolonial movements across the globe. The British Empire, already declining by the early 20th century, was effectively dismantled after World War II. The independence movement of India, led by the nonviolent strategies of Mahatma Gandhi, succeeded in freeing India from British control on August 15, 1947. Communists in China under the leadership of Mao Zedong defeated nationalist Chiang Kai-Shek nearly two years later. Revolution in Cuba in 1959 overthrew the Batista regime, placing Fidel Castro in control. In Africa, anticolonial resistance in Algeria secured that country's independence from France in 1962. Angola gained its independence from Portugal in 1975. Rhodesia became Zimbabwe in 1980 following armed resistance to the minority government that represented its colonial heritage. South Africa's racist apartheid government was overthrown through popular resistance and elections in 1994. The effects of World War II weakened European control of the global colonial system. This created the opportunity for resistance movements to dismantle colonialism and create their own sovereign countries.

In Vietnam, an anticolonial resistance movement against the French led the United States into a war that lasted 10 years. The French, weakened by World War II, were unable to quell the resistance led by Ho Chi Minh. The United States intervened, escalating its involvement after the Gulf of Tonkin incident, which led the U.S. Congress to authorize President Lyndon B. Johnson's escalation of military activity in Vietnam. The Vietnam War was justified by the United States as necessary to prevent Vietnam from falling under the influence of communism.

The Vietnam War drained the United States economically as the country had to operate under budget deficits to finance the war. It also caused social instability in the United States because of an unpopular military draft and mass public rejection of the war. This public rejection questioned the morality and necessity of the conflict. The Vietnam War killed over 58,000 U.S. soldiers. The number of Vietnamese killed is unknown, but conservative estimates place this number in excess of 1 million soldiers and civilians.

The Soviet Union, the People's Republic of China, and anti-colonial resistance movements placed limits on the global system led by the United States. The Soviet Union and China isolated themselves from the influence of the capitalist global economy. However, Deng Xiaoping initiated economic reforms in China in 1979 that allowed for China's integration into the global economic system. The collapse of the Soviet Union in 1991 did the same thing for the former Soviet Union.

The Era of Globalization: 1973–Present

It was clear by 1973 that the global system designed by the United States was in need of transformation. The global economic system, as designed at Bretton Woods, began to break down. In the 1970s, the United States was plagued by low economic growth combined with trade and budget deficits. The U.S. economy was shocked by an energy crisis caused when the Organization of Oil Producing Countries (OPEC) instituted an oil embargo in 1973. This embargo was retaliation for United States support of Israel during the Yom Kippur war of 1973. During this war, OPEC sided with Arab countries against Israel. OPEC used its economic leverage over international oil supplies to express its disapproval of U.S. foreign policy.

The combination of higher oil prices and the U.S. budget and trade deficits created a world awash with U.S. dollars (USD). The United States was unable, or at least unwilling, to honor the dollar under the gold convertibility system established in the Bretton Woods agreement. The Bretton Woods System utilized the USD as the global reserve currency; $35 was convertible to one ounce of gold. President Richard Nixon removed the USD from the gold standard in 1971. With this action, the United States unilaterally dismantled the international currency exchange mechanism. From this point forward, the system of a fixed exchange rate between the USD and gold was replaced by a system of free-floating currencies. Currencies were now determined by investor sentiment regarding their values. The USD retained the role as the global reserve currency, although it was not pegged to gold.

By the late 1970s the United States economy was suffering from "stagflation," a term reflecting monetary inflation combined with economic recession. The United States was also experiencing economic competition from the resurgent economies of Europe and Japan. This created a trilateral economic system that replaced the unilateral economic system dominated by the United States. In 1979, Federal Reserve chairman Paul Volcker implemented a stern monetary policy to defend the falling value of the USD. The Federal Reserve raised long-term interest rates in the United States to a peak of 14.17 percent in 1981. The debt burden of the developing world increased greatly. Many developing countries found that they could not repay their debts. This action also caused economic hardship for many people in the United States.

These new problematic realities created the environment for the rise of supply-side economics. Supply-side economics encouraged low taxes on business, free trade, and the deregulation of international finance. The 1980s ushered in supply-side economics as official economic policy in the United States, solidified by the elections of Ronald Reagan in the United States and Margaret Thatcher in Britain. Under the banners of "Reaganomics," and Thatcher's phrase "TINA" (There is no alternative), a push was made to implement supply-side economic policy. It is at this time that the neoliberal worldview came to dominate economic practice in the global economy.

This economic transition enabled investors to pursue higher returns without the threat of government regulation. High interest rates also lessened the danger of loss in monetary value due to inflation. With deregulated international finance, investment flows rushed into developing countries. Much of these flows were in the form of loans to developing countries made possible through petrodollars.

The OPEC oil crises of 1973 and 1979 pushed oil prices higher, causing a massive transfer of USDs from the United States to oil-producing countries. These excess funds, called "petrodollars," were reinvested by oil-producing countries in Western financial institutions and U.S. treasury bonds. Western financial institutions then recycled accumulated petrodollars to developing countries in the form of development loans.

The 1990s was characterized by widespread acceptance of neoliberal economic policies. In 1994, the Uruguay round of

GATT negotiations created the World Trade Organization (WTO) (see chapter 7). The WTO created a global system of trade governed under binding rules. Each country belonging to the WTO must conform to these rules in order to retain WTO membership.

The deregulation of capital altered the economies of developing countries as production shifted to those countries where labor was less expensive. This off-shoring of production displaced many workers in developed countries as they lost their high-paying manufacturing jobs. Off-shoring was beneficial to those who owned shares in the firms investing overseas. Access to cheap labor and resources benefited the multinational corporations and those who invested in their stocks.

During this time the percentage of international trade per global GDP grew dramatically. In 1973, the percentage of exports in goods and services was 15.3 percent of global GDP (World Bank 2007). This number rose to 18.3 percent in 1983, 19.4 percent in 1993, and 26.1 percent in 2004 (World Bank 2007). The rapid rise of international trade was accomplished through international trade agreements such as the North American Free Trade Agreement (NAFTA) and institutions such as the WTO.

All was not fine with the new global economy. Beginning in the 1980s, it began to experience massive and periodic instability such as the debt crisis of Mexico in 1982. The 1990s saw debt collapses in Mexico again in 1995, East Asia in 1997, Russia in 1998, and Argentina in 2001. The amount of external debt held by developing countries rose from nearly $566 billion in 1981 to more than $2 trillion in 2005 (World Bank 2007).

In the 21st century, it was made clear that debt crises were not limited to the governments of developing countries. In 2007, the collapse of the U.S. housing market is threatening to create a global financial crisis. Loose lending standards created through financial deregulation have rocked the financial world. In the United States, mortgage loans were widely approved for people who could not afford to repay them. Rampant housing speculation created a "wealth effect," encouraging lenders and buyers to escalate their risky speculative activity.

Loans were provided to home buyers who were purchasing homes at unsustainable prices. It became clear that with deflating home prices, many of these loans would not be repaid. Housing foreclosures skyrocketed as the housing bubble burst. Financial institutions holding mortgage-backed bonds realized they were overvalued. An international credit crisis ensued as holders of these bonds found they could not market them to others. Financial institutions around the world realized they possessed hundreds of billions of dollars of nonperforming investments. The collapse of the housing bubble coupled with trade and budget deficits in the United States have created the conditions for global economic instability. Although it began in August 2007, this crisis was still unfolding in early 2008.

In conclusion, the rise of the United States as the dominant world power began the modern era of globalization. The United States reconstructed the global system from the devastation of two world wars and the Great Depression. Although the United States built this system it is no longer the dominant economic power. The global economic system is now dominated by three economic blocs: the European Union (EU), the North American trading bloc, and Asia, led by Japan with the rapid emergence of China. Financial liberalization in the last 35 years has been characterized by instability and uncertainty. The future of the global economy is unclear, being a controversial dimension of globalization.

Actors of Globalization

This section outlines the major actors and forces that shape the current era of globalization. We explain major actors, including nation-states, central banks, international nongovernmental organizations, international governmental organizations, multinational corporations, international financial institutions, and free trade agreements. Together these actors and forces make up the institutional backbone of globalization. The actions of these actors compose the globalization process.

Nation-States

Nation-states are what are commonly referred to as countries. Nation-states are the central and most powerful actors in globalization, which could not exist without their support (Waltz 1999). Nation-states exist to govern social relations within geographically defined borders; they maintain social order within their borders by executing laws and monopolizing the use of violence. These qualities of a nation-state reflect its sovereignty, or its possession of legitimate and independent authority.

Globalization has affected the sovereignty of nation-states. Many scholars, however, argue that the nation-state remains the most important form of human social organization. Nation-states make up the basic units of the international state system. As stated in the history on globalization, the nation-state system began in Europe in the 17th century. With the collapse of European colonialism the international state system expanded to encompass the entire globe. Newly freed colonies were transformed into independent nation-states. Globalization, however, has made the sovereignty of nation-states a contentious issue.

Central Banks

Countries rely on central banks to coordinate monetary policy. Prominent central banks in the global economy include the Board of Governors of the Federal Reserve System in the United States, the Bank of England in Britain, the European Central Bank, the Bank of Japan, and the People's Bank of China. Central banks print money and regulate the banking system of their respective countries. Central banks also act as a lender of last resort to troubled domestic banks.

Central banks control the money supply of their respective countries to promote economic stability. They have the power to issue government debt in the form of treasury bonds. They also set interest rates for the domestic economy. Through open market transactions, central banks increase the money supply by buying treasury bonds and shrink the money supply by selling treasury bonds. A current example of this process is the Federal Reserve of the United States selling treasury bonds to finance the U.S. government's budget and trade deficits. The Federal Reserve can "soak up" USDs around the world by issuing treasury bonds. In the process, the United States acquires the money it needs to spend beyond its revenue.

The Bank of Japan and the People's Bank of China buy these treasuries to prop up the USD. By doing so, they keep their exports to the United States inexpensive and competitive. This example shows that even though the particular goals of central banks may differ, they coordinate their activities. This coordination has the collective goal of stabilizing the global economy.

International Nongovernmental Organizations

International Nongovernmental Organizations (INGOs) are international networks of people organized around specific issues and representing the interests of many diverse groups. INGOs are formed around business interests, the environment, peace groups, human rights, scholarly pursuits, and many other issue areas. They can be found throughout the global system. International leaders of business meet at forums such as the Trilateral Commission and the World Economic Forum. Human rights groups such as Amnesty International and Oxfam operate international organizations to promote human rights and social justice. Greenpeace operates on a global basis to protest about and publicize pressing environmental problems. The Carnegie Endowment for International Peace assembles scholars to focus on problems of global security and peace. INGOs form because important issues transcend geographical borders. This is a result of increasing globalization.

There are thousands of INGOs operating around the globe. In the era of globalization, they have become an important voice, often able to pressure countries to pursue their goals in the international arena. Although this is the case, some INGOs are more successful in having countries willingly address their concerns. Chapter 7 provides information on INGOs that focus on issues of globalization.

International Governmental Organizations

Since World War II, the global system has seen a dramatic rise in international governmental organizations (IGOs). IGOs are organizations composed of sovereign countries. Some are considered legal entities created through the ratification of treaties. Countries that join IGOs do so because they see their membership in particular IGOs as providing for their national interest. When a country complies with the rules and norms of an IGO, it can be said to be following international law. There are currently more than 250 IGOs. Well-known ones associated with globalization are NATO, the World Bank, the International Monetary Fund, the EU, and the United Nations (UN). The UN is considered to be the one truly global IGO, representing most countries in the global system. These important IGOs are explained in further detail in chapter 7.

IGOs actively take the form of international regimes. International regimes are defined as "sets of implicit or explicit principles, norms, rules and decision-making procedures around which actors' expectations converge in a given area of international relations" (Krasner 1995). A similar definition of international regimes states that these are a "bundle of formal and informal rules, roles, and relationships which define and regulate international practices and so constrain state and non-state actors" (Tabb 2004). International regimes foster open communication, cooperation, and good faith negotiation among countries.

International regimes are an important factor in the era of globalization. International trade regimes such as the WTO provide global rules for conducting trade. The Kyoto Protocol calls for the reduction of greenhouse gases by the countries of the world. The Geneva Conventions place rules and duties on nation-states involved in conflict. It should be stated, however, that international regimes work best when countries willingly accept their rules. The global system of nation-states has no international authority to enforce rules.

Multinational Corporations

Most of the products we consume in the developed world are produced by MNCs. They make our clothing, our automobiles, the gasoline to power those automobiles, our food, and the natural gas used to heat our homes and cook. In the developed world, it is difficult to go about one's daily business without consuming a product of MNCs.

Most of the information we acquire through the media is provided by MNCs. They own and control the vast majority of our telecommunication services. These services include the Internet, cable, and satellite television. MNCs provide us with our nightly news, our newspapers, and our various forms of entertainment. They record our music, create our video games, and provide us with our computers. In the era of economic globalization, MNCs play a central role.

By sheer size, MNCs have become a dominant force in the global economy. Of the 100 largest economies in the world, 52 of them are MNCs (Anderson and Cavanagh 2005). When comparing the GDP of nation-states with the sales of MNCs, many MNCs possess more economic power than some countries. For example, in 2002 Wal-Mart Corporation was the 19th largest economy in the world. Wal-Mart had sales totaling nearly $247 billion USDs. This was more than Sweden, the 20th largest economy in the world, with a GDP of $229.7 billion USDs (Anderson and Cavanagh 2005). General Motors, the 24th largest economy in the world, had sales of $186.7 billion USDs in 2002. This was larger than Saudi Arabia, the world's 25th largest economy. Saudi Arabia had a GDP of $186.4 billion USDs in 2002 (Anderson and Cavanagh 2005).

International Financial Institutions

Global financial markets are dominated by large banks and private investment groups. The top 10 largest banks ranked by assets are these (2004 numbers in USDs):

1. United Bank of Switzerland (UBS): $1.53 trillion
2. Citigroup: $1.48 trillion
3. Mizuho Financial Group: $1.29 trillion
4. HSBC Holdings: $1.27 trillion
5. Crèdit Agricole: $1.24 trillion
6. BNP Paribas: $1.23 trillion
7. JP Morgan Chase & Co.: $1.15 trillion
8. Deutsche Bank: $1.14 trillion
9. Royal Bank of Scotland: 1.19 trillion
10. Bank of America: $1.11 trillion

(*The Economist* 2006)

Along with these large banks, private hedge funds, insurance companies, and pension funds scour the planet searching for the highest return on their investments. Whether we realize it or not, saving for our retirement depends on the stability of the global financial system. Our futures are directly tied into the globalization process.

Free Trade Agreements

Along with the WTO (see chapters 6 and 7) a number of regional free trading blocs have been negotiated. Regional trading regimes also have the impact of increasing international trade flows but within prescribed geographies among participant nation states. Regional free trade agreements include NAFTA (see chapter 6), the Association of Southeast Asian

Nations (ASEAN) (see chapter 7), Asia-Pacific Economic Cooperation (APEC), and the South African Development Community (SADC). Regional trade agreements operate within the global economy as cooperative ventures between nation-states to increase regional trade.

Scholars of regional trade agreements argue that regional trade agreements have been underestimated in the context of economic globalization. Regional trade agreements express development policies employed by diverse nation-states to meet their own particular circumstances and needs (Stallings 1995). In 2001, the number of regional trade agreements was 220 (Dembinsky 2003, 88). Given disputes that have erupted at the Seattle and Doha rounds of WTO negotiations, the United States has pursued bilateral and regional trade agreements to extend its economic interests. This practice is discussed in more detail in chapter 3.

Conclusion

This chapter introduced globalization by defining it and providing metaphors useful for conceiving its complexity. It then offered a history explaining long-term processes that have led to the current era of globalization. Finally, this chapter identified major actors of globalization and the forces that result from their actions. In the next chapter, the focus shifts to the controversies, problems, and solutions related to globalization.

References

Anderson, Sarah, and John Cavanagh. 2005. *Field Guide to the Global Economy*, 2nd ed. New York: New Press.

Arrighi, Giovanni. 1994. *The Long Twentieth Century. Money, Power, and the Origins of Our Times*. New York: Verso.

Boulding, Kenneth E. 1996. "The Economics of the Coming Spaceship Earth." In *Valuing the Earth. Economics, Ecology, and Ethics*, edited by Herman E. Daly and Kenneth N. Townsend, 297–309. Cambridge, MA: MIT Press.

Cato Institute. 2006. "Definition of Globalization." Available online at www.cato.org/current/globalization/index.html (accessed October 27, 2006).

Chomsky, Noam. 1993. *Year 501. The Conquest Continues.* Boston, MA: South End Press.

Dembinsky, Paul H. 2003. *Economic and Financial Globalization. What the Numbers Say.* New York: United Nations Institute for Training and Research.

The Economist. 2006. "Survey, International Banking. Thinking Big." May 18. Available online at www.economist.com/surveys/displaystory.cfm?story_id=6908408 (accessed November 5, 2006).

Hardin, Garrett. 1996. "The Tragedy of the Commons." In *Valuing the Earth,* edited by Herman E. Daly and Kenneth N. Townsend, 127–143. Cambridge, MA: MIT Press.

Held, David, Anthony McGrew, David Goldblatt, and Jonathan Perraton. 1999. *Global Transformations. Politics, Economics, and Culture.* Stanford, CA: Stanford University Press.

Herman, Edward S. 1999. "The Threat of Globalization." *New Politics* 7, no. 2 (new series), no. 26 (Winter). Available online at www.wpunj.edu/newpol/issue26/herman26.htm (accessed March 5, 2008).

International Monetary Fund (IMF). 2006. "Definition of Globalization." Available online at www.imf.org/external/np/exr/ib/2000/041200.htm (accessed October 27, 2006).

Krasner, S. D. 1995. "Structural Causes and Regime Consequences: Regimes as Intervening Variables." In *International Regimes,* edited by S. D. Krasner. Ithaca, NY: Cornell University.

Matthews, Roy, T. Platt, and F. Dewitt. 1992. *The Western Humanities.* Mountain View, CA: Mayfield.

Morgan, Gareth. 1997. *Images of Organization,* 2nd ed. Thousand Oaks, CA: Sage.

Nye, Joseph S., and John D. Donahue. 2000. *Governance in a Globalizing World.* Washington, DC: Brookings Institution.

Stallings, Barbara. 1995. "Introduction: Global Change, Regional Response." In *Global Change, Regional Response. The New International Context of Development,* edited by Barbara Stallings. Cambridge, UK: Cambridge University Press.

Tabb, William. K. 2004. *Economic Governance in the Age of Globalization.* New York: Columbia University Press.

Waltz, Kenneth N. 1999. "Globalization and Governance." *PS Online.* December. Available online at www.mtholyoke.edu/acad/intrel/walglob.htm (accessed November 12, 2007).

World Bank. 2006. "Definition of Globalization." Available online at www.worldbank.org/economicpolicy/globalization/ (accessed October 27, 2006).

World Bank Development Data Group. 2007. *2007 World Development Indicators Online.* Washington, DC: World Bank. Available online at go.worldbank.org/3JU2HA60D0. (accessed December 15, 2007).

2

Problems, Controversies, and Solutions

This chapter examines the problems, controversies, and solutions related to globalization. Technology has had an incredible impact on the globalization of economic activity, the relationship between our species and the global environment, and the ability to execute war on a global scale. This chapter examines these issues by analyzing each controversy and problem and addressing it through worldviews of globalization. Solutions provided by the worldviews show it to be a contentious issue. This discussion will be better informed with an explanation of the different worldviews.

Differing Worldviews to Interpret Globalization

Students of globalization should keep in mind that this is a hotly contested and divisive concept. As Gerald Helleiner explains, the word itself "has now become so slippery, so ambiguous, so subject to misunderstanding and political manipulation, that it should be banned from further use, at least until there is precise agreement as to its meaning" (Helleiner 2001, 242). The authors of this book understand this view and can sympathize with its message. However, our intention is to show that globalization is a useful concept. This book addresses the problems associated with Helleiner's observations by looking at the ways globalization is interpreted in contending worldviews.

To understand globalization as a controversial concept, it must be examined from multiple worldviews. Worldviews consist of the ideas that inform our perceptions of the world in which we live. Individual viewpoints concerning globalization depend on the content of the worldview held by the individual. This book identifies three major worldviews employed in interpreting the impacts of globalization. Each one offers a different theoretical "lens" through which to view the controversies and problems of globalization. Worldviews also provide the solutions that address problems of globalization. The three worldviews offered in this book are divided into the categories as seen by neoliberals, institutionalists, and critics.

These categories are ideal types, or simplified groupings used to delineate the theories that explain globalization. It should be understood that variation and nuance exist among the individual views contained within these distinct categories. Admittedly, many viewpoints will intersect two or more of these ideal categories; some individual viewpoints may not be sufficiently represented by any one of them. Acknowledging these limitations, the authors believe these worldviews are effective in providing a basic understanding of globalization.

The Free Market Enthusiasts: The Neoliberals

Neoliberals regard globalization in its current form to be beneficial to humanity. Globalization is the result of rational and natural processes. The current form of globalization is based in the economic system of capitalism—an economic system in which productive power is privately owned. The goal of production is to realize a profit. Unfettered capitalism, according to neoliberals, is the ideal economic expression of human freedom and ingenuity. Economic growth produced through market transactions provides benefits for everyone. Neoliberals admit that global markets may disrupt the lives of some in the short term, but in the long term, markets provide for better standards of living for those who participate in them.

Neoliberals believe government intrusion into the global marketplace is damaging to efficient market operation. Government intervention is a violation of free market principles. Globalization, though it may create unpredicted problems, should be left to the "free hand" of the marketplace as this free hand contains self-correcting mechanisms to deal with short-term externalities, the unintended consequences of market transactions. Neoliberals are aware of the short-term problems that economic change can produce. They are also aware of the unequal benefits and problems that markets have on different people. Neoliberals argue, however, that these problems are a by-product of change, or "creative destruction." Problems associated with change eventually work themselves out, leading to a new era of increased wealth and prosperity for all.

Neoliberals vigorously defend the rights people enjoy by owning private property. Owners of private property should be free to utilize and dispose of their property as they see fit. They should be free to enjoy the maximum benefits derived from the ownership of property. Neoliberals argue that undue tinkering with property rights distorts market mechanisms. Investors rely on markets to provide the information needed to make informed decisions. Market-based decisions are important because they help property owners to know where to allocate their resources in the most efficient and profitable manner. Regulating property rights is viewed as an infringement on personal freedom by neoliberals. Governments and nonmarket actors should refrain from interfering with the globalization of the market economy.

Regulating Globalization: Institutionalists

Institutionalists agree with the neoliberals that globalization is a positive benefit to humanity. Institutionalists, however, do not believe that markets are self-sufficient in attaining the common good. Imperfect knowledge, argue institutionalists, can lead to irrational decisions. Imperfect knowledge and irrational decisions lead to market failures when dominant beliefs do not match well with actual conditions (Soros 1998, 47–58). As our knowledge is never perfect, we need effective public regulation to ensure that globalization provides benefits, not problems. Institutionalists believe that regulation and international cooperation are essential to retain the stability of the global system.

Institutionalists argue that globalization has created a world characterized by complex interdependency (Keohane and Nye 1977). Given complex interdependency, institutionalists argue that countries must create mechanisms to enhance cooperation and understanding to solve collective problems. These problems include economic decisions, environmental problems, conflict and security, and other issues that affect more than one country. Institutionalists recommend international agreements, and institutions to provide for better cooperation and understanding of globalization. These mechanisms offer a way to increase communication among actors to deal with collective issues associated with globalization.

Globalization as Destructive Imperialism: Critics

Critics of globalization come from a vast array of movements and worldviews. Collectively, the global movement of critics is known as the "global social justice movement." Critics of globalization work to achieve dramatic social change through the promotion of social justice. The critical worldview is not against the idea of globalization per se, but is opposed to the contemporary form of capitalist globalization. The critical worldview differs from the neoliberal and institutionalist worldview. It denies the potential for capitalist-led globalization to create prosperity for the world's people.

Critics argue that capitalist globalization represents injustice, domination, and exploitation. Capitalist globalization oppresses the majority of the world's people; it also destroys the Earth's natural environment. Many critics argue that economic globalization is a form of imperialism. Under imperialism, "core" capitalist countries exploit the labor and natural resources of "periphery" countries. Globalization is the process of capitalists enriching themselves at the expense of human rights and environmental health.

Some critics, though they resist the contemporary form of globalization, believe that globalization does not have to be a negative process and that it can increase understanding and acceptance of cultural diversity. Globalization could be pursued to enhance universal humanism and collective solidarity. With increased interaction and understanding, humanity may relieve itself of xenophobia (fear of foreigners). These fears often serve as a catalyst and justification for conflict, war, and oppression.

Now that this chapter has briefly explained the three worldviews that interpret globalization, the focus can shift to discussion of the controversies, problems, and solutions. This discussion begins with technology because it is a central factor in globalization.

Technology: Benefits and Problems

Technological progress is a defining characteristic of the human species. Prehistoric humans fashioned primitive tools out of the offerings of the natural world to help them survive nature's challenges. Stone-tipped spears, sinew-strapped bows, and animal skins fashioned for protection from the elements are all examples of prehistoric technological advancement. The human ability to make tools from nature's product through innovative thinking provided prehistoric humans with a mechanism to alter nature to fit their needs.

The major advancements of technological progress began in Europe with the Scientific Revolution in the 16th century. During this period the scientific method, or the systematic examination of nature through observation and experimentation, provided European society with the means to manipulate natural processes on an unprecedented scale to meet human needs. The works and imagination of Leonardo Da Vinci serve as a primary example of using the human intellect to devise machines for human use through the understanding of natural processes. The Scientific Revolution of the 17th and 18th centuries, fueled by the discoveries of Copernicus, Kepler, Galileo, Newton, Bacon, Descartes, and Pascal, further opened the way for the systematic examination of the natural world. The discovery of the scientific method led to the sciences of chemistry, biology, and engineering that provided the foundations for the most important social transformation in human history, the Industrial Revolution.

Technology is and has always been the central catalyst making globalization possible. Advances in communication and information technologies have expanded the scope of human interaction to unprecedented levels. Advances in transportation have made humanity more mobile than ever before, increasing trade and the migration of people. Technology is rapidly changing our lives. The Internet, laptop computers, cell phones, and MP3 players are all high-tech products that have become very popular. The rate of technological change is staggering when one considers that only 25 years ago people did not use many of the technological innovations we rely on today.

Technology has spread benefits to many people, but not equally. Although globalization has diffused technology it has also unfolded with an increasing technological gap. With globalization, the privileged few enjoy technological innovations while the majority do not.

For example, in developed countries only two people per thousand accessed the Internet in 1990. This number jumped to 439 people per thousand in 2005 (ITU 2007). In developing countries the Internet was nonexistent in 1990. In 2005, only 83 people per thousand had accessed the Internet (ITU 2007). Another example is the use of mobile phones. In 1987, in developed countries two people per thousand used mobile phones. This number increased to 780 per thousand by 2005 (ITU 2007). In contrast, developing countries had fewer than one person per thousand who used a mobile phone in 1987. By 2005, this number increased to 225 per thousand (ITU 2007). Technology is being diffused in the era of globalization, but not equally among all people.

Although technological advances have brought benefits, they have also created problems. Humans possess the ability to alter and exploit the natural environment in ways not possible in the preindustrial age. Technology has enabled humans to alter nature beyond the natural carrying capacity of Earth's ecosystems. This means that Earth's natural systems can no longer assimilate the results of human activities. This is the cause of pollution and breakdown in ecological stability. Technological advances have also increased the destructive capacity of warmaking capabilities. This has created a security dilemma for all of humanity. In the past, it was difficult for warring countries to eliminate their enemies en masse. Today this can be engineered quite easily, if the situation were to arise.

The advancement of technology has been a catalyst for globalization. Technology has enabled distant peoples to interact with one another. This process has created the controversial issue of cultural globalization.

Cultural Globalization

Globalization is important because it affects people. It does so in diverse ways, some beneficial, some not. The cultural dimension of the globalization process is immense and incredibly important. This section addresses some central concerns raised within the dynamic of cultural globalization. The discussion begins by explaining what is meant by cultural globalization.

There is little doubt that globalization is having an impact on the cultures of the world. Through technology, information, symbols, images, values, and beliefs can be transmitted across the globe nearly instantaneously. Thanks to satellite communications, computers, and the Internet, information possesses a global reach.

The rise of global communication has led to an increase in cultural interaction. Diverse and distinct cultures now come into contact with cultural messages and norms that were once beyond their perception. Cultural interaction can have the effect of altering the beliefs and norms of others. Cultural interaction and the cultural change produced by it have created a situation of "cultural hybridization" (Beynon and Dunkerley 2000). An example of cultural hybridization is the way much of the world's population has embraced American pop culture. Blue jeans, soft drinks, movies, music, and celebrity icons have become popular the world over. The spread of American pop culture is a form of cultural globalization that has resulted in cultural hybridization.

The impact of globalization on culture is contentious. Neoliberals argue that the globalization of culture leads to improved standards of living provided by a modern consumerist lifestyle. Institutionalists believe cultural globalization can lead to better networks of understanding and cooperation. Critics argue that cultural globalization leads to cultural homogenization and is a process of cultural imperialism.

Neoliberals on Cultural Globalization

Neoliberals consider cultural globalization to be a positive process allowing free markets to diffuse the best ideas. These ideas are the best because they compete in a global "marketplace of ideas." This view contends that individuals have freedom of choice in deciding what ideas to consume and which to ignore. It follows that if imported cultural norms are embraced by a particular culture, this culture has expressed its preference in embracing new norms over traditional ones. Neoliberals believe consumers should be allowed to choose what cultural norms they will embrace for it represents an expression of individual freedom.

Neoliberals also cite the progressive nature of free market capitalism in providing better incomes and higher standards of living. Cultural globalization can export free market capitalism to people who have yet to fully embrace its premises. Cultural globalization can help others understand how free markets can be beneficial. In this view, cultural globalization can export the "American dream." This provides the poor with the hope for a better future in an economy that allows for social advancement and upward mobility through the social classes (Gersemann 2004).

To neoliberals, cultural globalization can lead people out of poverty by allowing them to embrace the ideals of modern capitalist consumer culture. This culture is characterized by higher standards of living created through the increased consumption of high-technology goods. The cultural hybrid that results from cultural globalization instills the acceptance of the modern lifestyle. Successfully adopting the modern lifestyle encourages other cultures to participate and become more deeply interconnected with economic globalization.

Institutionalists on Cultural Globalization

Institutionalists regard the spread of information as an overall benefit to humanity. Communication between diverse cultures has the positive effect of creating a better environment for cooperation among distant peoples. Intercultural communication could lead humanity to a basic understanding of a "world ethic" achieved through intercultural dialogue (Nuscheler 2002). This is a cosmopolitan view. Cosmopolitanism is a hopeful view that increased communication and understanding can create universal values among diverse populations.

Some institutionalists have a more pessimistic view of the effects of cultural diffusion on globalization. Samuel Huntington, for example, argues in *The Clash of Civilizations* that cultural incongruity in the age of globalization will be a primary source of international conflict in the future (Huntington 1998). This thesis argues, for example, that Islamic fundamentalists may be motivated by a rejection of what they perceive as a decadent Western culture. A founding philosopher of the radical Islamist movement, Sayyid Qubt (whose brother was a teacher of Osama Bin Laden), considered Western culture an expression of schizophrenia that infected the Islamic mind (Berman 2003). Islamic fundamentalists see the globalization of American culture as an infection that is a threat to Islam itself. These ideas have gained support in the post–9/11 world.

Cultural conflict, however, does not have to take the dramatic and violent form of terrorism versus a "war on terrorism." Cultural conflict can be seen in the rejection of many French people of the fast-food culture exported by the United States. Many French citizens consider fast food a culturally based culinary disaster. This being said, however, many fast-food companies based in the United States have gone global and have experienced great success. One can now buy a McDonald's Big Mac in Moscow, Shanghai, and Paris.

Institutionalists are also skeptical of the real impact and importance of cultural globalization. The diffusion of American pop culture may not be as important as is often claimed. Cultural globalization may be surface level and trivial. This view argues that cultural artifacts diffused by globalization are mere tokens that do not affect the basic foundations of diverse cultural traditions (Nye 2002). The spread of blue jeans, pop culture, and celebrity icons may not be very important at all. These cultural exports may be mere fads that have little effect on the cultures of the world. This may be true, but it begs the question of what effect these cultural artifacts and norms have on the United States itself.

In short, institutionalists disagree about the actual impact and importance of cultural globalization. Cultural globalization can have negative or positive impacts. Most institutionalists stress the importance of promoting and advancing intercultural connections that foster greater understanding and cooperation among global actors. It is cultural interaction that can diminish the threat of conflict and offer solutions to collective problems.

Critics on Cultural Globalization

Critics view cultural globalization through a more negative lens. The critical view regarding cultural globalization focuses on two primary concepts: cultural imperialism and cultural homogenization. Cultural imperialism refers to the efforts of dominant cultures to control information and communication in an attempt to subvert diverse cultural norms and traditions. Cultural imperialism causes cultural homogeneity, or a decrease in cultural diversity. Cultural diversity is replaced by global cultural standardization and uniformity. Cultural imperialism and homogenization, according to critics, are strategies intended to dominate the meaning and interpretation of social, economic, and political forces. The goal is to minimize cultural rejection of foreign norms.

Critics argue that modern information and communication is controlled by multinational corporations (MNCs). These corporations have an interest in privileging certain interpretations of social reality over others. Those based in developed countries consciously pursue cultural globalization as a mechanism to dominate others. This domination of social reality is designed to diminish and thwart resistance to economic globalization.

In previous eras, cultural imperialism took the form of coerced education of indigenous peoples and religious missionary work. The intent of these strategies was to impose the dominant culture's values on those whom it had colonized. In the era of globalization, modern satellite technology, radio, and television allow MNCs to control interpretations of social reality that best fit their interests (Petras 2006). Cultural imperialism takes place by means of ideological indoctrination. Beliefs and attitudes are instilled in the culture, affecting its norms, values, and aspirations.

Cultural homogenization, according to critics, favors modern consumerism over traditional knowledge. The emphasis on modern consumerism diminishes global cultural diversity while creating a world of homogenous cultural clones (Clarke 1996). The global media dominated by MNCs exports homogenizing symbols and images meant to create a passive and obedient culture. This type of culture accepts its own domination as good, natural, and even necessary. This critique implies that a fantasy world is created where people's thoughts and actions are diverted from meaningful issues. Those subjected to homogenized culture spend their days speculating on the lives of movie stars and other pop icons, so caught up in a fantasy world that they seldom concentrate on the political and social reality in which they exist.

Cultural globalization is a complex issue characterized by disagreement and uncertainty. It is an ongoing process; its effects on diverse cultural realities are still unfolding and remain uncertain—with positive and negative aspects, depending on one's point of view.

The next section focuses on economic globalization—what is usually referred to when one speaks of "globalization." Many works exist on this subject, but its importance demands attention.

Economic Globalization

Capitalism is now a widespread economic system in which production and distribution take place on a global scale. In the past, economic activity was centered in local communities. Fixed capital, such as land and factories, implied long-term investment and social stability. With advances in technology and liberalized markets, economic production can flow where it can produce most efficiently.

Technology is a driving force behind economic globalization. Due to technological advancement, global gross domestic product (GDP) increased from nearly $9.5 trillion U.S. dollars (USDs) in 1965 to $36.3 trillion USDs in 2005 (World Bank 2007). The growth in world GDP has produced wealth on a magnitude never before experienced, but this bounty has not been distributed evenly among the world's people. The advanced industrial countries belonging to the Organization for Economic Cooperation and Development (OECD) accounted for 80 percent of global economic production in 2000. OECD countries represent only 18 percent of the global population (Dembinsky 2003).

Economic globalization spurred by technological advancement has been characterized by an increase in human inequality between and within countries. In the era of globalization, migration has been a result of global inequality. Many people have to migrate to find work in order to live. Examples of this migration are international guest worker programs and flows of illegal immigration. It is estimated that from the years 2000 to 2005 nearly 11.5 million people migrated to developed countries from developing countries (UNDESA 2005). This is nearly double the amount from the years 1975 to 1980 (UNDESA 2005). Much of this migration is to find work, but some is to escape political persecution and violent conflict. In the era of globalization, people are on the move.

The Globalization of Production

The production and distribution of goods and services reach every corner of the planet. This fact can be seen every day by the products we consume. Think about the blue jeans that you wear. It is possible that the cotton to make up your jeans was grown on one continent. The cloth made from that cotton could have been produced on another continent. The labor that sewed that cloth into blue jeans took place on another continent. Once produced, those same blue jeans were likely exported to another continent (possibly where the cotton was grown!). Although this is a hypothetical example, a simple pair of jeans today is likely to be the collective result of human activities across the globe.

A similar practice takes place with the food we eat. Take, for example, the fresh produce we in the Northern Hemisphere enjoy during the winter months. This produce is grown hundreds if not thousands of miles from where it is consumed. In a complex pattern of international trade, modern agricultural inputs such as machinery, chemical fertilizers, and pesticides are imported from developed countries to developing countries. In turn, agricultural products grown in developing nation-states are exported to developed countries. This example shows the increase in the intensity and extensity of global agricultural production.

In the age of globalization MNCs have become a productive force greater than many countries. The economic power and leverage enjoyed by MNCs is a central feature of the global economy. The 800 largest MNCs produce 11 percent of the total global GDP while employing only 1 percent of the global population (Dembinsky 2003). In comparison, the 144 poorest countries produce 11 percent of global GDP employing 1 billion people (Dembinsky 2003).

MNC production networks are global. It is estimated that MNC global production networks account for up to 70 percent of global trade (Held et al. 1999, 282). According to political economist William Tabb, up to one third of international trade is intra-firm production by MNCs. This means that one third of international trade does not represent economic transactions between different economic actors. These goods and services are not traded but are the result of MNCs operating with a global production network (Tabb 2001, 146–147). Given these statistics it is difficult to overestimate the influence of the MNC in the global economy.

Capital investing in productive capacity can now move globally to lower costs of production and increase profits. This is accomplished through foreign direct investment (FDI). FDI is long-term investment in foreign productive capacity such as factories, shipping ports, pipelines, power plants, and other economic infrastructure. Such investment allows MNCs to tap into the nearly 2.5 billion strong labor force in developing countries (FAO 2006). FDI is important to developing countries for owners of such infrastructure have a vested interest in the long-term stability of their productive capacity.

This means that investors in FDI are often concerned about maintaining a literate workforce that enjoys a standard of living that ensures they can produce efficiently. For example, owners of FDI do not want an illiterate workforce that cannot understand the technical manuals that teach workers how to properly operate machines. Similarly, they do not want a starving and diseased workforce because such workers are not productive. Multinational corporations have increased foreign direct investment in developing countries from $10.4 billion USDs in 1979 to $272.9 billion USDs in 2005 (World Bank 2007).

However, FDI does not always raise the standards of living for the world's poor. Labor that requires technical training is privileged to the process described previously. Uneducated workers that provide unskilled labor in areas such as the sewing of garments and agricultural harvesting often work under miserable conditions with low wages. These workers can be replaced if they become sick through malnourishment and disease. It is estimated that 1.4 billion people around the world struggle to live on less than $2 USDs a day (ILO 2004)

The Global Financial System

Global financial markets are conducted from the world's financial centers of London, New York, Tokyo, Hong Kong, Frankfurt, and Paris. The rise in information technology and telecommunications allows financial transactions to take place across the globe in mere seconds. The ability for financial funds to be transferred nearly instantaneously has given rise to an explosion in what is called "hot money." Hot money is speculative funds that search the globe for the highest profitable returns. According to David Korten (2001), "From 1.5 to 2 trillion dollars now change hands daily in the world's foreign exchange markets. Only some 2 percent is related to trade in real goods and services" (288). This means that the vast majority of money being traded on international markets is used to speculate, or gamble, on the value of economic assets. Only a slight percentage of these funds is actually used for the production of commodities.

Much of this investment takes the form of portfolio investments, or investment in the stock and bond markets of foreign countries. Portfolio investments can be pulled from a country's economy as fast as a computer can transfer them. This provides a great deal of leverage for those who control these monies. Countries need a stable investment environment to implement effective state policy. If the private owners of portfolio investment disagree with a country's economic or public policies, they can remove their investments. A sudden loss of investment funds leads to an economic crisis in the country subjected to a "capital strike" of portfolio investors.

Portfolio investment is much more destabilizing than FDI, which is less liquid than portfolio investment. The money tied up in direct investment cannot be transferred via computer in mere seconds; something purchased with FDI money must be placed on the market until it finds a willing buyer. Selling factories and other infrastructure is much more troublesome than exchanging a currency or trading stock and bonds. FDI is long term, focusing on the production of actual goods and services.

The business of international finance is conducted through a vast array of financial instruments. These instruments include derivatives, international bonds, domestic bonds, overseas bonds, Eurobonds, Yankee bonds, Samurai bonds, dragon bonds, subordinated bonds, senior bonds, convertible bonds, callable bonds, zero-coupon bonds, inflation-indexed bonds, mutual funds, and global deposit receipts (Singh 1998). The rise of complex and exotic financial instruments is a new feature of economic globalization. The impact that such financial instruments will have on the global economy is yet to be determined.

This era of financial globalization was spawned by the United States' unilateral disengagement from the Bretton Woods monetary system of pegged exchange rates. The breakdown of the Bretton Woods monetary system created a global currency market. Many currencies, including the USD, have their value determined by investors in international currency markets. The value of these currencies is subject to change in value due to investor sentiment. An exception to this is the Chinese yuan which is pegged to a "basket" of other currencies. Currently, China does not allow its currency to be traded in international currency markets.

Rather than being based on a gold standard, currencies are now fiat currencies. The value of a fiat currency is based on the legitimacy of the government in authority and the soundness of its economic system. A country lacking in either of these areas will have its currency sold, or devalued, by international investors. In the past, financing countries was considered a safe investment. It was thought that providing loans to countries was safe because countries did not go bankrupt. This idea has lost much of its validity with the financial crises of the last three decades. Countries can go bankrupt if their debt is not renegotiated by their creditors. Investors are very concerned about the ability or willingness of a country to repay its debt obligations.

As noted in chapter 1, financial globalization has experienced periodic instability. The Mexican debt defaults of 1982 and 1995, the East Asian financial crisis of 1997, Russia's default in 1998, the collapse of the hedge fund Long Term Capital Management in 1998, the 2001 debt crisis in Argentina, and the 2007 debt crisis spawned by the United States housing slump all serve as examples of financial instability found within economic globalization. It is not surprising that financial crises often result from debt burdens in developing countries. The total amount developing countries paid to service their debt obligations was $8.4 billion USDs in 1970 (World Bank 2007). This amount exploded to $355 billion USDs in 2005 (World Bank 2007).

Financial speculation is global. Financial chaos in one region of the world can quickly lead to chaos in distant financial markets. Developed countries have also accumulated a great deal of debt in the era of globalization. In 1974, the developed world paid only $800 million USDs to service its debt (World Bank 2007). This number had increased to nearly $160 billion USDs by 2005 (World Bank 2007). It is uncertain whether financial speculators may one day pull their portfolio investments out of heavily indebted developed countries, such as the United States.

These financial crises have exposed the threat of "financial contagion." This is the result of financial panic that spreads to other markets in other countries due to investor herd mentality. International investors, when they get spooked, start pulling their investments from foreign markets out of fear. Even if the economic fundamentals in a country are sound, frightened investors can change this soundness very quickly.

The Controversy over the World Trade Organization

Free trade agreements (FTAs) have become a controversial aspect of globalization. As explained in chapter 1, the WTO is a powerful free trade organization. An example of the power that the WTO yields was its binding decision that United States environmental laws were unfair restraints to free trade. Environmental laws in the United States restricted the importation of seafood caught with nets that also trapped sea life such as sea turtles and dolphins. The WTO ruled that these laws were unfair barriers to free trade. This case elicited much concern about the sovereign rights of the United States to make its own environmental laws.

The WTO is much more powerful than the General Agreement on Tariffs and Trade (GATT). The WTO contains mechanisms to enforce compliance to its standards. This newly created power of the WTO has generated considerable controversy, culminating in protests by a wide range of activists including trade unions and environmental nongovernmental organizations. The WTO protests in Seattle, Washington, on November 30, 1999, were joined by thousands of activists. Hundreds were arrested and downtown Seattle was effectively placed under martial law. Police drove protesters from downtown into surrounding neighborhoods where local residents got caught up in the turmoil. This event was considered the "coming out party" for the anti-WTO movement and resistance to neoliberal globalization.

After the Seattle protests, the WTO moved its negotiations to Doha, Qatar. In 2006, WTO negotiations failed due to a trade dispute concerning agricultural subsidies. Developed countries such as the United States and those of the European Union use agricultural subsidies to protect their agribusiness. Developing countries argued that these subsidies are unfair trade practices that manipulate global agricultural prices in favor of developed countries. Developing countries argued that developed countries treated WTO rules as "do as we say, not as we do." As of 2007, WTO negotiations have stalled and reached an impasse. Chapter 3 and chapter 6 provide more information on FTAs.

Worldviews on the Global Economy

Neoliberals

The neoliberal worldview is expressed by International Monetary Fund (IMF) and World Bank policy emphasizing structural adjustment policies for developing countries (see chapter 7). Neoliberals advocate the deregulation of the national economies of developing countries and the liberalization of their economic markets. These policy prescriptions are sometimes called the "Washington Consensus" as the IMF and World Bank are based in Washington, DC.

Neoliberals believe trade should have minimal restrictions for it brings people together. The transfer of technological innovation provided through trade leads to higher standards of living for those in developing countries. FTAs are helpful in ensuring that the benefits of free trade flow to as many people as possible. Neoliberals support the ability of these agreements to regulate trade and the conduct of governments. This may sound contradictory to the neoliberal worldview, but neoliberals believe the protection of trading rights through enforceable rules in FTAs is acceptable.

Neoliberals believe the same protection should be provided for international financial investment. Finance should be free to search for its most profitable allocation. Rules that protect finance are warranted in so far as they protect private property from illegitimate regulations. This idea was expressed in the proposed Multilateral Agreement on Investments (MAI). The MAI was leaked to the public, failing due to its controversial nature. It proposed that any law of any country that restricted the rights of international investment should be considered illegitimate and subject to removal.

The logic of the neoliberal view is that if one allows trade and investment to search for the highest returns, it will be put to its best use. Ernesto Zedillo, former president of Mexico and neoliberal advocate, argues that even though the global economic system has experienced many disruptions in recent years, the system remains stable. This stability, coupled with continued economic growth, provides evidence that economic globalization under neoliberal strategy is the best path to follow. Zedillo admits that economic growth is not even across regions or peoples, but he argues that the benefits of economic globalization outweigh its limitations (Zedillo 2006).

Institutionalists

Institutionalists are generally optimistic about the prospects of economic globalization. However, they believe that governments should play an active role to lessen the negative impacts produced by the global economy. In short, institutionalists believe economic globalization is good, but active governance of the global economy is necessary to ensure the stability of the global system.

Institutionalists argue that measures should be taken to stabilize the turbulence of the global economy. For example, institutionalists argue that IMF policy should be reformed from the neoliberal emphasis placed on structural adjustment programs (SAPs) (see "IMF," Chapter 7). Heribert Dieter offers three specific reforms for the IMF. The first reform is to drop the conditions imposed by SAPs for a country to receive support from the IMF. The second reform is to improve democratic control of the IMF. This would allow more input from donor countries other than the United States in formulating IMF policy. The third reform offered is to separate the IMF's financial power from the economic policy advice the IMF provides. This would involve separating the IMF's lending policy from its advisory role to countries in need of balance-of-payment help (Dieter 2002, 90–91).

Institutionalists also argue that to rein in volatile hot money flows, a Tobin tax should be implemented to tax financial speculation. The Tobin tax, named after economist James Tobin, would tax short-term portfolio investment transactions. This would curb financial speculation by decreasing the rate of profits. To further stabilize the global financial system, institutionalists call for an increase in regulation. Increasing regulation would provide for greater transparency in the global financial system.

Institutionalists such as Joseph Nye argue that individual countries cannot form effective economic policy in the era of globalization. Nye argues that countries will have to coordinate their economic activities if they wish to achieve the results they desire. This reality will require the creation of layers of governance in the form of international treaties and informal agreements among country's economic ministries. Cooperation, not unilateralism, is the key to success in the era of economic globalization (Nye 2002).

Nye argues that neoliberal policy is inherently destabilizing and must be regulated through cooperative activities. He promotes global governance but believes that global government is neither realistic nor desirable. Citing the instability found with economic globalization, Dani Rodrik proposes a form of quasi-global government through the implementation of "global federalism." Global federalism would not do away with the sovereignty of countries but would curtail it. Sovereignty would remain but would be limited by supranational legislation and authority. This authority would be institutionalized under a global executive and judiciary framed on the governmental system of the United States (Rodrik 2000, 353).

Critics

Critics contend that economic globalization is more correctly defined as global imperialism. Capitalism, with its engines of finance and industry, has escaped the bounds of national economies. Capitalism searches the globe for the highest returns on capital investment. Imperialist expansion makes problematic the assumption that capitalist interests coincide with national interests. Neoliberals and institutionalists assume that the success of capitalist enterprise is beneficial to the country as a whole. Critics argue that the global search for profits can, and does, hurt the national interest.

For example, the liberalization of labor markets proposed by the IMF has left many workers behind in developed countries. They can no longer compete because workers in developing countries will perform the same tasks for less money. This process has been called "de-industrialization." De-industrialization happens when manufacturing jobs and factories are exported to low-wage countries in the developing world. De-industrialization can create social and political instability within developed countries. This process, according to some critics, makes the concept of national interest problematic. These critics argue that if a country cannot act to defend the interests of its own citizens over the interests of global investment, then the country is better described as operating for the benefit of international investment, not its citizens.

These observations are similar to Marxist arguments put forth in the early 20th century. In *Imperialism, the Highest Stage of Capitalism*, Vladimir Lenin (see chapter 5) wrote that capitalist industry was controlled by monopolies and a financial oligarchy. Lenin argued that the entire world was being integrated into the capitalist mode of production through the export of finance capital. This was a necessary process, according to Lenin, because competition had been reduced among monopolies. Added to the problem of monopoly was an overabundance of finance capital. These forces led capitalists to export capital across the globe to stabilize decreasing rates of profit. By exporting capital, costs of production could be decreased. This was accomplished by gaining the right to exploit abundant natural resources and cheap labor in foreign lands. Capitalist development in foreign lands also created new markets for the goods produced by the industry in developed countries. Lenin provided a Marxist explanation for colonialism.

Contemporary critics follow a similar reasoning today. William Greider (see chapter 5) argues that the power of international finance has transcended the political boundaries of countries. International finance now dictates the fiscal and monetary policies of even the richest countries and has only one imperative: to grow and realize profit. International finance ignores the political stability of countries created through social agreements between labor and capital in the 20th century; it can hurl a country's economy into chaos if it does not agree with that government's economic and public policies. According to Greider, no country on Earth is immune from this danger (Greider 1997).

Recent critical scholarship argues that economic globalization is governed by the interests of an international rentier class (Greider 1997; Robinson 1998, 2004). Rentiers, in this sense, are composed of an elite capitalist class who live exclusively from the profits of their investments. In economic globalization, capitalist elites have more in common with their peers in other countries than with the working classes in their native countries. This critical view implies a type of global class warfare. International wealth is actively promoting policies to gain political and economic control of the world's population for its own purposes. In this view, the political power of working class citizens in developed countries and the political independence of developing countries are seen as threats to international economic elites.

Critics argue that to solve these issues, countries need to become more democratic. Critics disagree with how to achieve a more vibrant democracy and what institutional form it should take. They do agree, however, that democracy would require the participation of all citizens. Citizenship requires a political space to voice one's interests and needs. The economic system should be responsive to democracy, not vice versa. In short, critics argue that economic globalization is rotten to the core. The only way to fix it would be to abandon it and build a new global system.

It is quite clear that economic globalization is a controversial issue. The problems associated with it are many, and solutions to these problems differ. In this sense globalization is not only a concept but also a debate. This debate, however, does not end with economic globalization. The next section explores the controversies, problems, and solutions of global environmental problems.

Global Environmental Problems

Economic globalization, with its massive need for energy and natural resources, is negatively impacting the global environment. As modern economic processes spread throughout the world, these negative impacts increase as well. The globalization of environmental problems requires us to understand that the Earth is by and large a closed system. The only input of matter and energy that comes from outside the closed Earth system is energy from the Sun and meteorites. Other than the Sun's energy and meteorites—which usually break up in Earth's atmosphere—nothing else that scientists know of is added to the Earth's biosphere. Also, nothing escapes the Earth's closed biosphere other than the Sun's energy radiating from the Earth's atmosphere and the occasional satellite or spacecraft. There is no place on the Earth where we can escape the effects of our activities. The impact that human activity has on the environment affects us all. This is an important fact when considering the impacts of globalization on the natural environment.

Considering the Earth as a closed system has been expressed by environmental scholars in different ways. As discussed in chapter 1, Kenneth Boulding informs us that humans can no longer relate to the Earth like cowboys on the open frontier. Humans have to treat the Earth like astronauts on a spaceship. British scientist James Lovelock argues that the Earth is a single system composed of complex interactions between the biosphere, the atmosphere, the oceans, and the soil. Lovelock calls this holistic Earth system the Gaia hypothesis. Gaia is the interaction among these subsystems, creating optimal conditions for life on Earth. The Gaia hypothesis sees the Earth as a living entity that continually evolves according to the condition of its subsystems.

The Gaia hypothesis is controversial and has its critics. The idea does remind us, however, that as humans alter the Earth's biosphere, the biosphere will react and change accordingly. These changes will not necessarily be beneficial to humanity and could be very destabilizing, if not terminal, to much of the life on Earth, including humans. Lovelock recently announced his opinion that human activities have broken critical ecological thresholds and that humanity is well on its way to ecological catastrophe (Powell 2006).

This following section examines global environmental problems. Following this, these problems are analyzed through the different globalization worldviews. This section begins with a discussion of climate change, which represents an environmental problem that cannot be considered to be anything but global.

Climate Change

Climate change is the premier common pool environmental problem in the era of globalization. The gaseous content of the atmosphere is not limited to political boundaries and geographical space. Combating the threat of climate change will require cooperation among all countries. Developed and developing countries will have to cooperate to stop the pollution of the atmosphere with greenhouse gases. This section looks at the history of the discoveries of climate change, citing scientific understanding and international conventions and agreements.

Although theories of climate change have existed for about 100 years, scientific understanding of how Earth's climate works has made dramatic leaps in the last 30 years. Climate change is based on the theory that human activity powered by the combustion of fossil fuels is altering the makeup of Earth's atmosphere.

A denser atmosphere created through the introduction of greenhouse gases (GHGs) leads to an increase in the amount of the Sun's energy that is trapped by the Earth's atmosphere. The trapping of the Sun's energy in the atmosphere is called the "greenhouse effect." The greenhouse effect is a natural process that supports all life on Earth. Human activity, however, has increased the greenhouse effect through the introduction of greenhouse gases. Scientists have acknowledged that carbon dioxide (CO_2), methane, chlorofluorocarbons (CFCs), water vapor, and nitrogen oxides are the principal GHGs that result from human economic activity. Governments across the global system are aware that climate change is a real threat. In 2006, Britain issued the Stern Report, which estimated that attempts to stop climate change might cost 1 percent of global GDP while inaction will ultimately cost 5–20 percent of global GDP (Harvey 2006).

In 1760, prior to industrialization, the CO_2 level in the Earth's atmosphere was 208 parts per million (ppm). In 1960 this level rose to 316.9 ppm and in 2004 it was 377.4 ppm (WWI 2005). The years 1995–2005 were the 10 hottest years on record (GISS 2006). Of the 6.5 billion tons of carbon released into the atmosphere annually, only half is removed by nature, mainly by vegetation and the Earth's oceans (Brown 2003, 95).

The combustion of fossil fuels, coupled with deforestation, has saturated the carbon cycle, a principal system in Earth's ecology. With the carbon cycle saturated, it is unable to absorb, or fix, excess CO_2. The saturation of the carbon cycle leads to the accumulation of CO_2 in the atmosphere, resulting in the warming of the planet. This warming in turn leads to an alteration of Earth's climate and disrupts the stability of its ecosystems.

Symptoms of climate change are occurring across the globe. In 2002, the Larsen B ice shelf broke from Antarctica. Larsen B was larger than the state of Rhode Island and contained 120 billion tons of ice. Scientists believe the missing ice shelf could increase land ice melt, resulting in rising sea levels. In 2003, deadly heat waves devastated Europe killing as many as 30,000 people. In 2005, the United States experienced a record hurricane season, characterized by category 4 and 5 storms. In 2007, scientists warned that the Artic ice cap could disappear during summer months by the year 2012. Add to these events the possibility that climate change could "flip the switch" on the oceanic thermo-haline conveyor belt that carries the atmospheric jet stream to Northern Europe. The shutting down of the thermo-haline conveyor belt would rapidly plunge the Northern Hemisphere into an ice age (Taylor 1999). This theory was dramatized in the Hollywood movie, *The Day after Tomorrow* in 2004.

Stratospheric Ozone Depletion

Stratospheric ozone protects the Earth from much of the Sun's harmful radiation. Without the ozone layer much of the life on Earth would be unable to survive. Scientists discovered that an ozone hole over Antarctica had been created through the widespread use of CFCs, commonly used in aerosol cans and as a refrigerant. Other human-created chemicals that deplete ozone are carbon tetrachloride and methyl chloroform. Stratospheric ozone depletion is dangerous to humans because it increases the amount of ultraviolet radiation from the Sun that reaches the Earth's surface. In humans this causes skin cancer, is damaging to the eyes, and suppresses the immune system (EPA 2007).

In 1987, the Montreal Protocol on Substances that Deplete the Ozone Layer was signed banning the use and production of CFCs among signatory nation-states. The Montreal Protocol has been a successful international environmental agreement for two reasons. First, alternatives to CFCs were available, meaning that economic disruption caused by the ban was minimal. Second, there was agreement among signatory nation-states as to the cause of ozone depletion and the importance of reducing the use of CFCs. To solve the problem of stratospheric ozone depletion, international cooperation was essential.

Long-Range Transboundary Air Pollution and Acid Rain

Problems of long-range transboundary air pollution (LRTAP) and acid rain remind us there is no "away" for our pollution. It must go somewhere. This type of pollution is not global in scale per se, but it does cross international political boundaries, requiring international cooperation to solve the problem. Problems caused by LRTAP exist across the planet where industrial production is found, as it is largely caused by factories, incinerators, and coal-fired electrical power plants. These sources release air pollutants high into the Earth's atmosphere. The atmosphere transports these pollutants hundreds if not thousands of miles from their source. Three of the major LRTAP pollutants include sulfur dioxide, nitrogen oxides, and mercury. Atmospheric mercury is deposited into water sources in the form of rain. There it is transformed into methyl mercury, which enters the aquatic food chain. For those of us who fish, this is a prime reason we get mercury warnings along with our fishing registration guides.

Nitrogen oxides and sulfur dioxides cause acid rain, another example of LRTAP. Acid rain kills forests and aquatic life by acidifying ecosystems. It is produced largely by nitrogen and sulfur dioxide emissions from coal-fired electrical power plants. Globally, nitrogen oxide emissions have increased from 99.2 million metric tons in 1990 to 126.6 million metric tons in 2000 (The Netherlands National Institute for Public Health and the Environment/The Netherlands Environmental Assessment Agency [RIVM/MNP] 2005). Sulfur dioxide emissions have decreased from 154.2 million metric tons in 1990 to 150.3 metric tons in 2000 (RIVM/MNP 2005).

Declining Fishing Stocks

Oceans cover 71 percent of Earth's surface and contain 97 percent of the planet's total water (Middleton 2003, 85). Oceans serve as an important resource for humans, being a primary source for human economic activity and nutrition. For instance, fish are the number one source of protein for humans, and oceans provide much of the fish for human consumption (Middleton 2003, 85). The oceans are a global commons where all nation-states are free to exploit fish stocks as they see fit. At the same time, fish do not respect political boundaries in their life of spawning and feeding.

Open exploitation of fish stocks has created a classic commons environmental problem. Each actor engaged in fishing takes from the ocean commons as much as possible to maximize individual self-interest. The common pool problem arises as the combined activity of individual actors ends up depleting fish stocks beyond their ability to regenerate.

In 1961, a global human population of 3.1 billion people consumed 28 million metric tons of fish and fish products. In 2002, the 6.2 billion global human population consumed 101 million metric tons of fish and fish products (FAO 2004). World fishing harvests increased fourfold from 1950 to 1989 (Middleton 2003, 85). Humans, being reliant on 13,000 fish species, began to see a decrease in fish catches in the 1990s (Middleton 2003, 85). It is estimated that by the 1990s, 35 percent of all fish stocks were decreasing while another 25 percent showed no growth. Only 40 percent of fish stocks today provide increasing catch yields (Middleton 2003, 86).

The human reliance on fish as a source of protein is being supplemented with aquaculture. It is uncertain whether aquaculture can substitute for declining natural fishing stocks as the human population grows. If it cannot, declines in fishing stocks combined with a rising human population could cause food shortages for much of the Earth's population. This is a problem of globalization that must be addressed.

Ocean Pollution

Another common pool environmental problem associated with oceans is pollution. Seventy percent of marine pollution comes from land-based sources (Jacques and Smith 2003, 39). Ocean pollution is caused by the runoff of pesticides from agriculture and contaminants produced by industrial activity. According to Jacques and Smith, humans also dump 5.8 million gallons of oil into the oceans, half of which comes from transatlantic oil tankers (42). These authors note that this problem has increased dramatically due to the increase in size of transatlantic oil tankers. In 1929, the largest oceangoing oil tankers held only 18 tons of oil. By the 1950s, tankers could hold 50,000 tons of oil and today tankers can hold 100,000 tons of oil. Further, it is estimated that 60 percent of oil is transported by transatlantic tankers. Ocean pollution affects fish stocks where "contaminants can have a direct effect on the reproduction and development of the fish that use them" (Jacques and Smith 2003, 40). Ocean pollution caused by oil tankers is a good example of the impact technology has had on the global environmental commons.

Loss of Biodiversity

Biodiversity refers to the variety and variability of life forms found on the planet Earth. This diversity is determined by the genetic makeup of individual life species. Scientists do not yet know how many species of life forms are on the planet, but 1.75 million have been identified and the total number may be near 14 million, most of which are found in tropical rain forests. In

2006, 1,093 mammals, 1,206 birds, 1,811 amphibians, 1,173 fish, 341 reptiles, and 8,390 plants were species threatened with extinction (IUCN 2006). Although the evolutionary process regularly makes many species extinct, human activities have increased the rate of extinction among Earth's species. Even though much extinction takes place in local and regional settings, such as the Amazon rain forest, loss of biodiversity is a global environmental problem.

The problem is serious globally because science has much to learn about the impact that humans have on biodiversity, biomes, and ecosystems. Scientists know that human activity has transformed ecosystems and that this has led to species extinction. However, they are uncertain about what effect this will have on the ecosphere. They know that humans adversely affect ecosystems through the increase in human population, monocropping techniques of agriculture, suburban sprawl, and the addition of pollution and invasive species into ecosystems. A good example of this can be found by examining how human development has affected the Everglades in southern Florida.

The energy-intensive global economy has the side effect of altering ecosystems as its processes increase in intensity, extensity, and velocity. In the contemporary era of globalization, humans have the ability to dramatically modify ecosystems on a worldwide scale. The effects of such modification are uncertain, but scientists warn us that knowing the effects of some of our actions on the biosphere implies that continuing massive changes can pose potential dangers humanity should not ignore. The next section turns to the way these problems are interpreted by the globalization worldviews.

Worldviews on Global Environmental Problems

Neoliberal View on Global Environmental Problems

The neoliberal worldview is generally skeptical about the dangers of global environmental problems. Neoliberals promote market-based mechanisms to solve environmental problems if and only if environmental problems can be proved to represent an imminent danger to humanity (Bailey 1993). They insist on conclusive evidence and certainty regarding the dangers of environmental problems before action is taken. Neoliberals argue that unnecessary and burdensome economic regulations designed to solve environmental problems are likely to hurt the global economy (Michaels 1992, 2004; Bolch and Lyons 1993).

For example, as climate change science improved and public consciousness of the problem rose, neoliberals worked to counteract the new understanding. In 1989, the Global Climate Coalition (GCC) was formed as a business lobbying group by MNCs involved in the energy sector. The goal of the GCC was to reject all mandated reductions in greenhouse gas emissions. The GCC position supported market-based incentives and technological advances to confront climate change, but only if climate change could be proved to represent a threat to humanity. The organization argued that climate science was currently too uncertain to justify any action toward addressing climate change. In 2002, the GCC disbanded, noting that their lobbying efforts in setting the political agenda in the United States had been effective enough to warrant shutting down their operations.

This neoliberal view is often labeled "cornucopian," meaning that it is based on an optimistic belief in human innovation and technology. Made popular by the late economist Julian Simon (see chapter 5), this view contends that human ingenuity can ensure that the Earth has unlimited capacity to provide for human wants. Cornucopian thought rejects the need for government intervention in regulating the economy to protect the environment. Neoliberals as cornucopians see themselves as a vanguard (front line), protecting the liberty and freedom of property rights against a world tricked by big government ideology and unsubstantiated environmental concerns.

Institutionalist View on Global Environmental Problems

Institutionalists argue that global environmental problems represent complex challenges that are best addressed through international environmental regimes (IERs) created through international governmental organizations (IGOs). The past three decades have witnessed the growth of IERs and related agreements. Along with these IERs, global conferences on the environment have been held, such as the Stockholm Conference in 1972 and the Earth Summit in Rio de Janeiro in 1992. The Stockholm Conference led to an increase in international cooperation in global environmental matters including the creation of the United Nations Environmental Programme.

In 1992, Rio de Janeiro, Brazil, hosted the United Nations Conference on Environment and Development, known informally as the Earth Summit. This conference had the participation of 172 nations, with 108 heads of state present. The Earth Summit developed a definition of sustainable development that "meets the needs of the present without compromising the ability of future generations to meet their own needs" (Brundtland 1987, 40). The conference also produced Agenda 21, a 300-page comprehensive plan to promote sustainable development. It was agreed upon, however, only after negotiations led by the United States weakened its provisions.

The common pool nature of global environmental problems and the substantial cooperation necessary to address them creates a very complex regulatory environment. Given this reality Daniel C. Esty and Maria Ivanova have taken on the ambitious task of devising a framework for a global environmental mechanism (GEM) that they argue will be necessary to create a "policy space" for global environmental issues (Esty and Ivanova 2003). These authors recommend a GEM, citing the inefficiency of current IERs that are at many times ineffective, unenforceable, and put together in a piecemeal fashion. They admit that the challenges to the formation of a GEM will be daunting, for global regulations on economic activity will have serious impacts on hundreds of billions of dollars' worth of industrial capital whose value is based on the use of fossil fuels.

Al Gore's *Earth in the Balance: Ecology and the Human Spirit* asserts that human society is destroying Earth's natural environment and that the world's nation-states need to take part in a "global Marshall plan" that will help industrial economies become more environmentally friendly but will also be good for production and investment in the United States (Gore 1992). The global Marshall plan would initiate policies to transform the global economy into a sustainable mode of development. Wealthy states, Gore argued, will have to undergo a massive transformation that will not be easy because "powerful establishment patterns will be disrupted" (Gore 1992, 298).

In recent years Gore has taken up the issue of climate change as a personal crusade, producing the film *An Inconvenient Truth* in 2006 (see chapter 8), which explains the science of climate change to the public. In 2007, Gore promoted a series of music concerts called "Live Earth" that were performed on all seven continents. A number of well-known performers participated in these concerts whose purpose was to inform the public about the dangers of climate change.

Institutionalists argue that IGOs will be necessary to solve worldwide environmental problems. The common pool nature of these problems transcends the ability of nation-states to solve them on their own. Given the diffusion of modern industrial activity among an ever-increasing human population, the pressures exerted on the Earth's environment are bound to escalate. To institutionalists, these problems must be addressed now for they represent real threats with potentially catastrophic consequences. To the institutionalist, a healthy natural environment and global system stability cannot be separated.

Critics on Global Environmental Problems

Critics argue that so long as globalization persists and grows under capitalist assumptions the global environment will suffer. Capitalism is destructive to the environment because it commodifies nature in the pursuit of short-term profit maximization. To critics, the profit motive will always trump environmental sustainability. When a decision is to be made between ecosystem integrity and making a profit, the profit motive will win out. Administrative measures, IERs, and IGOs may reduce the harmful effects of economic globalization on the environment, but they will not solve continuing environmental degradation. Ecological economist Herman Daly argues this point by denying the possibility of sustainable growth. Daly reminds us that capitalism requires economic growth to continue the process of capital accumulation. To him, the notion of a sustainable capitalism based on growth is contradictory nonsense:

In its physical dimensions the economy is an open sub-system of the earth ecosystem, which is finite, nongrowing, and materially closed. As the economic subsystem grows it incorporates an ever greater proportion of the total ecosystem into itself and must reach a limit at 100 percent, if not before. Therefore its growth is not sustainable (Daly 1996, 267).

Daly states that eventually economic growth must come to an end. The question is whether, and if, natural limits to economic growth have already been reached. Critics believe the global economy has already transcended the Earth's natural capacity to assimilate human economic activity.

The critical view, like the institutionalist view, argues that if environmental degradation is not stopped it will be a catalyst for destabilizing economic globalization. World systems theorists argue that capitalism is facing a systemic crisis due to the irreconcilable contradictions that lie at the core of capitalist economics. The necessity for capitalists to reduce costs by pushing externalities onto others leads them to make ecologically insensitive ideas. Such ideas have culminated in an ecological crisis that threatens the very survival of modern society (Grimes 1999). The pursuit of profits derived from the logic of economic growth through the combustion of fossil fuels has led capitalists to deny scientific consensus concerning environmental problems for it contradicts their power and their interests (Wallerstein 1999).

Critics argue that ecological destruction caused by poverty in the developing world is the result of poor countries having their wealth taken from them by developed countries. Critics cite that while the poor suffer dire poverty, their governments pay off debts to the international financial elite based in developed countries (Bello 1999). Since there is little money to increase the standard of living of the poor, the poor are forced to exploit and degrade their environment to survive.

In this sense many critics reject Garrett Hardin's metaphor of the tragedy of the commons. Critics argue that the privileged few are using the impoverished many to exploit the commons for them. The privileged few, enriched by the ruined commons, then blame the impoverished many for this destruction, claiming that the population rate of the poor needs to be reduced to protect the environment.

Globalization of War, Conflict, Security, and Arms

War and Conflict: Global Security and the Global Arms Dynamic

The rise of Western powers from the 15th through the 20th centuries was extremely violent. Wars and the consistent competition for acquiring military domination over other powers is a constant theme in history. Seeking advantages through advanced weaponry has always been an inducement for technological innovation. In short, nation-states operating within the nation-state system have always been involved in a technological arms race. In the era of globalization, the quest for power is now truly global, and the arms race has diffused advanced weaponry across the planet. The Earth is now considered one geo-strategic arena, where nation-states compete for markets, power, and wealth through the advantage of possessing weaponry that is more advanced than the arms of their competitors. Total global military expenditures were estimated to be $1.2 trillion USDs in 2006, or 2.5 percent of global GDP. This number is a 37 percent increase from 1997 (SIPRI 2007). In 2006 there were also 17 major conflicts being fought around the globe (SIPRI 2007).

In the era of globalization, however, warfare has become problematic. Modern technology in weaponry, the rise of terrorism, and resistance to the domination of external powers has altered the dynamic of violence between and within countries. European countries realized this following World War II. They had learned that war between developed countries was not good public policy. War did not bring favorable results and did produce unintended consequences. Given this realization, the United Nations was formed in 1945 to act as a forum for resolving conflicts before they reached disastrous dimensions.

In the latter part of the 20th century the outcome of warfare between developed countries and less powerful adversaries has not always been characterized by clear victory. For example, the United States failed to pacify the agrarian peasant society of Vietnam and was unable to consider itself victorious in the Vietnam War. Although the United States had military successes against much less powerful opponents such as Libya, Grenada, and

Panama, and succeeded in expelling Iraq from Kuwait and in the extensive bombing of Serbia, it is finding much more difficulty in pacifying Iraq and Afghanistan following the invasions and occupations undertaken in the "war on terror." Similarly, the Soviet Union was unsuccessful in its invasion of Afghanistan, being forced to withdraw after 10 years of occupation from 1979 to 1989.

Globalization and Political Realism

The first controversial theme that must be addressed when discussing the globalization of war and conflict is the theory of political realism. At the center of nation-state foreign policy is the notion of "hard power" as informed by the theory of political realism. Hard power is the use of force by nation-states to attain their interests. Political realism is derived from the classical works of Thucydides, Niccolò Machiavelli, and Thomas Hobbes. Thucydides, in his *History of the Peloponnesian War,* wrote that political conflict was derived through competing interests. In writing about the conflict between the ancient Greek city-states Sparta and Athens, Thucydides said that there are times when violent conflict is unavoidable given irreconcilable and conflicting interests between military powers. Machiavelli's *The Prince* informed those with power of necessary strategies that must be employed to retain and strengthen their power.

Machiavelli's political theory separated ethics from politics. Ethics, argued Machiavelli, was ill suited to guide the individual seeking power. He believed that ethics was not a necessary subject for those seeking power at all costs. Hobbes's book *Leviathan* legitimized the modern nation-state as the necessary political organ to maintain social order and stability. The sovereign was to contain total power over social affairs necessary to preserve law and order. This ruler, or Leviathan, monopolized the use of violence and was legitimized by no less than the will of God. These classical theories of political realism have had an enormous impact on the formation of the modern nation-state system and the foreign policies pursued by nation-states within the system.

Modern theorists of political realism assert that the international state system is characterized by anarchy, or the lack of an institutional authority that enforces rules and norms for the entire system. With the condition of international anarchy, the foreign policy of a nation-state is geared toward its survival. To realists, nation-states compete for power in zero-sum scenarios. Gains made by one nation-state imply losses for others. The international state system is characterized by a hierarchical framework, where powerful nation-states dominate less powerful ones. In short, the rule of "might makes right" is the essence of political realism.

Political realism is important because it is an often overlooked political reality in the era of globalization. The principles of political realism are topics little discussed outside academic and foreign policy establishments. Even liberal democracies operate on the basic assumptions of political realism. Nation-states pursue policies to achieve their security interests by expanding their power. In understanding war, conflict, and security in the modern era of globalization, it is important not to ignore the assumptions of political realism. Sometimes, nation-states sell weapons to pursue their security interests. This is now a global enterprise. The next section focuses on the global arms trade.

Global Arms Trade

Economic globalization has led to the increase in the transfer of weapons. The global arms trade is thriving, providing a source of revenue to countries that have developed advanced weapons systems. This trade is also a lucrative business for arms manufacturers. According to the Stockholm International Peace Research Institute (SIPRI), global arms transfers were worth from $44.2 to $53.3 billion USDs in 2004 (SIPRI 2006). This is an increase from 1998 when the total worth of the global arms trade was estimated at $37.7 to $48.8 billion USDs (SIPRI 2006). The global arms trade is largely controlled by five nation-states: the United States, Russia, France, Germany, and Great Britain. From 1997 to 2004, the United States accounted for about 40 percent of the global arms trade ($108 billion USDs) while Russia accounted for 16 percent ($41.7 billion USDs); France, 10 percent ($26.7 billion USDs); Germany, 7 percent ($18.4 billion USDs); and Great Britain, 5 percent ($12.9 billion USDs) (Grimmett 2005).

Countries with advanced military technologies export many of their weapons to the developing world. Official arms sales are undertaken for reasons of national interest such as strengthening security by arming developing nation-states allied with advanced military powers. This being the case, however, not all international arms sales are officially sanctioned transfers. Many are clandestine and underground transactions that are many times criminal operations.

Examples of underground arms sales are the secret and illegal transfer of weapons from the United States to Iran and Contra rebels in Nicaragua during the 1980s. Other examples include the suspected transfer of weapons from Iran and Syria to Hezbollah. In Africa, arms are sold to obtain "blood diamonds," transactions in which rebel factions are armed by underground entrepreneurs. Underground arms transfers are also associated with the international drug trade. In Colombia it is believed that both right-wing paramilitary groups and leftist FARC rebels use revenue from the international cocaine trade to purchase weapons illegally. The underground arms trade was dramatized in the Hollywood movie *Lord of War* in 2005.

The underground arms trade is global, representing an obstacle and challenge to worldwide stability. The official and unofficial arms trade is an important aspect of globalization because it diffuses weaponry throughout the world. Although the increase in transfers of advanced weaponry is problematic in the era of globalization, the next section discusses an even more worrying issue, nuclear proliferation.

Nuclear Weapons and Globalization

The bombing of Hiroshima and Nagasaki in 1945 with nuclear weapons opened Pandora's box. Nuclear weaponry is an issue of globalization because the diffusion of nuclear technology leads to nuclear proliferation. As nuclear technology spreads across the globe, more countries are able to enrich uranium into the materials needed to produce nuclear weapons. Since 1945 it is estimated that 128,000 nuclear weapons have been built, with the United States and the former Soviet Union producing 97 percent of these (Norris and Kristensen 2006).

Though the security dilemma produced by the Cold War induced the United States and the Soviet Union to produce the vast majority of the world's nuclear weapons, other nation-states have joined the nuclear club. Currently, known nuclear powers other than the United States and Russia are Britain, France, China, Israel, India, and Pakistan. Israel is widely suspected of having a nuclear arsenal, but as of 2007 it has yet to publicly acknowledge being a nuclear power. Further, on October 9, 2006, North Korea claimed to have tested its own nuclear weapon, although there is still disagreement over the validity of this claim. With the realist foundation of the international nation-state system, many nation-states believe it is in their interest to join the nuclear club. Chapter 6 contains more comprehensive data related to the globalization of nuclear proliferation.

Deterrence, Mutually Assured Destruction, and Nuclear Utilization Theory

The possession of nuclear weapons by both the United States and the Soviet Union created a condition of threatened mutually assured destruction (MAD)—a theory created during the Cold War assuming that due to the massive amount of nuclear weaponry possessed by each foe, no winner could emerge from nuclear conflict. MAD assumes a nuclear stalemate, where neither side is willing to utilize a first strike because it is deterred by its opponent's lethal arsenal. This theory resulted in multiple nuclear agreements meant to limit the number of nuclear weapons and to stop their proliferation; these are listed in chapter 6.

In the era of globalization and after the fall of the Soviet Union, however, speculation into the offensive capabilities of nuclear weapons has been revived. Some foreign policy experts now subscribe to the nuclear utilization theory (NUT). Advocates of this theory argue that technological innovation can enable a nation-state to win a nuclear war. Space-based nuclear weapons are an example of the replacement of MAD with NUT. Space-based nuclear weapons could strike targets in seconds, not hours, offering no warning to the nation-state that would be destroyed by the space-based strike. NUT is an attempt to gain nuclear advantage, destabilizing the deterrence offered by the balance of MAD. NUT is very controversial and demands much more attention than it has received. The national security policy of the United States contains components of this idea; thus, it is discussed more fully in chapter 3.

Globalization and the Closing Gap in Firepower

The European countries' ability to colonize and conquer the world was the result of technological innovation in warfare and the willingness to be ruthless to those who resisted their hegemony. The late Carroll Quigley, an influential historian who taught at Princeton, Harvard, the Foreign Service School at Georgetown University (where he became future president Bill Clinton's intellectual mentor), and the United States Naval College, stated succinctly in his 1966 book, *Tragedy and Hope:*

> The most important parts of Western technology can be listed under four headings:
>
> 1. Ability to kill: development of weapons
> 2. Ability to preserve life: development of sanitation and medical services
> 3. Ability to produce both food and industrial goods
> 4. Improvement in transportation and communications
> (Quigley 1966, 15)

According to Quigley, superior technology derived through the scientific outlook enabled the European powers to become the world's hegemons. His statement is oddly cold, but it does reflect an uncomfortable truth. When European powers met resistance to their colonizing projects they were able to ruthlessly crush such resistance. These instances make up much of world history since the beginnings of European expansion in the 15th century. In the contemporary age of globalization, however, the gap in firepower, though enormous and growing, has become problematic and in need of discussion. In the era of globalization, conflict between a military hegemon and much less powerful actors can become very destructive, creating an uncertain situation with no clear-cut winners. This is a fairly new occurrence in human history.

In the era of globalization, military superiority still relies on possessing weaponry utilizing cutting-edge technology. Developed countries possess militaries and advanced weapons systems far more destructive than those of rogue states or terrorists. However, the diffusion of advanced weaponry and asymmetrical tactics has made "weak" enemies much more competent in the violent arts (Brzezinski 2004). For instance, rebel groups, though they may have much less military might, still possess destructive power that is problematic for advanced militaries. For example, the Mujahadeen successfully expelled the Soviet Union from Afghanistan with hit-and-run tactics. Similarly, the North Vietnamese and the Viet Cong successfully fought the United States until it was forced to abandon its war in the former French colony.

This fact can be seen today in the Middle East, where the Iraqi resistance to the United States occupation has successfully deployed guerilla tactics utilizing improvised explosive devices. These are commonly made from artillery shells left over from Saddam Hussein's Baathist regime. In 2006, the Israeli Defense Forces were repelled by Hezbollah fighters in southern Lebanon. Hezbollah utilized guerilla tactics combined with advanced weaponry such as cruise missiles and antitank weapons. Israel was stunned as one of its warships was hit by a cruise missile, possibly of Iranian origin. The Israeli Merkava tank, thought to be one of the most advanced designs in the world, was found vulnerable to Hezbollah's antitank weapons (Steele 2006).

Though these fighting forces were generally out-armed, out-manned, and in possession of less sophisticated weaponry, their tactics and possession of sufficient advanced weaponry enabled them to contest the military dominance of premier military powers. These examples represent the consequences of the globalization of technically advanced weaponry. In the past, European powers and the United States enjoyed a large firepower gap. Rifles, maxim guns, and artillery easily defeated foes wielding less technical and lethal weaponry. Today this gap has closed as the weapons of weaker opponents often include antitank weapons, AK-47 automatic rifles, and powerful explosives. These weapons, when combined with willful fighters whose motivations are not easily deterred, create dangerous foes.

Technology and Terrorism

Asymmetrical warfare combining guerilla tactics with modern technology increases the potential for destructive terrorism. Terrorism is the use of violence against civilians to achieve political ends. The terror attacks of 9/11 in New York and Washington, DC would not have been possible 50 years ago: Boeing 757 jetliners had not been invented so they could not be utilized as missiles. Second, flying commercial airliners requires technical expertise. The training required to fly such jets was not available to the global population.

A similar example is the Oklahoma City bombing in the United States in 1995. Former army soldier Timothy McVeigh and his accomplice Terry Nichols successfully destroyed the Alfred P. Murrah Federal Building with a homemade bomb composed of racing fuel and chemical fertilizer. McVeigh fell under the influence of a racist version of Christian fundamentalist ideology. The military training he received from the United States allowed him to build a terrorist weapon aimed at the United States itself.

This event, though possible, was also not likely to have happened 50 years ago. First, chemical fertilizers were not in wide use until the green revolution. Second, large rental trucks able to haul 5,000 pounds of explosive material were not easy to obtain. Third, procuring hundreds of gallons of high-octane racing fuel was not a possibility 50 years earlier.

These examples show that asymmetrical warfare and terrorists influenced by radically violent ideologies have gained much power. As technology has progressed, it has also been diffused and used in violent ways globally—consider the United States embassy bombings in Africa, Islamic terrorist bombings in Indonesia, and the bombing of residential dwellings in Russia by Chechen rebels. The increase in destructive capacities of marginal groups is an unintended consequence of the globalization of technology, warfare, and weaponry.

In summary, the successful use of mass violence is not limited to powerful nation-states with advanced modern militaries. It is probable that this new reality will continue to be expressed globally, having devastating effects in coming years. The concepts of national interest, security, and foreign policy will require a thorough critique as violent resistance movements associated with the globalization process become more powerful and organized.

War and the Environment

War is very destructive to the environment. Environmental problems are also security issues because they can cause conflict among those fighting for survival under conditions of resource scarcity. Thomas Homer-Dixon identifies three types of environmental problems that can lead to international conflict. The first is caused by resource scarcity. These conflicts arise due to the increased need for natural resources when not all actors can procure what they need. The second type of conflict is group identity conflict, exacerbated due to scarcity of natural resources. The third is deprivation conflict, caused by the unequal access to natural resources and the sense of injustice that such a situation creates (Homer-Dixon 1993, 45–49). The idea is that nation-states will defend their national interests in being able to procure sufficient natural resources, be they at home or abroad.

There are examples of environmentally based conflicts. For example, "peak oil" theorists believe the United States' recent escalation of military posturing in the Middle East is a response to an imminent peak in oil production. Peak oil theorists argue that as oil becomes scarce, a rush to procure a dominant political position over global oil supplies will ensue (Leggett 2005, 138). The theory of peak oil and conflict is examined further in chapter 3.

Finally, the late Carl Sagan, a prominent scientist from the United States, informed humanity of the dangers of "nuclear winter." Sagan's theory stated that if nuclear powers were to unleash their nuclear capabilities, the Earth's natural environment would be effectively destroyed. The world's forests would be lit afire while dust from the explosions would block out light and heat from the Sun. The Earth would be radiated, poisoning all life. A nuclear world war would effectively end humanity, offering no possibility of a winner.

Conclusion

Technology has enabled the process of globalization to change our world economically, environmentally, and in the destructive art of war-making. These dimensions do not stand alone but are interrelated. Combined, they have a profound impact on one another. The economic, environmental, and war dimensions of globalization are issues of great importance that are characterized by much controversy. Each of these dimensions represents a topic demanding much more research, but this lies beyond the scope of this book. It is our hope that our introduction of these topics is helpful in informing future research into globalization.

Chapter 3 focuses on the United States in the era of globalization, discussing the nation's role in the global economy, the environment, and the globalization of war and conflict. Given the central role the United States plays in the globalization of war and conflict, the next chapter interprets this role through the globalization worldviews.

References

Bailey, Ronald. 1993. *Eco-Scam.* New York: St Martin's Press.

Berman, Paul. 2003. *Terror and Liberalism.* New York: W.W. Norton.

Bello, Walden. 1999. *Dark Victory. The United States and Global Poverty.* London: Pluto Press.

Beynon, John, and David Dunkerley. 2000. *Globalization: The Reader.* Edited by John Beynon and David Dunkerley. New York: Routledge.

Bolch, Ben, and Harold Lyons. 1993. *Apocalypse Not. Science, Economics, and Environmentalism.* Washington, DC: Cato Institute.

Brown, Lester. 2003. *Plan B: Under Stress and a Civilization in Trouble.* Earth Policy Institute. New York: W.W. Norton.

Bruntland, G., ed. 1987. *Our Common Future: The World Commission on Environment and Development.* Oxford: Oxford University Press, 40.

Brzezinski, Zbigniew. 2004. *The Choice. Global Domination or Global Leadership.* New York: Basic Books.

Clarke, Tony. 1996. "Mechanisms of Corporate Rule." In *The Case against the Global Economy and for a Turn toward the Local,* edited by Jerry Mander and Edward Goldsmith. San Francisco: Sierra Club Books.

Dembinsky, Paul H. 2003. *Economic and Financial Globalization. What the Numbers Say.* Geneva: United Nations Institute for Training and Research (UNITAR), United Nations.

Daly, Herman E. 1996. "Sustainable Growth: An Impossibility Theorem." In *Valuing the Earth. Economics, Ecology, and Ethics,* edited by Herman E. Daly and Kenneth N. Townsend. Cambridge MA: MIT Press.

Dieter, Heribert. 2002. "World Economy—Structures and Trends." In *Global Trends and Global Governance,* edited by Paul Kennedy, Dirk Messner, and Franz Nuscheler. Sterling, VA: Pluto Press.

Environmental Protection Agency (EPA). 2007. "Health Effects of Overexposure to the Sun." *The Sunwise Program.* Available online at www.epa.gov/sunwise/uvandhealth.html (accessed November 20, 2007).

Esty, Daniel C., and Maria H. Ivanova. 2003. "Toward a Global Environmental Mechanism." In *Worlds Apart. Globalization and the Environment,* edited by James Gustave Speth. Washington, DC: Island Press.

Food and Agriculture Organization of the United Nations (FAO). 2004. *FAOSTAT Online Statistical Service.* Rome: FAO. Available online at apps.fao.org (accessed December 2, 2007).

Food and Agriculture Organization of the United Nations (FAO). 2006. *FAOSTAT Online Statistical Service.* Rome: FAO. Available online at faostat.fao.org. (accessed November 19, 2006).

Gersemann, Olaf. 2004. *Cowboy Capitalism.* Washington, DC: Cato Institute.

Goddard Institute for Space Studies (GISS). 2006. *NASA GISS Surface Temperature Analysis (GISTEMP).* New York: GISS. Available online at data.giss.nasa.gov/gistemp/ (accessed December 15, 2007).

Gore, Al. 1992. *Earth in the Balance: Ecology and the Human Spirit.* New York: Penguin Books.

Greider, William. 1997. *One World Ready or Not: The Manic Logic of Global Capitalism.* New York: Simon and Schuster.

Grimes, Peter E. 1999. "The Horsemen and the Killing Fields: The Final Contradiction of Capitalism." In *Ecology and the World-System,* edited by Walter L. Goldfrank, David Goodman, and Andrew Szasz. Westport, CT: Greenwood Press.

Grimmett, Richard F. 2005. *Conventional Arms Transfers to Developing Nations, 1997–2004.* Report for Congress. U.S. Congressional Research Service, Library of Congress, August 29.

Harvey, Fiona. 2006. "Stern Report Gave Impetus to Climate Talks." *Financial Times.* November 29.

Held, David, Anthony McGrew, David Goldblatt, and Jonathan Perraton. 1999. *Global Transformations: Politics, Economic, and Culture.* Stanford, CA: Stanford University Press, 282.

Helleiner, Gerald K. 2001. "Markets, Politics, and Globalization: Can the Global Economy Be Civilized?" *Global Governance.* July/September.

Homer-Dixon, Thomas F. 1993. *Environmental Scarcity and Global Security.* Headline Series. New York: Foreign Policy Association.

Huntington, Samuel P. 1998. *The Clash of Civilizations and the Remaking of World Order.* New York: Simon and Schuster.

International Labor Organization (ILO). 2004. "Half the World's Workers Living Below US$2 a Day Poverty Line." Press release. Geneva. December.

International Telecommunication Union (ITU). 2007. *World Telecommunication Indicators 2006.* Geneva, Switzerland: ITU. Available online at www.itu.int/ITU-D/ict/publications/world/world.html

International Union for Conservation of Nature and Natural Resources (IUCN). 2006. *2006 IUCN Red List of Threatened Species.* Gland, Switzerland: IUCN. Available online at www.redlist.org/info/tables/table5; www.redlist.org/info/tables/table1 (accessed November 12, 2007).

Jacques, Peter, and Zachary A. Smith. 2003. *Ocean Politics and Policy. A Reference Handbook.* Santa Barbara, CA: ABC-CLIO.

Keohane, Robert O., and Joseph S. Nye. 1977. *Power and Interdependence: World Politics in Transition.* Boston: Little, Brown.

Korten, David C. 2001. *When Corporations Rule the World,* 2nd ed. Bloomfield: Kumarian Press.

Leggett, Jeremy. 2005. *The Empty Tank, Oil Gas, Hot Air, and the Coming Global Financial Catastrophe.* New York: Random House.

Michaels, Patrick J. 1992. *Sound and Fury.* Washington, DC: Cato Institute.

Michaels, Patrick J. 2004. *Meltdown.* Washington, DC: Cato Institute.

Middleton, Nick. 2003. *The Global Casino. An Introduction to Environmental Issues,* 3rd ed. New York: Oxford University Press.

The Netherlands National Institute for Public Health and the Environment/The Netherlands Environmental Assessment Agency (RIVM/MNP). 2005. *Precursors: NO_x (Nitrogen Oxides): Extended Emissions 2000 and Aggregated Emissions 1990/1995.* The Netherlands: RIVM. Electronic database available online at www.mnp.nl/edgar/ (accessed December 1, 2007).

Norris, Robert S., and Hans M. Kristensen. 2006. "Global Nuclear Stockpiles, 1945–2006." *Bulletin of the Atomic Scientists* 62 (4 July/August).

Nuscheler, Franz. 2002. "Global Governance, Development, and Peace." In *Global Trends and Global Governance,* edited by Paul Kennedy and Dirk Messner. London: Pluto Press.

Nye, Joseph S. 2002. *The Paradox of American Power. Why the World's Only Superpower Can't Go It Alone.* New York: Oxford University Press.

Petras, James. 2006. "The New Cultural Domination by the Media." In *The Post-Development Reader,* edited by Majid Rahnema and Victoria Bawtree. New York: Zed Books.

Petras, James, and Henry Veltmeyer. 2001. *Globalization Unmasked. Imperialism in the 21st Century.* New York: Zed Books Ltd.

Powell, Michael. 2006. "The End of Eden. James Lovelock Says This Time We've Pushed the Earth Too Far." *Washington Post.* September 2, C01.

Quigley, Carroll. 1966. *Tragedy and Hope: A History of the World in Our Time.* New York: Macmillan.

Robinson, William L. 1998. "Beyond Nation-State Paradigms: Globalization, Sociology, and the Challenge of Transnational Studies." *Sociological Forum* 13 (4): 562–593.

Robinson, William I. 2004. *A Theory of Global Capitalism. Production, Class, and State in a Transnational World.* Baltimore, MD: John Hopkins University Press.

Rodrik, Dani. 2000. "Governance of Economic Globalization." In *Governance in a Globalizing World,* edited by Joseph S. Nye and John D. Donahue. Washington, DC: Brookings Institution Press.

Singh, Kavaljit. 1998. *The Globalisation of Finance. A Citizen's Guide.* New York: Zed Books.

Soros, George. 1998. *The Crisis of Global Capitalism. Open Society Endangered.* New York: Public Affairs.

Steele, Jonathan. 2006. "There Are Burnt-out Tanks, but Few Israeli Troops." *Guardian Unlimited.* Available online at www.guardian.co.uk/syria/story/0,1838871,00.html (accessed March 20, 2007).

Stockholm International Peace Research Institute (SIPRI). 2006. "Financial Value of the Arms Trade." Available online at www.sipri.org/contents/armstrad/at_gov_ind_data.html#glo (accessed October 5, 2006).

Stockholm International Peace Research Institute (SIPRI). 2007. *Summary: SIPRI Yearbook 2007. Armaments, Disarmament, and International Security.* Available online at: www.sipri.org (accessed November 10, 2007).

Tabb, William K. 2001 *The Amoral Elephant. Globalization and the Struggle for Social Justice in the Twenty-First Century.* New York: Monthly Review Press.

Taylor, Kendrick. 1999. "Rapid Climate Change: A Primer." *The American Scientist* 87 (4 July–August).

United Nations Secretariat, Population Division of the Department of Economic and Social Affairs (UNDESA). 2005. *World Population Prospects: The 2004 Revision.* Dataset on CD-ROM. New York: United Nations. Available online at www.un.org/esa/population/publications/WPP2004/wpp2004.htm (accessed November 15, 2007).

Wallerstein, Immanuel. 1999. "Ecology and the Capitalist Costs of Production: No Exit." In *Ecology and the World-System,* edited by Walter L. Goldfrank, David Goodman, and Andrew Szasz. Westport, CT: Greenwood Press.

Wallerstein, Immanuel. 2003. *The Decline of American Power.* New York: New Press.

World Bank, Development Data Group. 2007. *2007 World Development Indicators Online.* Washington, DC: World Bank. Available online at go.worldbank.org/3JU2HA60D0 (accessed November 20, 2007).

WorldWatch Institute (WWI). 2005. "Climate Change Indicators on the Rise." *Vital Signs 2005:* 40.

Zedillo, Ernesto. 2006. "Give Globalization a Hand." *Forbes* 187 (6 October 2).

3

Special U.S. Issues

A point made clear in the last two chapters is that the global system was largely designed and built by the United States. The United States helped rebuild war-torn industrial powers following World War II and promoted investment in the developing world. The rebuilding and investment in the global system was not undertaken out of altruism. These were mechanisms by which the United States was able to pursue its interests. Following World War II, it was the only industrial power that had escaped widespread destruction of its economic infrastructure and so it found itself in the position of global hegemon. As such, it could shape the world to fit its security and economic interests, and although the United States has influenced the global system in this way, much has changed since the end of hostilities in World War II.

The role of the United States in globalization has become a contested issue with an uncertain future. It is important to understand that interpreting the role of the United States in the globalization process is done through study of ideology and theory. Differing ideologies and theories create disagreement and controversy in this interpretation. This chapter discusses the neoliberal, liberal institutionalist, and the critical view concerning the role of the United States in the era of globalization.

The future of globalization has become uncertain and contested. How these conflicts will be resolved is yet to be seen. Students of globalization can be confident that globalization will continue to transform itself into new forms that cannot yet be predicted. It has been popular in recent years to invoke the Chinese proverb "may we live in interesting times" when discussing globalization. Given the uncertainty of the future of globalization, this proverb serves as both a warning and a hope that globalization can be pursued in a fashion protective of human rights and dignity. This being said, it is now time to begin the discussion on the role of the United States in the globalization process.

The Role of the United States in the Global Economy

The United States is an important economic actor in the global economy. In 2005, the country's gross domestic product (GDP) was nearly, $11.05 trillion U.S. dollars (USDs). In the same year, the global GDP was nearly $36.35 trillion USDs (World Bank 2007). So the United States accounted for a little over 30 percent of the global GDP in 2005. This number certainly seems large, but in 1960 the U.S. GDP was nearly $2.6 trillion USDs, while the global GDP was $7.3 trillion USDs (World Bank 2007). In 1960, the United States produced nearly 36 percent of the global GDP. Although the U.S. GDP has dropped as a percentage of the global total, the United States economy remains a very powerful engine within the worldwide economy.

The United States also plays a central role in economic globalization as the global "consumer of last resort." In playing this global economic role, the United States has developed large trade deficits. This country consumes, or absorbs, more goods and services than it produces. In 1960, imports of goods and services made up only 4.4 percent of the total GDP in the United States. This number grew slowly, reaching 5.4 percent in 1970, but it accelerated in the 1970s, reaching 10.6 percent in 1980. U.S. imports remained stable until the early 1990s when they accelerated again. By 2004, U.S. imports had risen to 15.4 percent of GDP (World Bank 2007). In contrast, U.S. exports of goods and services grew from 5.2 percent of GDP in 1960 to 10.1 percent in 2004 (World Bank 2007). The United States has increased its imports at a faster rate than its exports.

The increase of imports in the United States was accompanied with rising trade deficits. In 1970, the United States had a current account balance surplus topping $2.6 billion USDs (World Bank 2007). This means that the United States exported $2.6 billion more USDs' worth of goods and services than it imported. This changed, however, when by 1990 the United States imported nearly $79 billion more USDs' worth of goods and services than it imported. By 2000, this number had reached more than $415 billion USDs, accelerating to nearly $792 billion USDs in 2005 (World Bank 2007).

Although continuous trade deficits alarm many economists, some see the trade deficit of the United States as an aspect of economic globalization that is beneficial to countries that export goods to the United States. This view argues that countries that are developing through export-oriented strategies rely on the United States to consume their products. This reliance compels exporting countries with a trade surplus to buy United States debt to continue this relationship. Those who export to the United States must help that country continue to consume more than it produces by extending its line of credit. This credit is produced through the recycling of USDs that end up in foreign countries by purchasing U.S. treasury bonds and other assets. This view was articulated by the vice president of the United States, Dick Cheney, when he stated that "Reagan proved deficits don't matter." Cheney's remarks referred to this interdependent situation (Phillips 2006). His view argues that if the rest of the world wishes to develop through economic globalization, then it must maintain the ability of the United States to buy the surplus product it exports.

The above process works along these lines. The United States consumes more than it produces; thus, it must import goods to meet the demand of excess consumption. In doing so, the United States places more USDs in foreign hands than it receives through exports to foreign countries. This relationship places pressure on the USD to depreciate in value since its global supply is greater relative to other currencies. If the USD depreciates, or is devalued, the purchasing power of the United States consumer is diminished. Foreign goods exported to the United States become more expensive. This in turn decreases sales of goods produced by exporting countries, harming the prospects for their development.

Countries that rely on exporting to the United States for revenue have been primary investors in U.S. treasury bonds, especially China and Japan. By February 2007, Japan held $617.8 billion USDs in United States treasury notes while China held $416.2 billion USDs (DOT, FRB 2007). Japan and China have built economies that are dependent on consumer markets within the

United States. If the United States consumer became unable to purchase goods produced by these countries, their economies would falter—a prime example of economic interdependence in the age of globalization.

This relationship has allowed the United States to continue to operate its trade deficits. How long this relationship can continue is uncertain and a point of contention among students of globalization. For example, a similar relationship exists between the United States and oil-exporting countries. The global oil market is priced in USDs; thus, a decline in the value of USDs hurts the profits of oil-exporting countries. The price of oil has risen in recent years as the value of the USD has declined. In January 2002, a barrel of oil had a global market price of $18.68 USDs (EIA 2003). On January 2, 2008, the global price of a barrel of oil topped $100 USDs for the first time.

The above data imply that the relationship between exporting countries and the United States as "consumer of last resort" may be unsustainable in the long term. Recent tensions between the United States and oil-producing countries such as Iran, Venezuela, and Russia have made the relationship between the USD and oil prices problematic. In the future, it is possible that oil could be traded in euros or another currency accepted by international oil traders. This would displace the central role the USD plays in the global oil trade. Were this to happen, the USD could experience devaluation, lessening the ability of the United States to consume the surplus global product.

The Neoliberal View

The United States pursues its global economic interests through the neoliberal free trade strategy by promoting bilateral and regional free trade agreements. It became clear at the Seattle, Cancun, and Doha rounds of World Trade Organization negotiations that this disagreement was stifling the neoliberal agenda for economic globalization. The United States decided that neoliberal strategies were best pursued with a bilateral and regional emphasis. Using the North American Free Trade Agreement (NAFTA) as the template to follow, the United States pursued and completed the Central American Free Trade Agreement (CAFTA) and supported the Free Trade Area of the Americas (FTAA), which has yet to be ratified by participating countries. CAFTA was joined by the United States, Honduras, El Salvador,

Nicaragua, Guatemala, Costa Rica, and the Dominican Republic. CAFTA can be viewed as an extension of NAFTA, through which neoliberal economic principles have been extended from North America into Central America. The FTAA, if ratified, would extend free trade from the Arctic Circle to the southern tip of South America, enveloping all countries within the Americas. The United States also completed a free trade agreement with South Korea and has pursued them with Middle Eastern countries (Hartnett and Stengrim 2006).

One of the most popular arguments for the neoliberal view of the role of the United States in the global economy was articulated by *New York Times* columnist Thomas Friedman. In his two best-selling books, *The Lexus and the Olive Tree* and *The Earth Is Flat*, Friedman explained the benefits the diffusion of technology and commerce has had for the world's people. The rise of the global economy has created a global middle class that in turn provides the foundation for the spread of liberal democracy. Economic globalization is created through the ingenuity of private firms being unleashed by liberalized markets. To Friedman, economic globalization is the "end of history" for economic theory (Friedman 2000, 70). Free market liberalism is the wave of the future, an unstoppable process that will inevitably transform the globe in beneficial ways.

The role of the United States in this process is (1) to allow its firms to compete freely in global markets, (2) to promote American consumer culture and lifestyles, and (3) to provide the military force necessary to open up the world's economies. The military should maintain this openness if individual countries decide to disconnect themselves from the global economy (Friedman 2000, 380–382). The last point is justified by Friedman because those who live in the "unflat" world suffer the consequences of being denied benefits derived by participation in the "flat" world. The "flat" world is one in which economic globalization operates freely, driven by neoliberal capitalism and the products and lifestyles it provides. The United States military can ensure the continuing "flattening of the world," which will open up societies, diminish Islamic terrorism, and offer a better life to the world's people (Friedman 2005). Friedman's view has been summed up as arguing that "neo-liberalism teaches the world how to live in peace, enjoying infinite consumer choices rather than waging endless wars" (Hartnett and Stengrim 2006, 34).

Friedman's view represents the goals and strategy of the United States as it relates to globalization. Since the end of the Cold War, the United States has focused on spreading productive capacity throughout the globe. The national interest of the United States is understood to be the success and growth of its multinational corporations and international finance institutions (IFIs). To defend this goal, the United States employs its military might to defend its economic interests, which are also considered the global economic interest. It may sound contradictory that neoliberals accept government intervention by providing military power as a guarantor of free and open markets. One should remember, however, that the protection of private property is a basic principle of free market operation for neoliberals. Utilizing the military as a global police force to open and extend global markets falls within the neoliberal worldview.

The Liberal Institutionalist View

In recent years it has become evident that much of the pro-capitalist globalization discourse has evolved from the neoliberal view to the liberal institutionalist view. The global economy, argue liberal institutionalists, should be based in free markets and liberal democracy. However, economic globalization must also be managed to prevent the system from destabilizing itself. Management is necessary, liberal institutionalists argue, because the benefits of economic globalization are not being distributed equally. Many people are being uprooted from traditional livelihoods while others are being severely exploited in the pursuit of private profit. Given such occurrences, regulation and rules must be constructed to ensure that economic globalization does not alienate the world's population on which it relies. Alienation spawns resistance to economic globalization, and this resistance is already visible and growing. Liberal institutionalists argue that such grievances are legitimate and merit concern. If policy is not pursued to lessen ill effects, resentment to economic globalization could turn into outright rebellion.

Liberal institutionalism is interesting in this way; in the era of globalization, liberal institutionalists sit between the neoliberals and the critics. They accept free market capitalism governed through liberal democracy but promote measures to keep the views of critics from being fulfilled and brought into reality. Liberal institutionalists see the United States as a crucial actor in pushing through the necessary reform and regulation of the global system. So far this hope has fallen on deaf ears in the early 21st century.

The economist Joseph Stiglitz provides a good representation of the liberal institutionalist argument. Stiglitz, a former World Bank (WB) economist and Nobel Prize winner in economics, has written that economic globalization contains a serious malfunction. Rather than wealth moving from the rich to the poor, it is moving from the poor to the rich. In short, all boats are not rising with the economic globalization tide. A few are rapidly rising while the vast majority have run aground or are sinking. This problem contradicts the claims of the neoliberals and offers a real challenge to the future stability of the global system. Stiglitz is critical of the International Monetary Fund (IMF), arguing that its structural adjustment policies are ill suited to foster development in developing countries.

Stiglitz reminds us that economic globalization is not inevitable. The globalization process has broken down before and it can break down again. Stiglitz lacks the optimism held by neoliberals such as Friedman. For those with an interest in maintaining the global system, he warns of potential dangers that should not be dismissed. Stiglitz argues that countries must have a social democratic system that emphasizes social justice and education. If globalization is not conducted within democratic institutions, those hurt by the process will continue to rebel, rejecting globalization altogether.

Stiglitz promotes the Scandinavian model of governance as an example for other countries to follow. This model supports social democratic values and a comprehensive social safety net to reduce social conflict and promote political stability. Stiglitz notes that the biggest challenge facing future globalization is the United States' current rejection of utilizing international organizations to address global problems (Stiglitz 2006). He argues that international institutions must be formed with democratic representation in mind and explains that government leaders must take care to use the appropriate level of governance toward specific issue areas, be they at the local, national, or international level. These ideas are further explained in his book, *Civilization and Its Discontents.*

David Held, a prolific writer on globalization, agrees with Stiglitz, arguing that the dominant American view of globalization is destabilizing the global system and producing a breakdown in consensus. Held argues that the neoliberal emphasis of the "Washington Consensus" does not address four crucial factors that will destabilize the global system. He claims that the Washington Consensus approach to globalization has not (1) led to development for much of the world's people who are plagued by poverty and disease, (2) addressed the troublesome double standards developed countries hold and defend regarding free trade, (3) addressed environmental dangers such as climate change, and (4) adequately questioned the use of force by the United States in world affairs (Held 2005, 6–7). Without addressing these problems, the opening up of markets through economic liberalization has had an overall destabilizing effect. This destabilization will threaten the viability of further economic globalization (Held 2005, 100).

The Critic's View

Critics argue that economic globalization was not designed to attain global social justice but to ensure global profiteering. Economic globalization hurts much of the world population because the global system operates under capitalist principles. Critics argue that reforms of economic globalization will not solve the social injustice perpetrated to attain profits. At best, critics claim, reforms could stall the demise of economic globalization but would not stop its eventual collapse. It is important to restate that critics are not against globalization as an idea but reject capitalist-governed economic globalization dominated by multinational corporations and IFIs. Economic globalization is currently pursued for the interests of political and economic elites based primarily in developed countries but with peers who govern the developing countries for their interests.

The political economist William Tabb argues that the United States designed the current global system with its own interests in mind by creating global state economic governance institutions (GSEGI). Tabb argues that GSEGIs, such as the IMF, the WB, and the WTO are intended to maintain the economic power of advanced industrial countries without regard for the interests of developing countries. The rules, norms, and beliefs embraced by capitalist elites are formed at private meetings such as the World Economic Forum in Davos, Switzerland, and the annual G-8 meetings. According to Tabb, these meetings are not conspiracy or evil intent but instead represent exercises of calculated self-interest employed to maintain the power of the global capitalist class. The governance of economic globalization is amoral. Tabb argues that the global system is governed by capitalists who are antisocial, lacking in true patriotism, and unwilling to think about the consequences of their actions (Tabb 2004).

In *Confessions of an Economic Hit Man*, John Perkins tells a sordid tale of personal life experiences that supports Tabb's view of economic globalization. Perkins's biographical work tells of being an "economic hit man." He claims he was recruited by the United States National Security Agency (NSA) to be an economic analyst for a private firm contracting with the NSA. Perkins states that it was his job to intentionally overestimate the future economic growth and infrastructure needs of developing countries. According to Perkins, this was done to justify loans from the WB and other development aid agencies that were not justified. Further, the development agencies knew the borrowing countries could not possibly repay the loans. The debt crises created throughout the developing world are the intended result of the activities of such economic hit men. Perkins states that this was the preferred strategy to gain control of the economic product of developing countries.

Other avenues, however, were open to the United States to achieve its economic interests. When economic hit men failed to convince a reluctant leader of the logic of their economic planning, the "jackals" were called in to perform political assassinations. If political assassination failed, the United States would resort to direct military intervention. Military intervention took the forms of supporting military coups or direct military invasion (Perkins 2006).

This book became a best seller and created quite a controversy. The United States Department of State has rejected Perkins's claims as "fantasy" and "misinformation." The State Department argues that there is no evidence that Perkins ever worked for the NSA, and the NSA is not involved in economic policy (United States Department of State 2006). On the other hand, investigative journalist Greg Palast has written about his experience with Perkins as an economic hit man, and although he does not address the specific evidence of Perkins's claims, he asserts that Perkins was ethically challenged and involved in questionable business practices similar to those Perkins describes in his book. Palast implies that given Perkins's past lack of ethics and amoral ambitions, his claims are believable and credible (Palast 2007). Whether Perkins's personal claims are credible or not, they directly reflect arguments made by many theorists who are critical of the United States' role in economic globalization.

In conclusion, the neoliberal and liberal institutionalist views support the use of U.S. power to stabilize economic globalization. These worldviews do not address the critical claims made by Tabb and Perkins. The controversy arises in the legitimacy and intent of the United States using its power to stabilize the global economic system. This controversy will be exhibited throughout this chapter. The next section focuses on the environmental dimension of globalization and the role of the United States within it.

The United States and the Global Environment

Environmental policy in the United States has gone through quite an evolution in the past four decades. In the late 1960s and early 1970s the United States was a global leader in environmental policy formation and environmental consciousness. By the early 21st century, however, the United States had become a reluctant and skeptical participant in international environmental policy formation. This evolution coincides with the United States' move from the New Deal social welfare state to the neoliberal emphasis that gained prominence in the 1980s. In the United States, neoliberal economics, coupled with environmental skepticism, has succeeded in challenging the legitimacy of United States involvement in international environmental policy formation.

The next section of the chapter discusses the evolution of environmental policy in the United States. Following this, an explanation of the United States' rejection of the Kyoto Protocol is offered with an interpretation of this rejection through the globalization worldviews. The role of the United States in the globalization of environmental problems such as climate change and its reluctance to lead in proposing policy to address such problems is a controversial aspect of the role of the United States in the global system. Discussing the evolution of environmental policy within the United States is important for it reflects the current view of the country in addressing environmental problems associated with globalization. The United States was once a global leader in environmental policy formation. Now it is widely seen as a global straggler in addressing such problems.

The neoliberal worldview does not believe the United States should be concerned with international cooperation in environmental policy formation. Liberal institutionalists argue that this lack of willingness to lead the world in international environmental policy formation is another missed opportunity for the United States to guide the world toward a stable global system. Critics argue that it is no surprise that the United States is unwilling to be a global leader in international environmental policy. In the era of globalization, critics argue, the United States no longer possesses the economic hegemony it once did, and in an effort to become more competitive, it is sacrificing environmental quality.

The Evolution of Environmental Policy in the United States

The golden years of environmental policy in the United States began in the 1960s and early 1970s. In these decades the United States passed the Clean Air Act (CAA) in 1963 (amended in 1970 and 1977), the Endangered Species Act in 1966 (amended in 1969 and 1973), and the National Environmental Protection Act (NEPA) in 1969. NEPA provided the legal basis for the creation of the Environmental Protection Agency (EPA) in 1970. The Clean Water Act was passed in 1972 (amended 1977). The Resource Conservation and Recovery Act of 1976 (amended in 1984 and 1986) gave the EPA cradle to grave regulatory power over the creation, transportation, storage, and disposal of hazardous waste. During the 1960s–1970s, the U.S. federal government played a powerful role in the formation, regulation, and enforcement of environmental policy within this country (Smith 2004).

The 1980s continued the central role of the federal government in environmental protection. The Safe Drinking Water Act was passed in 1986, creating requirements for drinking water quality. The dangers of asbestos insulation in homes and public spaces led to the passage of the Asbestos Hazardous Emergency Response Act in 1986. This was followed by the Federal Insecticide, Fungicide, and Rodenticide Act of 1988.

The 1990s witnessed the rise of the Republican Party to power when it gained control the House of Representatives in 1994. The Contract with America served as a blueprint for the Republican Party to reduce the size and scope of the federal government. A central emphasis was placed on reducing the federal regulation of states. This viewpoint became federal law with the passing of the Unfunded Mandate Reform Act of 1995. The growth of economic monetarism in the 1980s and the rise of Republican Party power in Congress in the 1990s led to a deemphasis on the federal role in environmental policy formation. Neoliberal economic arguments applied to environmental policy questioned federal command-and-control regulations. Command-and-control environmental regulations fell from favor as it was argued that they have a negative impact on the U.S. economy.

This trend extended into the 21st century with the election and reelection of President George W. Bush. Under the Bush administration, the emphasis on environmental protection has been founded on voluntary compliance and market-based incentives. The Bush presidency has also seen an increase of environmental degradation in the United States. For example, since the Bush administration took office in 2001, Superfund cleanups of toxic waste have fallen by 52 percent. Warnings about eating fish from rivers have doubled and warnings about fish from lakes have increased 39 percent. Beach closings were up 26 percent while civil citations for polluters declined 57 percent. Criminal prosecutions related to pollution have declined 17 percent while asthma cases increased 6 percent. It should be noted in all fairness, however, that during the Bush administration's tenure air emissions from smokestacks and tailpipes dropped 9 percent and total greenhouse gas (GHG) emissions dropped by 5 percent (Borenstein 2004; Moan and Smith 2005).

Note that as the neoliberal emphasis on reducing the federal government's role in environmental protection has gained prominence, it has been accompanied with a noticeable decline in environmental quality. There is, of course, disagreement among the globalization worldviews as to the importance and meaning of this fact. It can be said, however, that the evolution of domestic environmental policy in the United States reflects its attitude toward international environmental policy formation. The following sections assess what each worldview believes is important in assessing the role of the United States in the global environment by using the Kyoto Protocol as a case study.

The Rejection of the Kyoto Protocol

The United States' rejection of the Kyoto Protocol provides an example of its unwillingness to lead the world in the formation of international environmental policy. The rejection of the Kyoto Protocol is not limited to the Bush administration. It was also rejected by the Democratic Party in the United States. In July 1999, the Democrat-controlled Senate passed a resolution rejecting the Kyoto Protocol by a vote of 95 to 0. The Bush administration made its intent to reject the Kyoto protocol known in March 2001. Both the Democrat-controlled Senate and the Bush administration based their rejection on the basis that the protocol did not include reductions of GHG emissions for developing countries, notably China and India. The Democrat-controlled Senate and the Bush administration noted that the Kyoto Protocol was inherently unfair and would hurt the U.S. economy by burdening it with reductions of GHGs.

The Bush administration further justified its stance by claiming that climate change science is still too uncertain to warrant burdensome policies. The Bush administration thought it unwise to regulate energy prices in 2001 when energy prices were rising and California was experiencing energy shortages and rolling blackouts (Bush 2001b). It should be noted, however, that the collapse of Enron in October 2001 made it clear that energy shortages and rising prices were a result of energy market manipulation made possible through deregulation. The neoliberal view, embraced by both dominant political parties in the United States, supported deregulation of energy markets for reasons of economic efficiency and growth.

The next section discusses the policy regarding the Kyoto Protocol and climate change to show that the neoliberal worldview has largely captured the environmental policy agenda of the United States. In terms of globalization, this account suggests that the unwillingness of the United States to ratify the Kyoto Protocol implies that the country is currently unwilling to act as the leader in global environmental stewardship.

Climate Change Policy in the United States

The Neoliberal View

The rejection of the Kyoto Protocol by the United States could be considered the death knell for the effectiveness of this international environmental agreement—because the United States is the second largest carbon dioxide (CO_2) emitter on the planet. China replaced the United States for the top spot in 2007. The United States emitted 5,844,042 thousand metric tons of CO_2 in 2002 (UNEP 2002), accounting for 25 percent of the global total (EIA 2003). United States per capita CO_2 emissions were 20.16 metric tons in 2002, second only to those of Canada.

Rather than ratifying the Kyoto Protocol, the United States has formed the Global Change Resource Program (GCRP) whose purpose is to analyze the possibility and potential effects of anthropogenic climate change. The GCRP spans the United States federal government including 15 federal departments, government agencies, and research institutes. United States policy regarding CO_2 emissions and climate change is still in its infancy, with the EPA itself asserting that it has no legal basis to regulate CO_2. This assertion is based on an interpretation of the CAA that omits CO_2 as an air pollutant. This claim was overturned by the Supreme Court of the United States in 2007. In a 5 to 4 vote, the Supreme Court found that the EPA does have the power to implement regulatory policy on CO_2 emissions.

According to the Bush administration's Climate Vision plan, a new generation of innovative technologies will allow the United States to reduce its CO_2 emissions 18 percent per economic unit by the year 2012. This is equivalent to taking 70 million cars off the road (Bush 2002). Examples of such technologies are nuclear fusion reactors, carbon sequestration technologies, and hydrogen fuel. The Bush administration budget for fiscal year 2006 proposed $5.5 billion USDs toward addressing the issue of climate change, an increase of $1 billion USDs from 2002 (The Whitehouse 2005).

In 2003, the Bush administration was accused of covering up EPA findings regarding scientific research that revealed the serious impacts of anthropogenic climate change (Harris 2003). This accusation gained credibility when James Hansen, a National Aeronautics and Space Administration scientist and expert on climate change theory, noted that he had been pressured not to talk to the public about his scientific work regarding climate change. Other scientists have also claimed that they have been coerced by the Bush administration to remain silent on the topic.

In 2007, a congressional panel investigating such coercion questioned Philip A. Cooney, a Bush administration official. The investigation focused on Cooney's alteration of scientific reports provided by government scientists regarding climate change. Cooney, who does not have a scientific background, altered the findings of government scientists to downplay the urgency they recommended in addressing the threat of climate change. When asked of his intent, Cooney stated that his alterations represented the scientific view, a claim subsequently dismissed by government scientists. When further pressed, Cooney admitted that his job was to represent the views of the Bush administration regarding climate change and that his loyalties were with the president and his administration (Revkin and Wald 2007). Cooney's loyalty to the president took precedence over the scientific findings of government scientists.

In May 2007, President Bush announced his willingness to lead the 15 largest GHG–emitting countries in a global climate agreement. The Bush administration has made the United States a signatory to the Bali road map adopted at the United Nations (UN) Climate Conference at Bali, Indonesia. Although these are welcomed announcements, history and the Bush administration's adherence to neoliberal environmental skepticism warrants caution about assigning any seriousness to these proposals.

The Bush administration's strategy toward addressing climate change is based largely in market mechanisms, including cap and trade markets, tax policy, and government-subsidized research. With the creation of cap and trade markets, polluters have the incentive to decrease their emissions through technological innovation in order to sell their allotted credits they do not consume. Tax policy is geared toward consumers who purchase high-efficiency products. Research and development subsidized by the government help in creating alternative energy technologies, making these technologies competitive in the market (Jaeger 2005). It should be noted that even though these policies are considered market mechanisms, they ultimately require government involvement. This fact implies that it is difficult to retain the purity of the neoliberal worldview when discussing effective environmental policy.

Given the rejection of the Kyoto Protocol, it is clear that the economic interest of the United States is currently trumping international consensus on climate change. There are two principal reasons for this occurrence. First, the United States contains a powerful energy lobby that works to have its interests realized as the national interest. Second, the built environment (artificial surroundings) of the United States is energy intensive and geographically expansive. For example, there are 17.2 million miles of roads in the world. The United States possesses 3.9 million miles, accounting for over 22 percent of the global total (IRF 2002). The United States relies heavily on long-haul trucking, an inefficient automobile-based transportation sector, and the promotion of suburban sprawl to increase property valuations.

The United States is the largest consumer of energy on the planet. In 2003, the United States consumed 2,280,881 thousand tons of oil equivalents (ktoe) of energy. World consumption of energy was 10,571,717 ktoe (IEA 2006). The United States consumes roughly 21.5 percent of the world's total energy use. This is a striking fact given that the United States population accounts for less than 5 percent of the global total.

Considering the realities of its energy-intensive economy, the United States is currently rejecting any global leadership role toward addressing climate change. The rejection of the Kyoto Protocol, coupled with the environmental skepticism of the neoliberal worldview, implies that the United States is choosing to disengage from the global consensus regarding climate change. The disengagement of the United States could be problematic for the future stability of globalization. Liberal institutionalists are concerned with this possibility, leading us into their view concerning the appropriate role for the United States concerning climate change.

The Liberal Institutionalist View

Liberal institutionalists argue that neoliberal environmental skepticism is unwarranted. Citing Intergovernmental Panel on Climate Change reports and findings of the national science foundations of many developed countries, liberal institutionalists contend that there is scientific consensus on climate change. They are troubled by what they see as a lack of climate change policy in the United States. They are further troubled by the view of the Bush administration that since bureaucrats and most government scientists work for the executive branch of government, it is their duty to be loyal to the views of the executive in power. It is argued that with such loyalty, environmental policy is suppressed and limited to the views and interests of the Bush administration.

Liberal institutionalists argue that global environmental problems such as climate change offer an opportunity for the

United States to exert a leadership role in the global system. Similar to Al Gore's proposed environmental "Marshall Plan" (see chapter 2), Lester Brown of the World Watch Institute calls on the United States to take the lead in transforming the global economy into a sustainable framework to address environmental problems. Brown believes the global economy is a "bubble" that is feeding off of Earth's natural assets. This bubble, if not gradually deflated through effective policy, will eventually lead to a collapse of the global system, effectively ending globalization (Brown 2003). Brown cites climate change, soil erosion, deteriorating rangelands, collapsing fisheries, and falling water tables as signs of human activities transgressing Earth's natural carrying capacity.

Brown calls for an economic and social "Plan B" in which the United States must take the lead with a "wartime mobilization" similar in scale to the planning of World War II (Brown 2003, 205). The Plan B that Brown announced would include adopting realistic prices for limited and exhaustible resources. Plan B also calls for limiting the global consumption of beef and pork, which would be substituted with farmed fish and poultry (Brown 2003, 138–139). Plan B would transform the global economy into a hydrogen-fueled operation complemented by other alternative energy sources such as wind and solar power. Brown estimates that Plan B would cut global CO_2 emissions in half (Brown 2003, 153).

Brown's argument is similar to those of ecological economists. He argues that the global system is in trouble because humans are living off of the unsustainable depletion of Earth's natural resources. Brown believes in markets but argues that markets must be honest in pricing the Earth's natural capital and the ecological services (water filtration, forests protecting soil from erosion, extracting CO_2 from the air, etc.) it provides. Brown is optimistic that if countries of the world were to act, the transition to Plan B could take place. He notes, however, that for now the world does not possess the necessary leadership, given that the United States still focuses on its interests in the form of economic growth and military security.

Of course, not all liberal institutionalists have such a dramatic policy proposal for globalization intended to prevent the collapse of the global system itself. What liberal institutionalists do agree on is the need for international cooperation and institutional mechanisms to address global environmental problems such as climate change. The next section focuses on critical arguments regarding the role of the United States and global environmental problems.

The Critic's View

The critical worldview contends that the skepticism of the United States in global environmental policy formation is not surprising. To the critics, this skepticism is quite logical given the capitalist assumptions under which the United States and the globalization process operate. Critics argue that the neoliberal control of the environmental policy agenda of the United States is derived from the capitalist logic to expand the economy. In expanding the economy it is rational to provide as little interference as possible to increase the rate of profit and economic growth. The frustrations expressed by liberal institutionalists are derived from their disagreement that short-term economic concerns should be allowed to trump long-term environmental integrity. Critics do not accept the notion that capitalism can be reformed into an eco-friendly mode. Capitalism, with its need to accumulate or grow to achieve its primary goal of profits is at odds with the natural environment. Natural assets have yet to be replaced by technological innovation in providing the basic materials necessary for economic growth. According to critics, capitalism created global environmental problems. So long as economic globalization is pursued with capitalist logic, environmental degradation will continue on a global scale.

A good representation of this view comes from John Bellamy Foster, a Marxist sociologist and editor of *The Monthly Review*. Bellamy Foster argues that nobody should be surprised or shocked that the United States has rejected the Kyoto Protocol given that the United States is the largest emitter of GHGs. Operating under capitalist rationality, the country realizes that it cannot reduce these emissions without harming its energy-intensive economy (Foster 2002, 16). Foster's argument contends that so long as the economic goals of the United States are focused on short-term wealth accumulation, concern for long-term environmental health will not be realized.

Economic growth has yet to be de-linked from increases in GHGs even though technological advances have made economic production less energy intensive. Foster argues that since the basic assumptions of capitalist logic are not challenged by neoliberals or liberal institutionalists, they are limited to technological fixes and programs of capitalist regulation and reformation. These solutions do not address the underlying causes of environmental degradation. Market-based solutions to environmental problems reward polluters whereas reliance on future technologies that do not yet exist make the capitalist global system reliant on science fiction for its survival. In short, the built environment of global monopoly capitalism and the need to reproduce it through expansion has created an irreversible global environmental crisis (Foster 2002, 102).

Foster offers the interesting view that the neoliberal logic the United States is pursuing with regard to climate change is quite rational given the context of the capitalist goal of short-term profiteering. Operating under the framework of short-term profitability, the United States realizes that it must protect its competitive advantage against world competitors—and it is currently retaining its competitive advantage, in part, through insufficiently addressing the challenge of climate change.

Another critic, the late Murray Bookchin, offers a bleak assessment for the future of the global environment. Bookchin argues that human society operates under hierarchical social relationships. This, to Bookchin, is an unnatural process invented by humans that does not correspond to the workings of nature. Hierarchy is absent from the science of ecology. Nature is characterized by complex interdependencies between systems with no hierarchical order. Human civilizations are rigid organizations of ordered society based in power differentials among unequal people. Environmental destruction, in short, is caused by the application of unnatural hierarchic social relations to the natural world (Bookchin 1998, 422–423). Bookchin's observations contend that the global system is a hierarchical human construct whose essence destroys the environment. So long as the globalization process under United States leadership operates under hierarchical assumptions, the global environment will be imperiled.

In conclusion, the United States is currently pursuing the neoliberal worldview when it comes to global environmental problems such as climate change. Although this is the case, it is also true that public awareness of climate change has grown in the United States. Public opinion polls suggest that the majority of Americans support government action to diminish the dangers of climate change. According to an ABC News/*Washington Post*/Stanford University public opinion poll taken in April 2007, 70 percent of United States citizens stated that they believed their government should do more to address climate change (Polling Report 2007).

The Democratic Congress, achieved in the elections in 2006, has also begun hearings on the dangers of climate change. This being the case, however, it is unclear, and uncertain, what policy the United States will adopt toward climate change given its economic interests and its neoliberal-inspired policy agenda. It is possible that neoliberal environmental skepticism will remain dominant as economic concerns in the United States dictate its willingness to implement environmental policy. It is also possible that a Democratic Congress coupled with supportive public opinion may make the United States more open to international agreements such as the Kyoto Protocol. Unfortunately, it may also be the case that the future will be characterized by continual environmental degradation produced through the capitalist global system. Nobody knows what the future will hold, but in the era of globalization, pressing environmental problems will likely worsen while this dimension of globalization remains subject to controversy and uncertainty.

Global Security and the United States Military

The United States is the uncontested global military hegemon. It controls the oceans, operates a worldwide network of military bases, and possesses the most technologically advanced military on the planet. In recent years, the inclusion of outer space as a realm necessary to achieve "full-spectrum dominance" has gained in importance and controversy. The next section assesses the role of the United States military in the globalization process as seen through the globalization worldviews. The United States is currently pursuing a hawkish strategy of international relations based on explicit unilateralism, zero-sum definitions of power, and use of military power to achieve its objectives within the global system.

This discussion shows that neoliberals and liberal institutionalists believe the role of the United States military is vital in the maintenance of economic globalization. Conversely, critics are opposed to the use of the United States military in economic globalization.

Basic Facts on the United States Military and Globalization

Before assessing the role of the United States military in globalization it is necessary to provide some relevant data. The United States military operates 737 military bases in 130 countries (DOD 2005). The US military employs 1,840,062 military personnel (Johnson 2006, 140). This number does not include an additional 473,306 Department of Defense (DOD) civil servants who work to formulate and implement United States defense policy (Johnson 2006, 140). The official Pentagon (DOD) budget in 2007 was $439.3 billion USDs, although supplemental costs for the wars and occupations in Afghanistan and Iraq make the actual defense budget much higher. Although the costs of these ongoing operations are ultimately unknown and debatable, a study by Joseph Stiglitz and Linda Bilmes estimates that the Iraq war alone has already incurred a cost of $2 trillion USDs (Bilmes and Stiglitz 2006). Additional defense expenditures incurred from the Bush administration's proposed ballistic missile defense system is estimated to cost $1.2 trillion USDs.

The defense expenditures of the United States outweigh the defense spending by the rest of the world combined (see chapter 6 for a detailed account of defense spending by the United States as well as spending by other countries). The United States has not been reluctant in using its massive military power to achieve its interests. According to William Blum, "From 1945 to 2003, the United States attempted to overthrow more than 40 foreign governments, and to crush more than 30 populist-nationalist movements" (Blum 2004, 392).

Such defense spending by the United States was justified during the Cold War as a necessary cost to contain communism. With the collapse of the Soviet Union, the defense expenditures of the United States decreased under George H. W. Bush and Clinton administrations. During the George H. W. Bush administration's four years in office, defense spending decreased 4 percent per year. During the Clinton administration defense spending decreased by almost 10 percent over seven years, a per capita decline from \$1,034 per person in 1993 to \$871 in 1999 (Korb 2000; Burnham and Long 2001). Although defense expenditures decreased during this time, the United States maintained a large defense establishment and continued a military strategy based on global military hegemony.

After the terrorist attacks on 9/11, however, the Bush administration increased defense expenditures to levels not seen since the Cold War. The need for such defense spending by the United States is interpreted differently by globalization worldviews. The next section of the chapter takes a look at the foreign policy strategy of the Bush White House.

The Foreign Policy of the Bush Administration

Within the Bush administration and much of the Republican Party, economic neoliberals have embraced a hawkish (willingness to use force) view of international relations. This section explains this view and how it is realized in the global security policy of the United States. It must be noted, however, that not all economic neoliberals support hawkish security policy. In fact, some neoliberals, or advocates of free markets, do not believe the United States should maintain a large military establishment at all. This neoliberal view argues that freedom requires peaceful social relations. This being the case, however, most neoliberals do support the use of the United States military to protect private property and global economic markets.

Hawkish foreign policy relies on political philosophies that are a throwback to a unitary executive, akin to monarchism. Foreign policy hawks believe in a unitary executive unencumbered by democratic processes, possessing powers similar to those once held by monarchs. Influenced by the political philosopher Carl Schmitt, they argue that a competent executive requires a strong, unencumbered sovereign who must "decide the exception" without having to worry about political disagreement (Schmitt 2005, 5). Foreign policy hawks argue that democracy, pluralism, and governmental checks and balances put undue requirements on the executive in maximizing national security. When President George W. Bush proclaimed on April 18, 2006, that he is the "decider" concerning the future of then Secretary of Defense Donald Rumsfeld, he was invoking the view of the unitary executive.

Recent arguments based on the idea of the unitary executive are set in the belief that the presidency of the United States should be free from congressional meddling in matters of foreign policy, especially in a time of war. The war on terrorism waged against "radical Islamists" or "Islamic fascists" is justified by the Bush administration to necessitate a unitary executive. Alberto Gonzalez, former attorney general of the Bush administration and White House legal counsel John Yoo have written legal opinions supporting this notion. They argued that the president should not be liable to international law such as the Geneva Conventions and assert that United States history shows that executive power transcends the will of Congress in times of war.

This is important when considering globalization because the idea of the unitary executive relates not only to an all-powerful leader executive within a country but also to the global system and the trajectory of globalization. Foreign policy hawks in the United States believe the nation must be willing to act as it wishes, defining the nature of the global system. This group argues that in the era of globalization, the United States is the legitimate unitary executive to shape the trajectory of globalization according to its interests. The United States is to be free from restraints created by the interests of other countries. This idea is expressed clearly in the Bush Doctrine, announced as the National Security Strategy of the United States (NSSUS) in 2002.

The NSSUS: The United States as Global Unitary Executive

The NSSUS of 2002 informed the world that the global system would take a design focused on the interests of the United States. This design is to be enforced through military action at the country's choosing. Although the principles laid out in the NSSUS have always been present in United States foreign policy (i.e., unilateralism and preemptive conflict to diminish potential future threats), these principles had been implied rather than explicitly stated. President George W. Bush stated explicitly that the United States is undertaking a global conflict of undetermined spatial and temporal dimensions. Countries across the globe have the choice of either being "with us or against us in the fight against terror." Further, all countries need to know that "they will be held accountable for inactivity" (Bush 2001a).

The NSSUS of 2002 defines the nature of United States power as being based on cooperation with other countries.

However, this cooperation is defined largely as obedience and deference to the interests and actions of the United States. The NSSUS explicitly states that it is a priority of the United States to stop the rise of any potential rivalry to its hegemony (i.e., China or an independent European Union security regime) (NSSUS 2002, 30). Under this concept, the United States puts itself at odds with other countries when dissent from its interests is not accepted as being a legitimate talking point of diplomatic negotiation. To achieve these ends, the United States intends to project its military and economic power broadly, rewarding those who submit to its will and punishing those who do not.

The NSSUS of 2002 was an announcement to the world that according to the United States, the global system has changed, requiring a dramatic alteration in U.S. foreign policy. This alteration requires an increased willingness to use military power preemptively or to attack potential threats before they actually become a danger (NSSUS 2002, 15). The doctrine of preemption states that the danger of inaction in light of potential threats requires the United States to go on a global offensive to maintain its security. Further, the NSSUS announced to the world that the United States did not consider the International Criminal Court to be legitimate and would not be subject to any criminal findings by this body (NSSUS 2002, 31).

The NSSUS is an interesting policy paper because it speaks much of cooperation and consensus as being central to the power of the United States. However, the interpretation of what consensus means within the document is clearly geared toward other countries allying their interests to those of the United States. This document does not express an equal partnership of global interests but the hegemonic interests of the United States as the legitimate global interest. In the era of globalization, the NSSUS states quite clearly that the United States reserves the right to define the security of the global system to fit its own interests.

The NSSUS was updated in 2006, restating many of the basic principles in the 2002 document. The strategy promotes the expansion of democracy and free markets to be led by the United States. The 2006 NSSUS is very idealistic in its tone, focusing on the United States' mission to end tyranny in the promotion of freedom. The document is controversial, however, for it equates the interests of the United States with the interests of the entire global system itself.

The NSSUS in Action: The Iraq War

The invasion of Iraq in March 2003 was a statement to the world that the NSSUS was not just talking points but a course of action. To prosecute Operation Iraqi Freedom, the United States relied on what it called the "coalition of the willing"—consisting primarily of many small countries that approved of the United States' actions but offered little in material support in the form of troops and funding to pay for the conflict. Britain offered the most support by taking responsibility for invading and occupying southern Iraq. Spain, an initial ally, broke from the coalition of the willing after the Madrid train bombings on March 11, 2004, compelled the Spanish people to vote out the government of Prime Minister José María Aznar.

It should be noted that many allies in the coalition of the willing were allied without the consent of the population of these countries. Although many countries became participants of the invasion of Iraq, their citizens did not necessarily agree with these actions (Chomsky 2003, 131).

In the case of Operation Iraqi Freedom, the United States disregarded international consensus provided through multilateral institutions such as the UN and the North American Treaty Organizaiton (NATO). Rather than operating within international structures designed to complement and ensure the global power of the United States, the United States chose to announce a change in the rules of the global system itself.

It is widely believed that the invasion and occupation of Iraq is based on a foreign policy strategy intended to acquire and control a vital natural resource: oil. This idea is derived from evidence found in past United States foreign policy documents. For example, United States National Security Council (USNSC) resolution 5401 of 1953 makes clear that it is the geo-strategic aim of the United States "to keep the sources of oil in the Middle East in American hands" (USNSC 1953, 5401). The resource war theory is also evidenced by the Carter doctrine of 1980 in which the United States announced,

> An attempt by any outside force to gain control of the Persian Gulf region will be regarded as assault on the vital interests of the United States. It will be repelled by any means necessary, including military force. (United States National Security Council–63 1981)

The United States relies mostly on foreign oil from sources other than those in the Middle East. However, the invasion and occupation of Iraq has less to do with the consumption of Iraqi oil than the issue of who controls and profits from the second-largest known oil supply on Earth. Admittedly, however, there is much disagreement over the intentions of the United States in invading and occupying Iraq.

It has been argued the invasion of Iraq was intended to strengthen the economic position of the United States in light of "peak oil." Peak oil is a theory first proposed by M. King Hubbert who argued that eventually global oil supplies would peak and then decline. Hubbert correctly predicted that oil production in the United States would peak in the 1970s. He and other peak oil theorists argue that global oil production will peak sometime in the early to mid-21st century. The decrease in oil production coupled with rising global demand will cause rising prices and political instability, including war (Leggett 2005).

Other reasons have been given to explain why the United States invaded Iraq. For instance, it has been argued that the invasion was to defend the supremacy of the USD as the medium of exchange for global oil markets (Sharma, Tracy, and Kumar 2004). To further complicate matters, two prominent realist international relations scholars argue that the United States went to war in Iraq, in part, due to pressure from lobbyists representing influential political factions in Israel (Mearsheimer and Walt 2007).

It is unclear what policy planners had in mind when contemplating the invasion of Iraq. It is likely that control of Iraqi oil reserves was a major consideration. This assumption is supported by basic reasoning of mainstream realist theories of international relations, which inform us that countries do not readily expend vital resources such as lives and revenue for reasons other than national security and power. Although this premise is not openly espoused in polite conversation or by major media outlets, the quest for power currently guides the concept of national security.

Many realist theorists, however, reject the Bush administration's interpretation of realpolitik. They argue that the current foreign policy strategy of the United States is hurting the global interests of the United States. Two such views by leading realist international relations theorists, Kenneth Waltz and Stephen Walt, can be heard online in interviews conducted by the University of California Television webcast series, *Conversations with History.* Chapter 8 offers information on this series that contains many instructive interviews by experts on the topic of globalization.

In conclusion, the hawkish view expressed through the NSSUS focuses on the unilateral power of the United States. This power is to be projected to achieve the country's interests in the era of globalization. The NSSUS is based in realpolitik, or power politics, stating that the United States must rely on "self-help" to achieve its interests. These interests are to be pursued even if other countries disagree with the strategies employed. The foreign policy of the United States in the era of globalization is currently unilateralist in nature, seeing the globalization process as a reflection of its interests. The controversial nature of the Bush administration's security strategy leads us into the liberal institutionalist view of the role of the United States military in the era of globalization.

The Liberal Institutionalist View

Liberal institutionalists believe that international cooperation and consensus in matters of security are necessary in the era of globalization. They reject the Bush doctrine, stating that an aggressive security stance diminishes the chances that globalization will continue without instability and unnecessary disruptions. Liberal institutionalists note that immediately after the terror attacks of 9/11 the world expressed great sympathy for the United States. The attacks gave the United States a chance to unite the world against global terrorism, and most countries supported the United States' initial attack against the Taliban in Afghanistan. In just a few years, however, world sympathy had turned to scorn and distrust as the United States rejected international consensus in favor of a unilateral security posture with the invasion and occupation of Iraq. There are now serious contradictions between liberal institutionalist understandings of global security and United States foreign policy guided by assumptions held by foreign policy hawks. If the future shows that liberal institutionalists are correct, the role of the United States in all dimensions of globalization is uncertain.

Liberal institutionalists contend that rather than relying exclusively on hard power, or economic and military power, the United States must endorse, uphold, and adhere to international norms and rules. As described in chapter 2, Joseph Nye has labeled this "soft power," in which countries ally themselves with the United States not from coercion and threat but from a belief that their security interests are aligned with those of the United States. Nye argues that United States military power is central in holding the global system together, but without soft power, globalization can transform into a process that dilutes American power rather than reinforcing it (Nye 2002, 91).

Zbigniew Brzezinski, the former national security advisor to U.S. President Jimmy Carter, stated in 2007 that the global position of the United States was imperiled due to the hawkish unilateralism of the Bush administration. Speaking before the United States Senate Foreign Relations Committee, Brzezinski stated, "The war in Iraq is a historic, strategic, and moral calamity . . . one should note here that practically no other country in the world shares the Manichean delusions that the [Bush] Administration so passionately articulates" (Brzezinski 2007, 1).

It should be recognized that liberal institutionalists are not pacifists, nor do they reject the use of hard power by the United States. In fact, many liberal institutionalists are quite hawkish themselves. To the liberal institutionalist, military intervention is acceptable if sufficient international consensus can be achieved. This consensus can be attained by gaining approval from UN resolutions or from the willing participation of security regimes such as NATO. An interesting case in point reflecting sufficient consensus can be found in the United States' bombing of Serbia in 1999. The United States sidestepped the UN and used NATO as sufficient international consensus regarding the legitimacy of using force against Serbia. Similar to the invasion of Iraq in 2003, the United States was unable to get UN Security Council approval to bomb Serbia for its crackdown on civil disorder in Kosovo. International consensus does not mean that all countries have to agree with the United States, but powerful countries should be supportive if hard power is to be successfully employed.

Liberal institutionalists argue that if globalization is to continue under United States leadership, the foreign policy of the United States must be formulated and implemented with care. Those holding liberal beliefs rely on many realist concepts of international relations, including collective security, hegemonic stability, hegemonic decline, and deterrence. All of these concepts are interrelated—that is, one leads to another in a logical fashion. For instance, liberal institutionalists argue that the aggressive unilateral stance of the Bush administration destabilizes global security. This destabilization encourages other countries to pursue collective security strategies against the United States through the formation of collective security alliances. When such alliances are formed against the United State, its hegemony is threatened, creating a vicious cycle in the form of a security dilemma. This vicious cycle creates a condition in which the United States becomes less safe than it was prior to its effort to achieve its security interests unilaterally. Liberal institutionalists argue that this ever-increasing security dilemma forces the United States to spend more on security as it continually becomes less secure. As this process continues, the United States could overextend itself militarily and economically, leading to its eventual decline as a hegemonic power.

Thomas Barnett's *The Pentagon's New Map* is a good example of liberal institutionalist thinking in the dimension of global security. Barnett proposes that globalization consists of a Core that operates under international consensus, or a rule set. The Core consists of an "old Core" and a "new Core." The old Core includes Europe, North America, and Japan. The new Core is made up of China, India, Russia, Brazil, South Korea, and much of South America (Barnett 2004, 55). Opposed to this Core is the "Gap," or countries that are not sufficiently integrated within the networks of globalization. The Gap is composed of much of the developing world, including countries in Central and South America, Africa, Central Asia, the Middle East, and Southeast Asia. Barnett argues that human misery in the Gap is no surprise given that those living in the Gap are unable to enjoy the benefits derived from the Core's rule sets governing globalization. Those living in the Gap suffer from oppressive forms of government, not enjoying the benefits of modern liberal democracy. Barnett argues that in the era of globalization, the United States military should be used to integrate the Gap into the Core. This is achieved by defending and spreading global consensus found in globalization rule sets that result in a peaceful world with less misery (Barnett 2004, 383).

Liberal institutionalists support United States leadership in securing the global system. They argue, however, that the United States must work with other countries in a cooperative fashion. It cannot achieve these goals alone. This leads us to the critical view of the United States' role in global security. Critics argue that the country is selfishly pursuing its security interests under the guise of global security interests.

The Critic's View

The role played by the United States in global security is controversial. Critics argue the United States' posture as global military hegemon is not a rational or proper policy for the nation to pursue. This view is based on and informed by reflection on the disastrous conflicts that characterized the 20th century. In the era of globalization, all-out conflict among advanced industrial countries would end civilization as we know it. It is with this thought in mind that many scholars reject the utility of warfare and continuous preparations for it. The critics presented here point out that in the era of globalization, the strategy of achieving the interests of countries through military means does not stand up to cost-benefit analysis. Human history, critics admit, often shows that violence has utility, even in the promotion of injustice and domination. In the era of globalization, however, this idea may be out of date and a reconsideration of what constitutes national security may be necessary.

It is true that critical viewpoints regarding warfare often do not go beyond academic concerns or activist circles. These ideas are often dismissed as idealistic, unrealistic, and radical. Given that this is the case, such ideas can be left out of public policy formation since they rarely enter policy debate. Students of globalization must be aware of critical arguments and consider them on their merit. Critical viewpoints may be necessary to help prevent the use of destructive forces that humans can unleash upon one another.

The first critic of the role of the United States in the globalization of security is Gabriel Kolko. In his book, *Another Century of War?* Kolko argues that in the era of globalization the United States is the only nation-state with the political ambition backed by economic and military power to shape the world as it sees fit. The United States sees the world's interest as its interests; they are one and the same (Kolko 2002, 109). Kolko believes, however, that this ambition is destined to fail. He points out that the United States maintained a militarist economic and political posture throughout the Cold War to defeat communism, yet now that communism is largely extinct, the country finds itself as insecure as ever (Kolko 2002, 138). Further, the ambitions of the United States are beginning to "exceed its military, political, and moral resources for attaining them" (Kolko 2002, 140).

The United States, Kolko recommends, must realize the limits to its power in the 21st century or suffer the consequences of previous hegemons. The foreign policy of the United States, which is based on hard power, has been counterproductive, being an irrational policy that has produced more problems than it has solved. The reliance on hard power is not likely to change in the near future, for both Republicans and Democrats have failed to understand the long-term consequences that the ideology of warfare has brought to the world (Kolko 2002, 104). Kolko sums up his argument, "A foreign policy that is both immoral and unsuccessful is not simply stupid, it is increasingly dangerous to those who practice or favor it" (Kolko 2002, 138).

In 2000, Chalmers Johnson published the book, *Blowback.* Blowback is the Central Intelligence Agency term that "refers to the unintended consequences of policies that we kept secret from the American people" (Johnson 2000, 8). Blowback refers to violence directed at the United States and its global interests due to past policy that has made the United States many enemies. The year after *Blowback* was published, the terrorist attacks on 9/11 unfolded, and this book became a best seller.

In 2006, Johnson published *Nemesis, the Last Days of the American Republic.* Using a metaphor from ancient Greek mythology, he argues that the hubris the United States possesses and its reliance on hard power has brought the nation to a point that it will be punished by the Greek goddess Nemesis—the goddess of retribution who punishes those who become arrogantly unjust and reliant on domination. Johnson argues that the United States has been arrogantly militaristic in the expansion of its power in the post–World War II era. This militarism has led to a global empire that is now overextended and faltering. To save the global empire, the United States is being forced to give up the republican values on which it was founded.

Similar to Rome, the United States is evolving from a republic to an empire. Republics are based in popular representation, constitutional restraints on government power, and a balance of power realized through separate branches of government. Empires are governed by an unrestrained dictatorial executive. Johnson states that the United States can have a republic or an empire, but it cannot have both. The need to maintain empire erodes constitutional republican principles until they become mere shells of their former selves (Johnson 2006, 88). To Johnson, the United States was able to build a world empire by maintaining a constitutional republic at home while using its military abroad. Now that the United States has overextended itself and is facing repercussions of its past foreign policy, the constitutional republic will be replaced by an executive dictatorship that is necessary to maintain its global reach. Johnson is not optimistic about the future prospects of the United States and the world. If he is correct, the future of globalization will be one of conflict and strife, when a declining United States hegemon unleashes its military power in a futile attempt to maintain its global power.

Noam Chomsky, a longtime critic of United States foreign policy, published *Hegemony or Survival* in 2003. Chomsky, like Johnson, offers a bleak future for humanity. He argues that the ideology and policy framework of elites in the United States endanger the global system. This danger lies in the all-consuming quest for power as hegemonic power. Chomsky argues that the United States has no intention of giving up its hegemonic power and will fight for it at all costs. This has led the country to take the lead in the militarization of space, where enemies and potential rivals could be attacked by nuclear weapons without warning. This plan is laid out in *The Space Command Vision for 2020*, a policy paper written during the Clinton administration. *The Space Command Vision for 2020* spells out the strategy for the United States military to dominate outer space to attain "full spectrum dominance." This means the United States intends to control the land, sea, and now outer space—a strategy intended to protect U.S. interests and investments.

Chomsky notes that the United States intends to use its military to protect economic globalization (Chomsky 2003, 229). He argues that the United States is aware that economic globalization will produce "haves" and "have nots." Policy elites in the United States understand that they must prepare to crush the expected rise in resistance and opposition to economic globalization. The crushing of this resistance will be rationalized with noble intentions, just as prior powers have done in legitimizing their colonizing projects (Chomsky 2003, 230–231).

Chomsky's idea, when applied to the arguments put forth by Thomas P. M. Barnett, have much to say about the controversy that exists in the role of the United States military in the era of globalization. The United States is currently pursuing a hawkish foreign policy it declares is necessary to face security challenges to the globalization process. It remains to be seen to what extent the United States is willing to rely on force to maintain its dominance of the global system.

Conclusion

The role of the United States in the globalization process and the current global system is a contentious one. This country designed the global system and set the current trajectory of globalization with its own interests in mind. In the current era of globalization however, the interpretation of what constitutes the global interests of the United States is in dispute.

The research conducted by the authors of this book leads us to believe that the future prospects for globalization under its current form are uncertain, but likely dim. Given the problems associated with globalization in the dimensions of the economy, the environment, and security, it is likely the future will be characterized by conflict and resistance to processes and problems associated with globalization. It is yet to be seen how each worldview will impact the future trajectory of globalization and which one is most correct in explanatory power. Will globalization stabilize itself under free markets as neoliberals assume? Will liberal institutionalists gain an upper hand in advising policy makers and setting the globalization agenda? Will the warnings of critics come to pass? Only time will tell.

References

Barnett, Thomas P. M. 2004. *The Pentagon's New Map. War and Peace in the Twenty-First Century.* New York: G.P. Putnam's Sons.

Bellamy Foster, John. 2002. *Ecology against Capitalism.* New York: Monthly Review Press.

Bilmes, Linda, and Joseph Stiglitz. 2006. "The Economic Costs of the Iraq War: An Appraisal Three Years after the Beginning of the Conflict." National Bureau of Economic Research Working Paper 12054, February. Available online at www2.gsb.columbia.edu/faculty/jstiglitz/download/2006_Cost_of_War_in_Iraq_NBER.pdf (accessed March 15, 2007).

Blum, William. 2004. *Killing Hope. U.S. Military and C.I.A. Interventions since World War II.* Monroe, ME: Common Courage Press.

Bookchin, Murray. 1998. "Society and Ecology." In *Debating the Earth. The Environmental Politics Reader,* edited by John S. Dryzek and David Schlosberg, 415–428. New York: Oxford University Press.

Borenstein, Seth. 2004. "Environment Worsened under Bush in Many Key Areas, Data Show." Knight-Ridder. October 13. Available online at www.commondreams.org/headlines04/1013-12.htm (accessed March 20, 2008).

Brown, Lester R. 2003. *Plan B: Rescuing a Planet Under Stress and a Civilization in Trouble.* Earth Policy Institute. New York: W.W. Norton.

Burnham, David, and Susan Long. 2001. "The Clinton Era by the Numbers." *The Nation.* January 29.

Brzezinski, Zbigniew. 2007. Senate Foreign Relations Committee Testimony. February 1. Available online at www.senate.gov/~foreign/testimony/2007/BrzezinskiTestimony070201.pdf (accessed March 20, 2008).

Bush, George W. 2001a. "President Welcomes President Chirac to the White House." Office of the Press Secretary. November 6. Available online at www.whitehouse.gov/news/releases/2001/11/20011106–4.html (accessed May 10, 2007).

Bush, George W. 2001b. "Text of a Letter from the President to Senators Hagel, Helms, Craig, and Roberts." White House Press Release. Office of the Press Secretary, March 13. Available online at www.whitehouse.gov/news/releases/2001/03/print/20010314.html (accessed April 9, 2007).

Bush, George W. 2002. "President Announces Clear Skies and Global Climate Change Initiatives." Office of the Press Secretary. February 14.

Chomsky, Noam. 2003. *Hegemony or Survival. America's Quest for Global Dominance.* New York: Henry Holt.

Department of Defense (DOD), Office of the Deputy Undersecretary of Defense (Installations and Environment). 2005. *Base Structure Report.* Available online at www.defenselink.mil/pubs/20050527_2005BSR.pdf (accessed March 20, 2008).

Department of the Treasury, Federal Reserve Board (DOT, FRB). 2007. "Major Foreign Holders of Treasury Securities." Available online at www.ustreas.gov/tic/mfh.txt (accessed April 30, 2007).

Energy Information Agency (EIA). 2003. *International Energy Outlook, 2003.* Available online at www.eia.doe.gov/oiaf/1605/ggccebro/chapter1.html (accessed December 17, 2006).

Energy Information Administration (EIA). 2007. *All Countries Spot Price FOB Weighted by Estimated Export Volume (Dollars per Barrel).* Available online at tonto.eia.doe.gov/dnav/pet/hist/wtotworldw.htm (accessed January 2, 2008).

Friedman, Thomas L. 2000. *The Lexus and the Olive Tree.* New York: Anchor Books.

Friedman, Thomas L. 2005. *The Earth Is Flat. A Brief History of the Twenty-First Century.* New York: Farrar, Straus and Giroux.

Harris, Paul. 2003. "Bush Covers Up Climate Change. Whitehouse Officials Play Down Its Own Scientists' Evidence of Global Warming." *The Observer.* September 21.

Hartnett, Stephen J., and Laura A. Stengrim. 2006. *Globalization and Empire. The U.S. Invasion of Iraq, Free Markets, and the Twilight of Democracy.* Tuscaloosa: University of Alabama Press.

Held, David. 2005. "At the Global Crossroads: The End of the Washington Consensus and the Rise of Global Social Democracy?" *Globalizations* 2 (1): 95–113.

Held, David, et al. 2005. *Debating Globalization.* Cambridge, UK: Polity Press.

International Energy Agency (IEA), Statistics Division. 2006. *Energy Balances of OECD Countries (2006 edition)* and *Energy Balances of Non-OECD Countries (2006 edition).* Paris: IEA. Available online at data.iea.org/ieastore/default.asp (accessed December 15, 2007).

International Road Federation (IRF). 2002. *World Road Statistics 2002 on CD-ROM,* Table 1. Available online at www.irfnet.org/wrs.asp. Geneva, Switzerland: International Road Federation. (accessed December 23, 2007).

Jaeger, William K. 2005. *Environmental Economics for Tree Huggers and Other Skeptics.* Washington, DC: Island Press.

Johnson, Chalmers. 2000. *Blowback.* New York: Henry Holt.

Johnson, Chalmers. 2006. *Nemesis. The Last Days of the American Republic.* New York: Henry Holt.

Kolko, Gabriel. 2002. *Another Century of War?* New York: New Press.

Korb, Lawrence, et al. 2000. "Money for Nothing: A Penny Saved, Not a Penny Earned in the U.S. Military." *Foreign Affairs* 79 (2): March/April.

Leggett, Jeremy. 2005. *The Empty Tank. Oil, Gas, Hot Air, and the Coming Global Financial Catastrophe.* New York: Random House.

Mearsheimer, John J., and Stephen M. Walt. 2007. *The Israeli Lobby and U.S. Foreign Policy.* New York: Farrar, Straus and Giroux.

Moan, Jaina L., and Zachary A. Smith. 2005. "Bush and the Environment." In *A Bird in the Bush. Failed Policies of the George W. Bush Administration.* New York: Algora.

National Security Strategy of the United States of America (NSSUS). 2002. September. Available online at www.whitehouse.gov/nsc/nss.pdf (accessed March 20, 2008).

Nye, Joseph. 2002. *The Paradox of American Power. Why the World's Only Superpower Can't Go It Alone.* New York: Oxford University Press.

Palast, Greg. 2007. "John Perkins: Jerk, Conman, Shill." Available online at www.gregpalast.com/john-perkins-jerk-con-man-shill/ (accessed December 10, 2007).

Perkins, John. 2006. *Confessions of an Economic Hit Man.* London: Penguin Group.

Phillips, Kevin. 2006. *American Theocracy. The Peril and Politics of Radical Religion, Oil, and Borrowed Money in the 21st Century.* New York: Viking.

PollingReport.com. 2007. ABC News/Washington Post/Stanford University Poll. April 5–10. Available online at www.pollingreport.com/enviro.htm (accessed May 5, 2007).

Revkin, Andrew C., and Matthew L. Wald. 2007. "Material Shows Weakening of Climate Reports." *New York Times.* March 20.

Schmitt, Carl. 2005. *Political Theology. Four Chapters on the Concept of Sovereignty.* Chicago: University of Chicago Press, 5.

Sharma, Sohan, Sue Tracy, and Surinder Kumar. 2004. "The Invasion of Iraq: Dollar vs. Euro: Re-denominating Iraqi Oil in U.S. Dollars Instead of the Euro." *Z Magazine.* February.

Smith, Zachary A. 2004. *The Environmental Policy Paradox,* 4th ed. Upper Saddle River, NJ: Prentice Hall.

Stiglitz, Joseph. 2006. "Making Globalization Work. Economic Globalization Has Outpaced the Globalization of Politics and Mindsets—It's Time for Change." *The Guardian.* September 8.

Tabb, William K. 2004. *Economic Governance in the Age of Globalization.* New York: Columbia University Press.

United Nations Environmental Programme (UNEP). 2002. GRID-Arendal data. Available online at www.globalis.gvu.unu.edu/ 2002 (accessed December 10, 2006).

United States Department of State. 2006. International Information Programs (USINFO). "Confessions—or Fantasies—of an Economic Hitman?" Available online at usinfo.state.gov/media/Archive/2006/Feb/02–767147.html (accessed January 2, 2008).

United States National Security Council (USNSC). 1953. NSC–5401.

United States National Security Council (USNSC). 1981. NSC–63.

The White House. 2005. "Climate Change Fact Sheet" May 18. Available online at www.whitehouse.gov/news/releases/2005/05/20050518–4.html (accessed January 21, 2007).

World Bank, Development Data Group. 2007. *2007 World Development Indicators Online.* Washington, DC: World Bank. Available online at go.worldbank.org/3JU2HA60D0 (accessed December 18, 2007).

4

Chronology

This chapter offers a timeline that focuses on pivotal events related to globalization, exposing trends and anomalies in the development process. Globalization is a complex process that has been unfolding over the course of human history; consequently, this timeline cannot list all historical events related to globalization, but the events listed offer the reader a good starting point to understand the unfolding reality of globalization.

200,000 BCE Homo sapiens, or genetically modern humans, evolve from earlier forms of hominids in Africa and begin to increase in population through the successful use of tools in hunting and gathering survival strategies.

50,000 BCE Humans begin to displace other hominids and expand throughout Eurasia.

23,000 BCE The first humans cross from Asia into North America over the Bering Land Bridge—a large land mass between Russia and Alaska exposed due to lower ocean levels caused by an ice age.

3100– The Egyptian civilization arises with the unifica-
525 BCE tion of the Lower and Upper Nile River settlements. Humans begin the transformation from hunter–gatherer societies to the use of agriculture and domestication of animals.

3000– **1600** BCE	The Sumerian, Akkadian, and Babylonian civilizations arise between the Tigris and Euphrates rivers in what is now modern Iraq. The first writings by humans emerge in the form of Sumerian cuneiform.
3,000– **327** BCE	The Hittite, Assyrian, Medean, and Persian empires arise in the Middle East.
2000 BCE– **present**	China begins its nearly 4,000 years of history. Although many social, economic, and political transformations have transpired over this time, modern China can be said to represent a continuous and coherent historical evolution.
509–31 BCE	The Roman Republic arises, being the first civilization governed by separation of powers, checks and balances, and pluralist representation of diverse political interests. The United States Constitution is based on the ideals of the Roman Republic.
479–323 BCE	Hellenic Greek civilization appears. The Athenian Empire expands, controlling and influencing much of the land area surrounding the Mediterranean Sea.
323–31 BCE	Greek civilization reaches it peak and declines in the Hellenistic Age. Greek philosophy leads to modern mathematics (Pythagoras and Euclid), serving as the precursor to modern science and the use of systematic logical reasoning. Greek civilization culminates with the rise and fall of Alexander the Great's Macedonian Empire and the beginning of the Roman Empire.
31 BCE– **476** CE	The Roman Empire arises with the dissolution of the Roman Republic. The republican form of government is replaced by dictatorial executive power to administer an empire that stretches across the Mediterranean, Europe, North Africa, and the Middle East. The Roman Empire falls after decades of civil wars, its conversion to Christianity as official

state religion, and foreign invasions by Germanic tribes (the Visigoths and the Vandals).

250–900   The Mayan civilization is in its classical period. Located in Central America, the Mayans build a sophisticated civilization that made advances in architecture and writing. The Mayans also possess a sophisticated calendar utilizing astronomical observations. The reason for the collapse of the Mayan civilization is debated, but some archeologists believe that it is due to unsustainable agricultural practices leading to catastrophic environmental degradation (NASA 2004).

632–1362   The Arab Empire expands from the Middle East into Central Asia, North Africa, and southern Europe, including much of the Iberian Peninsula, which constitutes Portugal and Spain. The Arab Empire makes great advancements in literature, philosophy, medicine, and mathematics. The intellectual culture of the Arab Empire keeps the works of Aristotle alive, introducing his writings to Europe.

1000–1300   The historical period of the High Middle Ages provides the social, political, cultural, and economic foundations of Western Civilization. In this era, feudalism prevails as the dominant socioeconomic order. This era is characterized by the rise of towns, the first European monarchies, and the transition to an early form of capitalism.

1197–1592   The Incan Empire grows and expands, encompassing much of the territory that is now Peru. The Incan Empire falls due to a combination of civil war, conquest, and smallpox. The Spanish Conquest, undertaken by conquistadors Francisco Pizarro and Hernando De Soto, is central to the fall of the Incan Empire.

1271   Marco Polo, along with his father and uncle, sets out on the Silk Road to China. This wealthy merchant family spends the next 17 years with the Kublai

1271
(cont.)
Khan. This event represents one of the first documented accounts of international trade leading to cultural interaction between Asia and Europe.

1325–1521
The Aztec Empire rises in what is now central Mexico. Tenochtitlán, the Aztec capital, is on the site of modern Mexico City. The Aztec Empire falls with the conquest of Spanish conquistador Hernán Cortés.

1400–1520
Western Civilization revives classical thought with the Renaissance. Beginning in Italian city-states and spreading throughout Europe, the Renaissance revives Greek and Roman thought and culture leading to a flourishing in the arts and sciences. In this era the first nation-states form. Mercantilism emerges as the dominant economic strategy of the new European nation-states. The activities of modern finance also begin in Italian city-states.

1400–1600
The nation-state system solidifies as technological advancements in weaponry (such as the cannon and use of gunpowder) enable larger political units to overpower smaller political entities in Europe. In this era, decentralized political authority condenses into centralized nation-states ruled by absolute monarchs.

1492
Christopher Columbus sails west from Spain, landing in the Bahamas while looking for an oceanic trade route to India. This event begins the European conquest and colonization of the Western Hemisphere, having disastrous consequences for Mesoamerican civilizations and other native populations.

1498
Vasco de Gama sails around Africa and reaches India, discovering an oceanic trade route for the Portuguese. Only 54 out of an original 170 sailors return to Portugal in 1499.

1513   Niccolò Machiavelli publishes *The Prince*. Written as a strategy to maintain the power of the Medici family, *The Prince* serves as a template for modern political realism, disregarding moral concerns in favor of the rational pursuit of power. Political realists are concerned with the pursuit, preservation, and expansion of the power of nation-states.

1517   Martin Luther posts his Ninety-five Theses, documenting abuses of power within the Church of Rome. This event begins the religious reformation, giving rise to Protestantism. Max Weber, the great 19th-century sociologist, argues that the rise of the Protestant work ethic creates the social, cultural, and economic foundations of modern capitalism.

1519   Ferdinand Magellan, a Portuguese sailor, sets out to find an oceanic trade route to Asia for Spain. The desire to engage in the international trade of spices leads to the first circumnavigation of the globe by sea. The expedition returns to Spain in 1522 without Magellan, who dies in battle in the Philippines. Out of an original five ships with 270 sailors, only one ship returns with 18 sailors.

1530   Charles V unifies much of Europe under his rule forming the Hapsburg Empire. He abdicates his rule of the Hapsburg Empire in 1555, splitting much of continental Europe among his heirs. His son, Philip II, reigns over the Spanish Empire, enriching it through the extraction of precious metals from newly conquered lands in the Americas.

1607   The Jamestown Colony is founded by the Virginia Company of Great Britain. The intention of founding Jamestown is to find gold and an oceanic trade route to Asia.

1618–1648   The Thirty Years' War is fought, a European-wide conflict. The Thirty Years War involved Protestant nation-states versus Roman Catholic nation-states. The war ends with the signing of the Treaty of

Westphalia. This treaty begins the modern nation-state system, in which nation-state sovereignty is mutually recognized among European powers. The sovereignty of nation-states legitimizes spheres of influence, diplomacy, and agreements between nation-states.

1620   The Plymouth Colony is founded by the Pilgrims who land in what is now Massachusetts. They sail on the Mayflower across the Atlantic Ocean to escape religious persecution in Britain.

1651   Thomas Hobbes publishes *The Leviathan,* a political treatise emphasizing a mechanistic universe containing a humanity driven by fear and an unrelenting desire for power. Hobbes argues that a social contract is necessary to keep the lives within the political community from being "nasty, short, and brutish." Sovereign absolute monarchs, according to Hobbes, rule by divine right in executing the decrees of the social contract. This work influences modern political realism, which rejects theories focusing on human potential while observing how people actually act.

1687   Isaac Newton publishes *Mathematical Principles of Natural Philosophy.* This book is considered a monumental achievement of the scientific revolution in providing for the systematic and predictable investigation of the natural world.

1690   John Locke publishes *The Second Treatise on Civil Government,* which serves as a foundation of modern liberalism. Locke argues that property rights are central to political liberty and that a social contract devised among free men constitutes the legitimate sovereignty. Legitimate sovereignty, in turn, justifies the power of the nation-state. According to Locke, citizens of a free state based on private property rights can be self-governing.

1694   William Paterson founds the Bank of England. This bank employs fractional banking, creating and lending money to make a profit. Fractional banking is possible due to the fact that most depositors are unlikely to withdraw their savings at the same time. Although Italian city-states and the Dutch discovered fractional banking, it is Britain that first utilizes it as a primary tool of nation-state policy.

1750s   Britain begins its Industrial Revolution, a watershed event for human society. The Industrial Revolution replaces human and animal labor power with the use of machines, greatly increasing efficiency in economic production.

1765   James Watt improves the Newcomen steam engine, leading to a dramatic advance in mechanized production, which characterizes the Industrial Revolution.

1776   The Declaration of Independence is written by Thomas Jefferson and the American Revolution begins, leading to the formation of the United States of America. The Declaration of Independence is influenced by the political philosophy of John Locke.

Adam Smith publishes *The Wealth of Nations*, providing the theory of "the invisible hand" of the marketplace. Smith argues that individual acts found within market transactions serve the common good of society. His theory serves as the foundation of free market capitalism as promoted by neoliberals.

1789–1799   The French Revolution unfolds, shaking up the political world in Europe. The French Revolution is one of the most important events in political history due to its radical break from traditional forms of political and economic rule. The French Revolution leads to the demise of rule by landed aristocracy in France and to the empowerment of the middle class.

1799–1815	Napoleon Bonaparte attempts to unite Europe under the spirit of the French Revolution. He is defeated by allied European nation-states at Waterloo, Belgium, ending his plans that threatened traditional powers on the European continent.
1815	The Congress of Vienna is attended by European powers to settle interstate political problems in Europe. The Congress of Vienna is an early form of international institution building and diplomacy intended to maintain peace among European nation-states.
1848	Karl Marx and Frederick Engels publish *The Communist Manifesto,* arguing that the history of all society is that of class struggle. Marx and Engels predict that middle-class bourgeoisie rule will come to an end and a dictatorship of the proletariat will lead to the end of history as communism.
1864	The first Geneva Convention is signed, being the first international treaty codifying international humanitarian law.
1866	The first transatlantic telegraph cable is successfully laid, sending messages between Europe and North America. Although a transatlantic cable was previously attempted in 1858, it was largely unsuccessful, lacking in consistency and durability.
1867	Karl Marx publishes *Capital Volume 1. Capital* offers a critical view of classical political economy and serves as a foundation for future Marxist economic theories of imperialism.
1876	King Leopold I of Belgium hires Henry Morton Stanley to prospect the colonization of the Congo in Africa. The efforts to exploit the rubber trade lead to genocide in the Congo.
	Alexander Graham Bell is awarded a United States patent for the invention of the telephone. This

invention greatly increases the efficiency of communication between distant regions.

1914–1918   World War I begins when a Serbian nationalist assassinates Austrian Archduke Franz Ferdinand on June 28, 1914. The entrance of the United States into the war, coupled with the decline of British power, serves as the beginning of the United States' acquisition of the status of a global power. World War I ends with the Treaty of Versailles, whose harsh conditionalities help lead to the rise of fascism in Germany.

1917   The Bolshevik Revolution in Russia results in the formation of the Soviet Union. The Bolshevik leader Vladimir Lenin publishes *Imperialism, the Highest Stage of Capitalism* the same year, arguing that capitalist nation-states are compelled to extend economic activities beyond their borders. This expansion leads to competition and war.

1925   The Geneva Protocol bans the use of chemical weapons in warfare.

1929   The New York stock market crash leads to the Great Depression. The global economy experiences a rapid and massive deflation, jeopardizing global capitalism. The Great Depression causes political instability throughout the Western world and is not solved until the hostilities of World War II increase economic production through semi-command economies.

1933   The Nazis come to power in Germany under the dictatorship of Adolph Hitler. The rise of fascism represents a reactionary counterforce to the liberal ideals of the French Revolution. Fascism stresses allegiance to the nation-state over individual rights and promotes obedience to supreme executive power. Fascism also relies on the idea of national exceptionalism or the perceived right to expand political and economic power through violence.

1939–1945   World War II is fought between the Axis (Japan, Germany, Italy) and Allied (the United States, the Soviet Union, and Great Britain) powers. The conflict of fascism versus liberal democracy allied with authoritarian socialism ends with VE-Day in Europe and the dropping of nuclear bombs on Japan by the United States.

1944   The Allied Powers of World War II hold an economic conference in Bretton Woods, New Hampshire, to restore international trade and investment. The International Monetary Fund (IMF), the World Bank (WB), and the General Agreement on Tariffs and Trade (GATT) are created at the Bretton Woods Conference.

1945   Franklin D. Roosevelt, Winston Churchill, and Josef Stalin meet at Yalta on the Crimean Peninsula. This meeting ultimately divides the globe into spheres of influence under the United States and the Soviet Union.

The United Nations (UN) is founded to promote international dialogue and cooperation in matters concerning international law, security, economic development, and human rights.

1947   Led by Mahatma Gandhi and the philosophy of nonviolent resistance to colonial domination, Indian nationalists gain independence from Britain. This event ushers in the era of decolonization around the globe and the dismantling of the British Empire.

The Marshall Plan, named after U.S. General George Marshall, provides Europe with nearly $12 billion U.S. dollars (USDs) in aid to rebuild that continent's war-ravaged economies. The Marshall Plan is designed to be a conduit for finance and investment from the United States as well as a tool designed to pursue the anticommunist strategy of containment.

The UN adopts the Universal Declaration of Human Rights, which promotes comprehensive human rights for all nation-states to follow.

Britain pulls out of Palestine, ending the British Mandate for Palestine. Britain can no longer control this territory as resistance from both Jewish and Arab factions grows in the face of waning British power. The UN takes responsibility for the negotiated partition of the region.

The first Arab–Israeli war is fought. Israel captures most of the land the UN has set aside to be partitioned into a Palestinian nation-state.

1949   Chinese Communists led by Mao Zedong defeat Chiang Kai–Shek's nationalists. The People's Republic of China is created on October 1. The defeat of Chiang Kai–Shek is a setback to the interests of Western nation-states who ally themselves with the Chinese nationalists.

The North Atlantic Treaty Organization (NATO) is founded, creating a transatlantic alliance between the United States and West European nation-states. NATO is governed under the United States sphere of influence.

The Geneva Conventions are amended to include international rules concerning warfare, covering the treatment of prisoners of war and noncombatants.

The Soviet Union develops its first nuclear bomb. This development acts as a deterrent to the United States, leading to the Cold War reality of mutually assured destruction.

1950   North Korea invades South Korea. Under UN authority the United States and 16 of its allies send troops, halting the advance of the North Koreans. This begins over half a century of stalemated

1950 (cont.)	political tension between North Korea and the United States.
1953	The United States overthrows Mohammed Mossadegh, the democratically elected Prime Minister of Iran. The military coup, supported by the Central Intelligence Agency's (CIA's) Operation Ajax, successfully returns the Shah of Iran to power.
1954	The CIA overthrows the democratically elected government of President Jacobo Arbenz in Guatemala. Land reform undertaken by Arbenz is considered to be communist intrusion into the interests of the United States and the United Fruit Company, an agricultural multinational corporation based in the United States.
1955	The Warsaw Pact is founded, allying Eastern European nation-states under the sphere of influence of the Soviet Union.
1956	Egyptian leader Nasser takes control of the Suez Canal, which links the Mediterranean Sea with the Gulf of Suez. France, Britain, and Israel invade the Egyptian Sinai. The United States refuses to support its allies due to its interest in maintaining support among the oil-producing nation-states of the Middle East. The United States also disapproves of colonizing efforts by European nation-states in the Middle East, which it considers to be solely within its sphere of influence.
1958	Working for Texas Instruments, Jack Kilby invents the integrated circuit, or the first "computer chip." This invention leads to modern computers that transform the world, making globalization possible.
1960	The Organization of Petroleum Exporting Countries (OPEC) is founded. OPEC is created to pressure the foreign policy of Western nation-states toward Israel and to gain control over the price of

oil. OPEC member states set quotas on production to support the price of oil and to pursue their interests.

1961 The United States fails with its invasion of Cuba at the Bay of Pigs. The invasion is funded and planned by the CIA and perpetrated by Cuban exiles. The goal of the invasion is to overthrow the communist regime of Fidel Castro.

1962 The United States and the Soviet Union nearly come to a nuclear confrontation over the Soviet placement of nuclear missiles in Cuba. This event is known as the Cuban Missile Crisis.

1965 United States president Lyndon B. Johnson escalates the military involvement of the United States in Vietnam. This escalation takes place after more than a decade of support by the United States for French colonial interests. The United States and France are opposed by Vietminh nationalists led by Ho Chi Min.

1966 President of Indonesia Sukarno is ousted from power by General Suharto. Indonesia undergoes a purge of suspected communists, resulting in the deaths of 500,000 people. The CIA is instrumental in drawing up lists of names of suspected communists (Blum 2004, 194).

1967 The Six Day War ensues in the Middle East as Israel preempts Egyptian threats. Israel gains control of the Gaza Strip, the Sinai, the Golan Heights, and the West Bank. The Israeli victory persuades the United States to ally its interests to Israeli interests in the Middle East.

Israel becomes a nuclear power. Although the definite year is unknown, many analysts believe Israel produces its first nuclear weapon in 1967. Israel has never admitted to being a nuclear power.

1968   Paul Ehrlich publishes *The Population Bomb,* arguing that the rise in global human population will lead to mass starvation. Ehrlich argues that overpopulation will deplete Earth's natural resources, eventually making it unable to provide for human dietary needs.

1970   The Nuclear Nonproliferation Treaty (NPT) goes into effect. The intention of the NPT is to limit the possession of nuclear weapons to the permanent members of the UN Security Council, including the United States, the Soviet Union, Britain, France, and China.

1971   United States president Richard M. Nixon unilaterally removes the United States from the gold standard, eliminating the international currency regime set up at the Bretton Woods Conference. Removing the USD from the gold standard ($35 USD = 1 ounce of gold) results in the depreciation of the USD and debt denominated in USDs. Abandoning the gold standard leads to the floating of the USD against other currencies on international currency markets.

United States president Richard M. Nixon visits the People's Republic of China (PRC), beginning diplomatic relations between the United States and the PRC.

1972   United States president Richard M. Nixon travels to the Soviet Union and signs the first Strategic Arms Limitation Talks with Soviet General Secretary Leonid Brezhnev. This agreement places limits on the number of nuclear weapons to be possessed by each nation-state.

The UN holds its first conference on the environment in Stockholm, Sweden. The UN Conference on the Human Environment, known as the Stockholm Conference, focuses on international cooperation in solving the challenges humans present to the Earth's biosphere.

The Biological and Toxic Weapons Convention (BTWC) begins; it is signed by 155 nation-states by 2005. This convention bans the production and stockpiling of biological agents to be used as weaponry. The United States ratifies this convention.

1973   The Paris Peace Accords are signed, ending the involvement of the United States in the Vietnam War. Over 57,000 United States soldiers are killed in the conflict. The government of Vietnam claims that the Vietnamese suffered a total of 5.1 million casualties (Agence France Presse 1995).

The Yom Kippur War begins with Syria and Egypt attacking Israel. The UN brokers a cease-fire creating a buffer zone between combatants.

OPEC embargoes Western nation-states for supporting Israel in the Yom Kippur War. This embargo increases tension between OPEC and the multinational oil companies known as the "Seven Sisters." OPEC gains pricing power over international oil markets. The wealth and power accumulated from petroleum is now shared between multinational corporations and OPEC.

Chilean president Salvadore Allende commits suicide after being deposed in a military coup that gives dictatorial power to General Augusto Pinochet. Chile becomes a controversial experiment of political economy by combining repressive government policies with neoliberal economic strategies. These strategies are influenced by the ideas of University of Chicago economists, including Milton Friedman.

1974   India explodes its first nuclear device under Operation Smiling Buddha. India is not a signatory to the Nonproliferation Treaty of the Comprehensive Test Ban Treaty (CTBT).

1975   South Vietnam is overtaken by Vietminh (North Vietnamese) forces.

1979   The Soviet Union invades Afghanistan, beginning a decade-long occupation. The occupation meets successful resistance by Mujahadeen fighters trained and funded by the United States. This event is believed to have weakened the Soviet Union economically, being a catalyst for its eventual collapse.

Revolution in Iran overthrows the shah and ushers into power the Shiite leader Ayatollah Ruhollah Khomeini. Islamic revolutionaries take more than 60 American hostages from the United States embassy and hold them for 444 days. The Iranian Revolution sparks a sharp increase in the cost of oil, causing an energy crisis for the United States. This event provides justification for utilizing alternative energies in order to lessen the dependence of the United States on foreign sources of energy.

1980   After decades of violent resistance, the former British colony of Southern Rhodesia is overthrown through democratic elections, transforming the territory into the nation-state of Zimbabwe.

1982   Mexico experiences an economic crisis as rising interest rates make payment on its foreign debt untenable. This event is influenced by the raising of interest rates in the United States by Federal Reserve chairman Paul Volcker.

1983   The United States invades the island nation-state of Grenada.

1987   The UN undertakes the World Commission on Environment and Development (WCED), commonly known as the Brundtland Commission. The WCED issues the report, *Our Common Future*. This report concludes that environmental problems are global in scale and the global economy is environmentally unsustainable. The report defines sustainable development with an emphasis on intergenerational equity and justice.

The Montreal Protocol is signed. This international environmental agreement is designed to protect the stratospheric ozone layer from chlorofluorocarbons (CFCs). CFCs break down stratospheric ozone increasing the amount of ultraviolet radiation from the Sun that reaches the Earth's surface. The strategy to eliminate CFCs is based on graduated reductions over time.

1988   The United States and the Soviet Union sign the Intermediate-Range Nuclear Forces Treaty. The agreement eliminates ground-launched ballistic missiles with conventional or nuclear warheads with a range of 500–5,500 kilometers.

The Iraq–Iran war ends after eight years of conflict. The United States had allied itself with Saddam Hussein's Iraq while also arming the Iranians in covert operations uncovered during the Iran–Contra scandal.

1989   The Soviet Union withdraws from Afghanistan. The Soviet Union has suffered 13,000 military casualties after nearly 10 years of conflict (Saikal and Maley 1989).

The Cold War ends with the collapse of the Soviet Union. After decades of economic stagnation, the reforms of perestroika and glasnost initiated by General Secretary Mikhail Gorbachev lead to the dissolution.

The United States invades Panama under Operation Just Cause to depose Panamanian dictator Manuel Noriega. Although the invasion is successful, it leads to widespread looting. The invasion is condemned by many Latin American nation-states.

1990   The Intergovernmental Panel on Climate Change (IPCC) issues its first report warning about the dangers of climate change. This is the beginning of international scientific cooperation in studying the phenomenon of anthropogenic climate change.

1991   The United States and its allies execute Operation Desert Storm. Also known as the Persian Gulf War, the conflict is undertaken to expel Iraqi forces from Kuwait. Estimated Iraqi casualties of the Persian Gulf War range from 20,000–35,000 killed while coalition forces suffered 240 deaths. Following the Persian Gulf War, Iraq is subjected to UN-imposed economic sanctions to punish the Baathist regime of Saddam Hussein. It is estimated that the UN sanctions lead to the deaths of 500,000–1,000,000 Iraqis. Thousands of United States soldiers taking part in the conflict also experience "Gulf War Syndrome," a sickness whose cause is yet to be determined.

The Maastricht Treaty is signed, creating the foundation for the European Union. The unification of Europe is expressed in a common currency (the euro), a common foreign and security policy, and a common justice and internal policy (Ray and Kaarbo 2002). The Maastricht Treaty also leads to the formation of the European Central Bank.

The first Strategic Arms Reduction Treaty (START I) is signed between Russia and the United States. START I reduces the number of operational nuclear warheads maintained by each signatory nation-state.

1992   The Earth Summit, held in Rio de Janeiro by the UN Conference on Environment and Development, meets to discuss a global action plan to address environmental problems. The conference creates Agenda 21, setting nonbinding goals to be met by participating nation-states.

The Internet Society is formed, reflecting the rapid change in communication technology that inter-links continents. The Internet becomes the most revolutionary communication technology in history, advancing global human interaction and the spread of information.

1993   The second Strategic Arms Reduction Treaty (START II) is signed, banning all multiple independent warhead reentry vehicles. START II further reduces nuclear stockpiles held by the United States and the Soviet Union.

The World Trade Center is bombed by Islamic extremists. The truck bomb used fails to bring down the tower and does not disperse the cyanide gas contained within.

The Chemical Weapons Convention (CWC) is opened for signatures. The CWC is signed by 165 nation-states by 2007. The United States is among signatory nation-states.

1994   The World Trade Organization (WTO) is formed with the Uruguay round of GATT negotiations. The WTO strengthens rules concerning international trade with an emphasis on protecting the rights of those engaged in international trade, namely multinational corporations.

The genocide in Rwanda perpetrated by Hutus against Tutsis results in the death of 800,000 people over a three-month period. The genocide is an example of political and social upheaval derived from the legacy of colonialism.

Mexico experiences a currency crisis as international financial speculators lose confidence in Mexico's ability to repay its foreign debt. The collapse of the peso caused by capital flight leads to the Mexican stock market losing half its value. The

1994
(cont.)
economic crisis is mitigated with a $50 billion USD bailout in credit arranged by the United States. Contributors to this bailout include the United States, the IMF, the WB, and G-7 nation-states.

1995
The North American Free Trade Agreement (NAFTA) goes into effect, creating a free trade zone within North America among Mexico, the United States, and Canada.

The Zapatista National Liberation Army begins armed resistance in the southern Mexican state of Chiapas in response to NAFTA.

The CTBT goes into effect, banning the testing of all nuclear weapons. As of 2007, the CTBT is signed and ratified by 138 nation-states (CTBTO 2007). The United States rejects and fails to ratify the CTBT.

1997
The East Asian financial crisis begins with a speculative run on the Thai baht that spreads to surrounding East Asian nation-states. Through a process called contagion, the financial crisis leads to a dramatic drop in the standard of living for the majority of the populations in Malaysia, South Korea, and Indonesia.

The Kyoto Protocol is signed, calling for participating developed nation-states to reduce greenhouse gas emissions by 5 percent.

1998
General Suharto, president of Indonesia, is ousted from power after months of public unrest. The East Asian financial crisis destroys the livelihoods of Indonesians, causing massive political chaos.

Russia experiences a financial crisis caused in part by the fallout from the East Asian financial crisis. The IMF and WB provide loans to stabilize the Russian financial system. Russia regains financial stability but at the cost of increased political instability and social inequality.

The U.S. embassies in Tanzania and Kenya are bombed by Al-Qaeda. The Clinton administration responds with the firing of cruise missiles into Afghanistan and Sudan. The attacks are aimed at Al-Qaeda training camps in Afghanistan and a pharmaceutical factory in Sudan.

The hedge fund Long Term Capital Management (LCTM) loses $4.6 billion USDs in less than four months, requiring a bailout from its creditors. Without this bailout, it is feared the liquidation of LCTM to pay back the debts it used to leverage markets for profits could destabilize the global financial system.

Pakistan conducts its first nuclear tests, exploding five nuclear warheads.

1999   An estimated 50,000–100,000 anti–WTO protesters representing 1,400 nongovernment organizations successfully disrupt WTO negotiations in Seattle, Washington (University of Washington 2007). The protest is organized by labor unions, environmental activists, nongovernment organizations, and a wide variety of political dissidents. The Seattle protest is considered the "coming out party" for those opposing capitalist globalization.

Seventeen United States sailors die as the USS *Cole* is bombed while at port in Yemen.

2001   The United States is attacked by Al-Qaeda on September 11. Nearly 3,000 people are killed at the World Trade Center and the Pentagon. The event, commonly known as 9/11, is the most destructive and costly terrorist attack in history.

The United States is attacked with anthrax mailed through its postal system. The U.S. Federal Bureau

2001
(cont.)

of Investigation suspects that the attack was undertaken by a domestic terrorist with possible links to United States biological weapons programs.

The United States bombs and invades Afghanistan marking the beginning of the global "war on terrorism." The invasion of Afghanistan is supported by NATO and the Northern Alliance composed of Afghani warlords.

The WTO meets in Doha, Qatar, for its 4th Ministerial Conference. There are no reported protests. Many developing nation-states reject negotiations, citing that rules of free trade are geared toward the interests of developed nation-states. Much of the disagreement is centered on protectionist agricultural policies employed by developed nation-states.

2002

In Venezuela, a military coup backed by Venezuela's business community fails to topple President Hugo Chavez. Although there is no definitive proof of United States involvement, Chavez claims the coup was engineered and supported by the United States.

Argentina suffers an economic crisis caused by economic stagnation and capital flight from international investors. Argentina defaults on its foreign debt and suffers currency devaluation. Poverty, human mortality rates, and political chaos increase in Argentina. Argentina is able to restructure much of its foreign debt, lowering foreign-held liabilities. The IMF is reluctant to relieve debt it is owed and proposes structural adjustment policies to address the crisis. Argentina shifts its financial policy toward the purpose of freeing itself from IMF debt.

The International Criminal Court (ICC) is created and ratified by 60 nation-states. The intent of the ICC is to prosecute war crimes, crimes against humanity, and genocide. The United States rejects the authority of the ICC in the National Security Strategy of the United States (NSSUS) of 2002.

The United States withdraws from the START II. Russia soon follows suit.

The NSSUS is announced, altering the United States foreign policy posture to explicit unilateralism, preemption, and nonparticipation in the ICC.

2003 The United States bombs, invades, and occupies the sovereign nation-state of Iraq. The reasoning given by the United States to invade Iraq is that rogue nation-states possessing weapons of mass destruction cannot be tolerated. Evidence provided to the UN by Bush administration Secretary of State Colin Powell turns out to be false, including documented fabrications.

Anticorporate globalization protesters meet in Cancun, Mexico, to challenge the 5th Ministerial Conference of the WTO. An estimated 20,000 protesters (McGarr 2003) are met by 20,000 Mexican police and military personnel. South Korean farmer Lee Kyang Hae commits suicide at the protest to symbolize the plight of South Korean farmers.

2004 OPEC cuts oil production, limiting the global supply of oil. This cut is undertaken to influence the foreign policy of advanced industrial nation-states reliant on OPEC oil (Kegley 2007, 368).

2005 An estimated 10,000 anticorporate globalization protesters meet at the 6th Ministerial Conference of the WTO in Hong Kong, China.

2006 The flu virus (H5N1) commonly known as "bird flu" continues to spread in East Asia, potentially threatening all corners of the globe. With advanced

2006
(cont.)

transportation technologies in the era of globalization, deadly viruses and diseases are able to spread rapidly. Although bird to human transmission has not become a global pandemic, cases have been reported in Europe, Asia, Africa, the Pacific, and the Near East (CDC 2006).

2007

The IPCC issues its fourth report, finding that anthropogenic climate change will continue for centuries. Predictions of the consequences include a rise in sea level, increasing droughts, stronger and more frequent cyclones, higher tides, heat waves, and an increase in destructive heavy rainfall.

In South America, Venezuela and Argentina pledge foreign currency reserves to form the Bank of the South (Banco del Sur). Brazil, Ecuador, Bolivia, and Paraguay are set to join, as well as Nicaragua in Central America and many Caribbean nation-states. The Bank of the South is touted as an alternative to development to diminish reliance on the IMF and WB.

Beginning in August, the global financial system is rocked by the deflating housing bubble in the United States. Many bonds underwritten by mortgages in the United States are found to be overpriced and nonperforming. This financial crisis differs from previous crises in that it originates in the United States, the center of the global financial system.

In December, delegates from countries around the world meet at Bali, Indonesia, at the UN Climate Conference. The conference adopts a road map for further negotiations. Delegates agree that developed countries should reduce greenhouse gas emissions by 25–40 percent, but no binding measure is agreed to. The United States stalls in supporting the terms of negotiation but changes its stance to support the spirit of the road map.

References

Agence France Presse. 1995. News release concerning the Vietnamese government's release of official figures of dead and wounded during the Vietnam War. Available online at www.rjsmith.com/kia_tbl.html (accessed May 22, 2007).

Blum, William. 2004. *Killing Hope.* Monroe, ME: Common Courage Press.

Centers for Disease Control and Prevention (CDC). 2006. "Avian Influenza: Current Situation." Available online at www.cdc.gov/flu/avian/outbreaks/current.htm (accessed May 4, 2007).

Kegley, Charles W., Jr., 2007.*World Politics. Trend and Transformation,* 11th ed. Belmont, CA: Thompson Higher Learning.

Matthews, Roy T., and F. Dewitt Platt. 1992. *The Western Humanities.* Mountain View, CA: Mayfield.

McGarr, Paul. 2003. "'This Is Victory' Say Cancun Protesters." *Food First.* Available online at www.foodfirst.org/node/1200 (accessed May 12, 2007).

National Aeronautical and Space Administration (NASA). 2004. "The Rise and Fall of the Mayan Empire." Available online at science.nasa.gov/headlines/y2004/15nov_maya.htm (accessed February 6, 2007).

Preparatory Commission for the Comprehensive Nuclear Test Ban Treaty Organization (CTBTO). 2007. "Treaty Status." Available online at www.ctbto.org/ (accessed May 3, 2007).

Ray, James Lee, and Juliet Kaarbo. 2002. *Global Politics.* Boston, MA: Houghton Mifflin.

Saikal, Amin, and William Maley. 1989. *The Soviet Withdrawal from Afghanistan.* New York: Cambridge University Press.

University of Washington. 2007. "WTO History Project." Available online at depts.washington.edu/wtohist/intro.htm (accessed April 1, 2007).

5

Biographical Sketches

This chapter offers biographical sketches of important figures of globalization. The entries provide the ideas put forth by each individual and his or her education, career history, and personal achievements. At the end of each biographical sketch is a list of books written by the individual to provide the reader with important works in the study of globalization. These sketches show that different worldviews pertaining to globalization can lead to different perceptions of the benefits and problems associated with the globalization process.

Thomas P. M. Barnett (1962–)

Thomas P. M. Barnett is a military geo-strategist and liberal institutionalist scholar who has worked for both the Pentagon and the United States Naval War College. He received his Ph.D. in political science from Harvard University. Barnett is known for working on the "New Rules Project Set," which identifies U.S. national security interests in the era of globalization. This project was undertaken by the U.S. government in collaboration with Cantor Fitzgerald, a global financial services firm. Cantor Fitzgerald had its New York office in the World Trade Center and lost two thirds of its workforce in the terrorist attacks on September 11, 2001.

Following this event, Barnett worked for the Department of Defense in the Office of Defense Transformation. He became well known for a PowerPoint presentation that was published as a book, *The Pentagon's New Map* (2004). A year later he followed up this book with *Blueprint for Action: A Future Worth Creating* (2005).

These books reflect Barnett's view that globalization consists of rule sets that reduce violence and promote order under an interdependent system of norms and beliefs protected by the rule of law.

The "Core" of globalization consists of nation-states and actors that exist within the rule sets that serve as the foundation of the modern era of globalization. Opposed to the Core is the "Gap," or nation-states and actors that are not sufficiently integrated into the global system. Nations in the Gap do not adhere to the rule sets, and they suffer for it. Because the Gap is not integrated into the global system, those living in Gap nation-states exist under social conditions characterized by misery.

Barnett argues that the United States military should undertake strategic planning to "shrink the Gap." He believes the United States military is the central force to further globalization by expanding and enforcing the rule sets that define the Core. The United States military is the most viable option available to defend globalization, and this reality should be central in the considerations of United States security planning.

Walden Bello (1945–)

Walden Bello is a professor of sociology and public administration at the University of the Philippines at Diliman. He received his Ph.D. in sociology at Princeton University in 1975. He is a member of the nongovernmental organization Food First and executive director of Focus on the Global South, which he co-founded in 1995.

Bello is a critical scholar of globalization with a long personal history of political activism related to resisting capitalist globalization. He is against the United States presence in the Pacific, including the military presence in Okinawa and the Philippines. Born in Manila, Bello's political activism began as Ferdinand Marcos declared martial law in the Philippines in 1972. Bello worked tirelessly in restoring democracy to the Philippines.

Following this, his political activism focused on ending corporate-dominated economic globalization. He has been an active participant in antiglobalization protests, including Seattle in 1999 and the G-8 Summit in Genoa, Italy, in 2001. Singapore banned Bello from entering the city-state when the International Monetary Fund (IMF) and World Bank (WB) met for their meetings in

2006. For his activism and scholarship, Bello was awarded the Right Livelihood Award, Sweden's alternative to the Nobel Prize. As well as being an anticapitalist globalization activist, he is also an environmentalist, being a member of Greenpeace in Southeast Asia.

Much of Bello's scholarship argues that the World Trade Organization, the IMF, and the WB work to keep developing nation-states under the control of advanced industrial nation-states. This control is derived, in part, by advanced industrial nation-states pushing debt onto developing nation-states, debt that they cannot hope to repay. Defaults on loans require IMF assistance that in turn requires structural adjustment programs that harm the majority of the population in these developing countries. Repaying debt hinders domestic development and allows advanced industrial nation-states to control and profit from the labor and natural resources possessed by developing nation-states. Books explaining his critical views on globalization include *Dilemmas of Domination: The Unmaking of the American Empire* (2005), *The Anti-Development State: The Political Economy of Permanent Crisis in the Philippines* (2004), *Deglobalisation: Ideas for a New World Economy* (2004), *Global Finance: Thinking on Regulating Speculative Capital Markets* (2000), and *Dark Victory: The United States and Global Poverty* (1999).

Kenneth Boulding (1910–1993)

The late Kenneth Boulding was an economist, poet, peace activist, religious mystic, and pacifist Quaker. He is widely regarded as one of the most visionary thinkers of the 20th century.

Born in Liverpool, he went to Oxford University, earning an M.A. in 1939. He became a United States citizen in 1948 and pursued postgraduate work at Harvard and the University of Chicago. Boulding never earned received his Ph.D., but he became a very influential scholar at multiple universities. He was a professor of economics at the University of Michigan from 1949 to 1967 and the Distinguished Professor of Economics at the University of Colorado from 1967 to 1981. He published dozens of books and scholarly articles and received honorary Ph.D.s from over 30 universities. He was the president of multiple professional scholarly associations, including the American Economic Association, the American Association for the Advancement of

Science, the Society for General Systems Research, the International Peace Research Society, the Association for the Study of the Grants Economy, and the International Studies Association.

As a scholar, Boulding supported capitalism and the profit system but argued that human economic activity is not a self-sufficient end. He argued that human life is a subsystem of a complex Earth system and human actions must be complementary to the larger system in which it is contained. His scholarship focused on systems theory, especially the inputs, outputs, and feedback loops that characterize the homeostasis of any organism or organization existing within a larger physical environment. Humanity, argued Boulding, is out of sync with the Earth system in which it operates. He believed in a unification of the social sciences through an interdisciplinary approach. In order to understand human relationships with others and with nature, a holistic vision is necessary. Boulding pursued his visionary scholarship with explicit normative foundations, being a social philosopher interested in ethics, religion, ecology, and questions of conflict, war, and peace. He believed the human species continually evolves its values and understanding this evolution is of paramount importance.

Lester R. Brown (1934–)

Early in his life, Lester Brown was a farmer. As a young man who traveled and lived in rural India, he became concerned about the impact that population growth has on natural resources. Brown earned two master's degrees: one in agricultural economics from the University of Maryland in 1959 and another in public administration from Harvard in 1962. After his educational training he became an adviser to the U.S. secretary of agriculture, focusing on foreign agricultural policy. In 1979 he left government service to help in organizing the Overseas Development Council. Brown is the recipient of two dozen honorary doctoral degrees and has received dozens of scientific and literary awards. Currently, Lester Brown is a member and adviser to over two dozen public policy institutes focusing on economics, agriculture, ecology, sustainability, and population.

In 1974, Brown founded the World Watch Institute. This organization analyses the state of the global environment, publishing its findings in annual *State of the World* reports. The World

Watch Institute also publishes *World Watch Magazine* and the annual publication of *Vital Signs: The Trends that Are Shaping Our Future*. In 2001 he founded the Earth Policy Institute whose primary purpose is to envision public policy geared toward the creation of a sustainable global eco-economy. Brown's work focuses on the unsustainability of the current global economy, noting the depletion of natural resources and environmental degradation that result from a growing human population, poverty, and modern lifestyles.

Brown has authored and coauthored 50 books, including *Plan B 2.0: Rescuing a Planet under Stress and a Civilization in Trouble* (2006), *Outgrowing the Earth: The Food Security Challenge in an Age of Falling Water Tables and Rising Temperatures* (2005), *The Earth Policy Reader* (2002), and *Eco-Economy: Building an Economy for the Earth* (2001).

Noam Chomsky (1928–)

Noam Chomsky is a linguist and political activist who is considered one of the leading political dissidents in the United States. Born in Philadelphia and son of a scholar of the Hebrew language, Chomsky began his intellectual journey early in life. He has fond memories of working at his uncle's newsstand in New York City where political discussion and debate was a lively affair.

Chomsky received his Ph.D. in linguistics at the University of Pennsylvania in 1955. Much of the work on his dissertation was done while he was a junior fellow at Harvard University. In 1957, he published *Syntactic Structures*, revolutionizing the field of linguistics. Chomsky's work on linguistics asserts that humanity possesses a universal and innate ability to acquire and use language. Chomsky is Institute Professor at the Massachusetts Institute of Technology where he has been in residence since 1955.

As a political activist, Chomsky subscribes to an anarchist worldview founded in the classical liberal values of the Enlightenment. He is a critic of United States foreign policy and corporate globalization, arguing that they represent modern imperialism. He is critical of the corporate control of modern communication, citing its effect on indoctrinating populations subjected to its repetitious messages.

In 2006, Chomsky's book, *Hegemony or Survival* (2003), was promoted by Venezuelan president Hugo Chavez during his speech to the General Assembly of the United Nations. President Chavez told those assembled that Chomsky's book explained the imperial strategy of the United States in the current era of globalization. Other books by Noam Chomsky focusing on the U.S. role in globalization include *Interventions* (2007), *Failed States: The Abuse of Power and the Assault on Democracy* (2006), *9–11* (2002), *Rogue States* (2000), *Profit over People* (1998), *Year 501: The Conquest Continues* (1993), *Deterring Democracy* (1991), *Manufacturing Consent* (1988), and *Power and the New Mandarins* (1969).

Herman Daly (1938–)

Herman Daly is an ecological economist who critiques neoclassical economic assumptions based on growth. His ideas have been crucial to conceptualizing theories of sustainable economic development. In Daly's view, globalization based on infinite economic growth cannot continue indefinitely for the physical limitations of the Earth make such a notion impossible.

Daly received his Ph.D. in economics at Vanderbilt University in 1967. He pursued an academic career at Louisiana State University where he taught for 20 years. In 1988, he left Louisiana State and accepted the position of senior economist at the Environment Department at the World Bank. He held this position until 1994.

In his farewell speech, Daly admonished the bank for policies based on economic principles that were producing disastrous results worldwide. Daly argued that development policy must be sustainable. Sustainable development requires a steady-state economy, or an economy that does not grow. According to Daly, the reliance on growth to reduce global poverty is impossible. Humanity has already breached Earth's natural carrying capacity in providing for human needs and assimilating the wastes produced by human society. To Daly, economic globalization in its current form is imperiled and destined to be disrupted by resource scarcity and environmental degradation.

Daly is currently professor of ecological economics at the University of Maryland's School of Public Policy and cofounder of the International Society for Ecological Economics. He is a recipient of the Right Livelihood Award and the Heineken Prize for Environmental Science awarded by the Royal Netherlands Academy of Arts and Sciences. His books include *Ecological Economics and the Ecology of Economics (1999), Beyond Growth* (1996), *Valuing the Earth* (1993), *For the Common Good,* coauthored with John B. Cobb Jr. (1989, 1994), and *Steady-State Economics* (1977, 1991).

Cynthia Enloe (1938–)

Cynthia Enloe is a feminist scholar whose academic work focuses on the impact of globalization on culture and gender. She argues that the globalization process affects women though the militarization of their lives and the exploitation of their labor. These processes have an impact on the identity of women, for they are forced to either cooperate or resist the imposition of these dynamics of globalization. Enloe argues that globalization is a masculinist project whose goals and norms are based in a gendered discourse.

Cynthia Enloe earned her Ph.D. in political science from the University of California at Berkeley in 1967. She has served as Invited Fellow at the Bunting Institute and Schlesinger Library at Harvard University and Honorary Professor at the Department of International Politics at the University of Wales from 1996 to 2001. She is a recipient of the Ford Foundation's International Conflict Fellowship. In 2003, she was Visiting Professor at the Institute for Gender Studies at Ochanomizu University in Japan. She is currently research professor at Clark University's International Development program and Women's Studies.

Enloe is a recipient of the Ford Foundation's International Conflict Fellowship and is on the editorial board of the scholarly journals *Signs* and the *International Feminist Journal of Politics.* Books written by Enloe explaining her feminist perspective on globalization include *The Curious Feminist: Searching for Women in a New Age of Empire* (2004), *Bananas, Beaches, and Bases: Making Feminist Sense of International Politics* (2000), *Maneuvers: The International Politics of Militarizing Women's Lives* (2000), and *Does Khaki Become You? The Militarisation of Women's Lives* (1983).

Milton Friedman (1912–2006)

Milton Friedman was one of the most famous representatives of the neoliberal economic worldview. Friedman was known for rejecting the Keynesian economic theory that dominated economic theory and policy from the Great Depression to the 1970s. His views on monetary policy, taxation, privatization, and deregulation served as the intellectual foundation of economic policies pursued by the United States and Britain under the Reagan and Thatcher administrations in the 1980s.

Born in Brooklyn, New York, Friedman paid for his education by working odd jobs. He worked for the United States Treasury Department from 1941 to 1943 and earned his Ph.D. in economics from Columbia University in 1946. His academic work is known for utilizing sophisticated mathematical research designs known as econometrics.

Returning to government service in 1950, Friedman went to Paris to help administer the Marshall Plan. His free-market ideas earned him the position of economic adviser to Senator Barry Goldwater during his unsuccessful run for the presidency of the United States in 1964. In 1976, Friedman won the Nobel Prize for Economics, followed by the Presidential Medal of Freedom, which was awarded to him by Ronald Reagan in 1988. As a neoliberal activist and public intellectual, Friedman spread his ideas though his weekly column for *Newsweek* and created the 10-part series *Freedom to Choose* for the Public Broadcasting System in 1980.

Friedman is considered a central intellectual figure of the Chicago School of Economics at the University of Chicago, having taught there from 1946 to 1976. He served as president of the American Economic Association, the Western Economic Association, and the Mont Pelerin Society. He was also a member of the American Philosophical Society and the National Academy of Sciences. Friedman authored or coauthored more than 50 books, including *Why Government Is the Problem* (1993), *Money Mischief* (1992), *Free to Choose* (1987), *Tyranny of the Status Quo* (1984), *Monetary Trends in the United States and the United Kingdom* (1982), *There's No Such Thing as a Free Lunch* (1975), *Monetary History of the United States 1867–1960* (1963), and *Capitalism and Freedom* (1962).

Thomas Friedman (1953–)

Thomas Friedman is foreign affairs columnist at the *New York Times*. He earned a master's of philosophy in modern Middle East studies from Oxford University. Upon completion of his studies he served as the London bureau chief for United Press International. Friedman joined the *New York Times* in 1981, serving as bureau chief in Beirut and Jerusalem. He has received three Pulitzer prizes for his work and an honorary title from the queen of England, Elizabeth II. Friedman has received honorary degrees from four universities and is a member of the board of trustees of Brandeis University.

Friedman is a neoliberal-inspired writer, focusing on the inevitability of economic globalization and the power of free enterprise to benefit humanity by providing a global higher standard of living. He argues that globalization is the central organizing principle of human society, replacing the global system created by the Cold War. He argues that the spread of information, technology, and capital has created a global marketplace and a global village. Friedman has published two best-selling books expressing his ideas on globalization: *The Lexus and the Olive Tree* (2000) and *The World Is Flat: A Brief History of the 21st Century* (2005).

William Greider (1936–)

William Greider is a democratic activist and critic of global capitalism. Although he is not against capitalism as an idea, his investigative reporting focuses on contradictions within corporate capitalism as they relate to democracy, economic stability, and social justice. He has been a reporter for over 40 years and served as a former assistant managing editor for national news at the *Washington Post* and a columnist for *Rolling Stone* magazine. He is currently national affairs correspondent for *The Nation*, a progressive political weekly. Greider has also been an on-air correspondent for six *Frontline* documentaries on PBS.

Greider's investigative reporting has led to books that analyze the financial logic behind the Federal Reserve System policy of the United States, the impact of money on politics in the United States, and the uncontrolled trajectory of economic globalization. Some of his books that relate to his ideas on globalization include *The Soul of Capitalism: Opening Paths to a Moral Economy* (2003), *Fortress America: The American Military and the Consequences of Peace* (1998), *One World Ready or Not: The Manic Logic of Global Capitalism* (1997), and *Secrets of the Temple: How the Federal Reserve Runs the Country* (1987).

David Held (1951–)

David Held is a prominent scholar of globalization. He was born in Britain and educated in Britain, France, Germany, and the United States. He is the Graham Wallas Professor of Political Science at the London School of Economics and cofounder of the academic journal, *Polity*. His prolific authorship and coauthorship on topics of globalization include *Global Transformations: Politics, Economics, and Culture* (1999), *Globalization/Anti-Globalization* (2002), *Taming Globalization: Frontiers of Governance* (2003), *The Global Transformations Reader: An Introduction to the Globalization Debate* (2003), *Models of Democracy* (2006), *Globalization Theory: Approaches and Controversies* (2007), and *Global Inequality: A Comprehensive Introduction* (2007).

Chalmers Johnson (1931–)

As a scholar, Chalmers Johnson is critical of the role the United States military plays in globalization. He argues that the U.S. military is used to project the power of a global American empire. Johnson argues that the creation and maintenance of an American empire is transforming the United States from a constitutional republic to an executive-led dictatorship.

Johnson was a United States naval officer during the Korean War. Following his service he earned his Ph.D. in political science in 1961 from the University of California at Berkeley. He served as a consultant with the Central Intelligence Agency (CIA) at the Office of National Estimates (ONE) from 1967 to 1973. He was elected a member of the Academy of Arts and Sciences in 1976. He taught political science at the University of California at Berkeley and San Diego from 1962 to 1992. Johnson is currently president of the Japan Policy Institute. Books explaining his views on the role of the United States and its military in the globalization process include *Nemesis: The Last Days of the American Republic* (2006), *The Sorrows of Empire: Militarism, Secrecy, and the End of the Republic* (2004), and *Blowback: The Costs and Consequences of American Empire* (2000).

Immanuel Kant (1724–1804)

Immanuel Kant is considered one of most influential philosophers of the 18th-century Enlightenment. His ideas concerning the universal nature of human reason made him an optimist in his belief that humanity could end war. His ideas concerning human freedom inform many neoliberals, liberal institutionalists, and critics. Kant had a cosmopolitan vision of a global sovereignty composed of democratic republics. Two works explaining his cosmopolitan ideas are *Idea for a Universal History from a Cosmopolitan Point of View* (1784) and *Perpetual Peace: A Philosophical Sketch* (1795).

In the *Idea for a Universal History from a Cosmopolitan Point of View,* Kant stressed the importance of the potential for all humans to employ reason to reach moral conclusions. Morality, to Kant, is realized in society, not the individual. He argued that morality through reason leads to human happiness and perfection. Before this end can be realized, however, a law governing human behavior must be employed until all humans realize the moral powers they possess. To achieve global peace, this law would be employed globally to create a civic union among the people of the world.

In *Perpetual Peace: A Philosophical Sketch,* Kant put forth one of the first versions of what is known as "democratic peace theory." He argued that democracies, by their nature, are unlikely to go to war with one another. Kant's cosmopolitan vision is a world composed of democratic republics working together to promote global peace. These democratic republics would be autonomous sovereignties, free from the dominion of other nation-states. Kant argued that in such a system, standing armies would have to be abolished. Further, he warns of the possibility of international money power creating bondage for a free people through debt. Nation-states should not interfere in the constitutional governments of other nation-states, nor should they engage in acts of hostility against one another.

Although Kant influenced many students of globalization, his ideas are interpreted differently and are subject to many debates. Nevertheless, Kant serves as a primary example of the attempt by political philosophers to envision global peace within the global system.

Paul Kennedy (1945–)

Paul Kennedy is a British-born historian specializing in international relations and grand strategy research. He earned his Ph.D. in history from Oxford University in 1970. He is a former visiting fellow at Princeton University and has taught at Yale since 1982, where he is director of Yale's International Security Program. In 2007, he became the Phillipe Roman Professor of History and International Affairs at the London School of Economics.

His work focuses on projecting important trends in global economics and politics, offering his view of the challenges humans face in this era of globalization and what potential outcomes may ensue. In 2001, he was awarded the title of Commander of the Most Excellent Order of the British Empire, one of the most prestigious honors bestowed by the British government. Kennedy is a fellow of the British Royal Historical Society and a former visiting fellow at Princeton University.

Kennedy is best known for his book *The Rise and Fall of Great Powers* (1987), in which he analyzes the rise and decline of hegemonic powers throughout history. He argues that the power of a nation-state can only be determined in relation to the power of other nation-states within the nation-state system. Power is a collection of factors related to economic, military, and political capabilities. Kennedy argues that since the beginning of the modern world system, hegemons tend to experience military overstretch and a relative decline in power. Hegemons, or "Great Powers," are unable to reproduce and maintain their power within the nation-state system over a period of time. This process is caused by the inability of the hegemon to attain its interests given that available resources fail to adequately support policies designed to achieve desired ends.

Kennedy's books study challenges related to contemporary globalization. These books include *Global Trends and Global Governance* (editor; 2002) and *Preparing for the Twenty-First Century* (1993).

Robert O. Keohane (1941–)

Robert O. Keohane is a liberal institutionalist scholar whose work stresses cooperation and interdependence among nation-states and nonstate actors. Complex interactions among nation-states and nonstate actors provide for a collective interest in stabilizing globalization and maintaining the global system, for it is in the interests of these actors to preserve it.

Keohane earned his Ph.D. from Harvard University in 1966. He taught at Swarthmore College (1965–1973), Stanford University (1973–1981), Brandeis University (1981–1985), and Harvard University (1985–1996). He is currently professor of international affairs at the Woodrow Wilson School of Public and International Affairs at Princeton University.

In 1999–2000, Keohane was president of the American Political Science Association. He is a former editor of the academic journal *International Organization*. Books by Keohane include *Governance in a Partially Globalized World* (2002), *After Hegemony: Cooperation and Discord in the World Political Economy* (1984), and *Power and Interdependence: World Politics in Transition,* coauthored with Joseph S. Nye (1977).

Vladimir Ilyich Lenin (1870–1924)

Vladimir Ilyich Lenin was revolutionary leader of the Bolsheviks and first head of state of the Soviet Union. Lenin became a revolutionary because Czarist Russia executed his brother, an act he felt was unjust. He earned his law degree in 1891 from the Law University of St. Petersburg. He became a Marxist theorist and lawyer, living and traveling throughout Europe. Lenin wrote many revolutionary tracts intended to overthrow the Czarist regime in Russia as well as other capitalist nation-states in Europe. He was exiled to Siberia in 1895 for his revolutionary activities. Upon his release he continued his work as a committed revolutionary.

Lenin's best-known work is *Imperialism, the Highest Form of Capitalism* (1916). This work examines capitalist accumulation on a world scale, arguing that the export of capital by monopoly capitalists had become a central feature of modern capitalism. Capitalism, argued Lenin, had become dominated by cartels and trusts, where banking and merchant capital had merged into one entity. Monopolization, argued Lenin, had led to Karl Marx's predicted lowering of the rate of profit, forcing these monopolies to find new territories to cut costs of production and sell excess goods. Lenin argued that World War I was an intercapitalist war based on rivals attempting to control geographic regions for profit. Lenin's theory of imperialism informs arguments made by critics regarding the unjust nature of capitalist globalization.

Karl Marx (1818–1883)

Karl Marx is one of the most influential figures in social science and philosophy. His life was one of exile and poverty. He lived in France, Belgium, and Britain and was supported financially by his friend and academic colleague, Friedrich Engels. His works span many subjects, but he is best known as a critic of classical political economy. Marx was born in Prussia and attended the University of Bonn, where he studied law. He transferred to the University of Berlin, but due to his radical ideas and lifestyle he had to defend his dissertation at University of Jena, earning his Ph.D. in 1841.

Marx was influenced by philosopher Georg Wilhelm Friedrich Hegel. Marx used Hegel's concept of the dialectic to analyze the material unfolding of human socioeconomic history. Material dialectics contends that social relations based on economic processes determine human potential and choice. Marx argued that when analyzing human affairs, scholars must look at the institutional structures and social relations in which humans exist. Marx put forth his critical theory of capitalism in *Grundrisse* (1858) and *Capital, Vol.1* (1867). *Capital, Vols. 2 and 3* were published posthumously by Engels in 1885 and 1894. Together, Marx and Engels wrote the *Communist Manifesto* (1848), an important work in the socialist movements of the 19th and 20th centuries.

Marx's critique of capitalism is based on the social relations between the capitalist and the laborer. He argued that capitalists expropriate the value added to commodities by labor. This expropriation is realized in profits that are then employed to produce more goods through the further exploitation of labor. This creates a continuous cycle of profiteering and economic expansion. Within this social relation, laborers are alienated from the value of their work and become mere commodities to be invested in by the capitalist, who desires to achieve profits. Marx's economic theory serves as the basis of many theories of imperialism that inform the critic's worldview of economic globalization.

Joseph S. Nye, Jr. (1937–)

Joseph S. Nye Jr. is a liberal institutionalist scholar best known for his theory of soft power—the ability to get others to do what you want. In contrast to hard power, or power realized through the use of force, soft power is based in the voluntary acceptance of norms, values, and goals that are held in common. In the era of globalization, complex interdependence among nation-states and other actors serves as a catalyst for achieving the common goals necessary to stabilize the global system. Nye argues that without soft power, no nation-state is going to be able to achieve its interests.

Nye was awarded a Rhodes Scholarship to study at Oxford University. He received his Ph.D. in political science from Harvard University in 1964 and became a professor of government at Harvard in 1969. He was promoted to dean of the John F. Kennedy School of Government at Harvard in 1995.

As well as being an academic, Nye has spent much of his professional career in government service. He was deputy to the undersecretary of state for Security Assistance, Science, and Technology from 1977 to 1979. In 1993–1994 he was chairman of the National Intelligence Council and assistant secretary of defense for International Security Affairs from 1994 to 1995.

Nye is a fellow of the American Academy of Arts and Sciences and the Academy of Diplomacy. He is a former fellow of the Aspen Institute and has served as director of the Aspen Strategy Group. He is also a member of the Council on Foreign Relations and the Executive Committee of the Trilateral Commission. He is an editor of the academic journals *Foreign Policy* and *International Security*. Books by Joseph Nye include *Soft Power: The Means to Success in World Politics, Understanding International Conflict* (5th ed.; 2004), *Power in the Global Information Age* (2004), and *The Paradox of American Power: Why the World's Only Superpower Can't Go It Alone* (2003).

James Petras (1937–)

James Petras is a critical scholar of imperialism, capitalism, and the global ruling class. He argues that globalization is a code word and an ideological justification hiding an American-led imperial project. He is an expert and activist on Latin American politics, social movements, and development policy. Petras worked with the Brazilian Landless Workers movement for 11 years and was a member of the Bertrand Russell Tribunal on Repression in Latin America from 1973 to 1976.

Petras earned his Ph.D. in sociology from the University of California at Berkeley in 1967. In 1968, his dissertation won the Western Political Science Association's best dissertation award. He has published 36 books and over 300 articles on development in Latin America and global development. He is currently a professor emeritus at Binghamton University in New York, where he has taught since 1972. As a scholar of globalization he has written two books: *Globalization Unmasked: Imperialism in the 21st Century* (coauthored with Henry Veltmeyer; 2001), and *Empire or Republic: Global Power or Domestic Decay in the US* (coauthored with Morris Morley; 1995).

David Ricardo (1772–1823)

David Ricardo was a classical economist who was influenced by the free-market ideas of Adam Smith. He was born in London, and in his adult life became a wealthy businessman, landowner, and financier. Ricardo was a member of the House of Commons in Britain from 1819 to 1823. He was a founding member of the Geological Society and the Political Economy Club in Britain. Ricardo's personal friends included the famous philosophers James Mill, Jeremy Bentham, and political economist Thomas Malthus.

In 1817, he published *On the Principles of Political Economy and Taxation* in which he put forth the labor theory of value. This theory proposes that the value of a commodity is proportional to the amount of labor put into its production. Ricardo argued that wages should be determined by free markets, informing the modern neoliberal worldview. He also argued that profits decrease as wages increase, because the revenue derived from production must necessarily be split between the two. This idea influenced the political economic theory of Karl Marx.

Ricardo is best known for his idea of comparative advantage. Comparative advantage informs economic actors that international trade is beneficial if they can buy goods from others at a lower cost than it would take to produce the goods themselves. Economic actors should gear their activities toward goods they produce most efficiently and trade these goods for those others produce most efficiently. Comparative advantage is based on the concept of opportunity cost, or the cost of producing one good over another given a finite amount of resources. Comparative advantage provides a foundation for neoliberals to advocate unregulated free trade in the global economy.

William Robinson (1959–)

William Robinson is professor of the sociology of global studies at the University of California, Santa Barbara. He is also involved with the Latin America and Iberian Studies Program and the Global and International Studies Program. He received his Ph.D. in sociology from the University of New Mexico in 1994. He is a scholar of comparative sociology, globalization, political economy, development, social change, and political sociology. The central theme of his work is that globalization represents a new historical era of capitalism characterized by global class conflict and cooperation among elites. He argues that in this new historical era, class interest is now realized along international lines where global elites work together on an international basis to achieve their common interests. Economic globalization is now one system of production designed to profit those who own the global productive apparatus. His theory is put forth in the books *A Theory of Global Capitalism: Production, Class and State in a Transnational World* (2004), *Transnational Conflicts: Central America, Social Change and Globalization.* (2003), and *Promoting Polyarchy: Globalization, U.S. Intervention, and Hegemony* (1996).

Vandana Shiva (1952–)

Vandana Shiva is a leading activist and critical scholar of globalization. She is a physicist, having received her Ph.D. in particle physics in 1978. Shiva's criticism of globalization is based on environmental concerns including the political economy of food.

She is considered to be a leading philosopher among ecofeminists. She was born in Dehradun, India, and participated in the nonviolent Chipko movement in India in the 1970s. The Chipko movement was a women's movement in India that resisted deforestation through the tactic of hugging trees, making it difficult for loggers to cut them down. This is where the term "tree hugger" came from, a pejorative term applied to environmentalists.

As a critic of capitalist globalization, Shiva is a leader in the International Forum on Globalization along with consumer activist Ralph Nader and social critic Jeremy Rifkin. In 1993, she received the Right Livelihood Award. She is a recipient of the Global 500 Award from the United Nations Environmental Programme and the Earth Day International Award from the United Nations.

Shiva's scholarship and activism focus on women's issues, the environment, and biopiracy. Biopiracy is pursued through the patenting of indigenous knowledge and the genetic modification of biological organisms. She supports a bio-ethic of local food production using sustainable agricultural production techniques. Shiva argues that globalization is bad for the natural environment, local sovereignty, and traditional knowledge systems. Some of her books that express her ideas are *Earth Democracy; Justice, Sustainability, and Peace* (2005), *Breakfast of Biodiversity: The Political Ecology of Rain Forest Destruction* (2005), *Globalization's New Wars: Seed, Water and Life Forms* (2005), *Water Wars; Privatization, Pollution, and Profit* (2002), *Stolen Harvest: The Hijacking of the Global Food Supply* (1999), and *Biopiracy: The Plunder of Nature and Knowledge* (1997).

Julian Simon (1932–1998)

Julian Simon was one of the most influential scholars promoting the cornucopian view held by environmental skeptics. He had an unwavering belief, backed up by statistical economic analysis, that environmental problems are overblown and not supported by relevant data. He possessed optimism toward the ingenuity of the human species in continuously creating a better world for itself. Simon argued that human population growth will lead to more geniuses who will help technological progress innovate and substitute our way out of potential problems.

Given this view, Simon did not consider pollution and resource scarcity to be major concerns.

Simon earned his Ph.D. in business economics from the University of Chicago in 1961. He was a professor of business administration at the University of Maryland. He was also a former visiting fellow at the Heritage Foundation and wrote policy reports for the Cato Institute, an influential libertarian think tank. Two of his most influential books explaining his optimism toward free markets and environmental skepticism are *The Resourceful Earth* (1984), coedited by Herman Kahn, and *The Ultimate Resource* (1981).

Adam Smith (1723–1790)

Adam Smith is widely considered to be the most important figure in economic theory. A lesser-known fact is that he was an important moral philosopher of the 18th-century Scottish Enlightenment. Being a bright young man, he entered the University of Glasgow at the age of 13. His work, *An Inquiry into the Nature and Causes of the Wealth of Nations* (1776), is a central work in the formation of the modern academic field of economics. *Wealth of Nations* stressed the importance of the division of labor in the production process. Using an example of the production of pins, Smith showed that one worker making a pin by himself is much less efficient than a number of workers specializing in distinct portions of the pin-making production process.

The idea Smith is most famous for is the "invisible hand of the marketplace," where self-interest leads to the common good. The invisible hand is realized by the laws of supply and demand, a self-regulating pricing mechanism that leads to the greatest efficiency in the production process. This promotes laissez-faire economics, where individuals should be free to pursue their self-interest rather than being controlled by restraints imposed by government. Smith was a critic of mercantilism, the favored economic theory of his era.

Although an advocate of free-market economics, Smith was also guided by his moral philosophy, which was founded in the importance of human sympathy. He believed that free markets could not work if humans did not possess an ability, or willingness, to care about others in a genuinely sympathetic fashion.

He was wary of public policy proposed by businessmen and was aware of the dangers economic monopolies posed for free markets.

George Soros (1930–)

Born in Budapest, Hungary, George Soros graduated from the London School of Economics, earning a B.S. in 1952. He immigrated to the United States in 1956 and became a financial trader who amassed a great amount of wealth through financial speculation. Soros is an interesting figure in globalization because he is a financial speculator who argues that the rise of financial speculation within economic globalization is unsustainable. He predicts massive disruption of economic globalization if public policy is not pursued to regulate and manage it.

Soros is chairman of Soros Fund Management and has a net worth of $8.5 billion U.S. dollars (USDs). He formerly operated the Quantum Fund, one of the first hedge funds. He is best known for speculating against the Bank of England's ability to prop up the value of its currency, the pound. On "Black Wednesday," September 16, 1992, Soros made over $1 billion USDs in profit in one day because he gambled correctly that the Bank of England could not protect the value of the pound against speculative attack.

Soros operates the Open Society Institute (OSI), which is designed to promote democracy, human rights, and the rule of law around the globe. The philosophy of Soros and the OSI is based on the concept of the "open society" proposed by the philosopher Karl Popper. The theory of the open society states that societies are healthy only when they are open, free, and democratic. It is the open society that leads to the acknowledgment and defense of human rights.

Soros's critique of economic globalization is informed by his theory of reflexivity. Reflexivity focuses on the idea that human perception lags behind reality or actual conditions. This lag creates financial bubbles, social crises, and other unexpected occurrences that destabilize the global system. Soros is a critic of neoconservative foreign policy in the United States and warns that the global system is unstable and in danger of potential collapse. His ideas are expressed in *The Age of Fallibility:*

Consequences of the War on Terror (2006), *The Bubble of American Supremacy* (2005), *George Soros on Globalization* (2002), *Open Society: Reforming Global Capitalism* (2000), and *The Crisis of Global Capitalism: Open Society Endangered* (1998).

William K. Tabb (1942--)

William K. Tabb is one of the leading critical scholars of economic globalization. As a political economist, he argues that the International Monetary Fund, World Bank, and World Trade Organization constitute international governance institutions designed to protect and extend the power of capitalist elites. He labels these institutions "global state economic governance institutions" (GSEGIs). GSEGIs institute policies designed to maintain the power of global capitalist elites.

Tabb earned his Ph.D. from the University of Wisconsin in 1968. He is currently professor of political science at Queen's College in New York. He is a frequent contributor to *Monthly Review* and the author of books critical of economic globalization, including *Economic Governance in the Age of Globalization* (2004), *Unequal Partners: A Primer on Globalization* (2002), *The Amoral Elephant: Globalization and Capitalist Development in the Early 21st Century* (2001), and *Reconstructing Political Economy: The Great Divide in Economic Thought* (1999).

Immanuel Wallerstein (1930–)

Immanuel Wallerstein is a sociologist who founded world systems theory. He is a macrolevel theorist and historian of the global capitalist economy. His academic expertise is in postcolonial African politics. Wallerstein earned his Ph.D. from Columbia University in 1959, spending much of his academic career as distinguished professor of sociology at Binghamton University in New York where he taught from 1976 to 1999. He founded the Fernand Braudel Center at Binghamton University in 1976 and served as president of the International Sociological Association from 1994 to 1998.

Wallerstein's world systems theory is based on the idea that the current world system is unified under capitalist governance.

The modern global system began in Western Europe in the 16th century and has evolved to encompass the entire globe. Inspired by the economic theory of Karl Marx, Wallerstein believes the world system is characterized by a conflict between capital and labor, where the Core dominates the Semi-Periphery and the Periphery. The Core consists of advanced industrial nation-states, the Semi-Periphery consists of newly developed nation-states, and the Periphery consists of what is commonly known as the Third World, or the poorest nation-states. Economic wealth generated by the Semi-Periphery and Periphery is expropriated by the Core, although the Semi-Periphery plays an essential role in managing the world system.

Wallerstein argues that the current world system is in the process of disintegration and will be replaced by a yet unknown system of human social organization. This disintegration is caused by a lack of the necessary geographical and human resources needed to counteract the contradictions of capitalist overproduction. Wallerstein has written many books explaining aspects of the world system, including *Decline of American Power: The U.S. in a Chaotic World* (2003), *Historical Capitalism, with Capitalist Civilization* (1995), *Geopolitics and Geoculture: Essays on the Changing World-System* (1991), *Transforming the Revolution: Social Movements and the World-System* (coauthored with Samir Amin, Giovanni Arrighi, and Andre Gunder Frank; 1990), *Antisystemic Movements.* (coauthored with Giovanni Arrighi and Terence K. Hopkins; 1989), and *The Modern World System,* Vol. I (1974), Vol. II, (1980), and Vol. III (1989).

Kenneth Waltz (1924–)

Kenneth Waltz is an international relations theorist known for being a principal founder of the school of neorealism. Neorealism is similar to classical realism in arguing that the world system is characterized by anarchy, or no central governance structure to impose order. Nation-states operating within this anarchic system must rely on themselves to achieve their perceived interests. Neorealism differs from classical realism in that neorealism does not rely on a view of human nature to explain international conflict and war. To the neorealist, war and conflict are not functions of human psychic pathology but of the structural reality of the global system. Neorealists analyze the behavior and actions of nation-states as being a function of their power relative to that of other states. This relative power is found within institutional structures that nation-states hold in common. Relative power defines the limits and possibilities in which nation-states can act to achieve their interests within the global system.

Waltz argues that globalization is a current challenge to nation-states. However, the globalization process does not remove the central importance of the nation-state within the global system. He argues that the United States is more secure than previous global powers and that perceived threats to the United States in the era of globalization are commonly blown out of proportion. Waltz argues that the danger of rogue nation-states possessing weapons of mass destruction (WMDs) is not a realistic threat given the survivalist nature of rogue regimes. Rogue regimes may consist of horrible people, but they do not commit acts that will hasten their self-destruction. Attacking the United States with WMDs is such an act, leading not to an increase in the power of the rogue regime but its immediate liquidation. Waltz puts forth the controversial argument that nuclear proliferation has been a catalyst for peace given that it has limited the utility of offensive force in world affairs.

Waltz earned his Ph.D. in political science from Columbia University in 1954. During his academic career he taught at many universities, including Swarthmore College, Brandeis University, Harvard University, the London School of Economics, Peking University, the United States Air Force Academy, and the University of California at Berkeley from which he retired in 1994. He was president of the American Political Science Association from 1987 to 1988 and a fellow of the American Academy of Arts and Sciences. In 1999, he was recipient of the James Madison Lifetime Achievement Award in Political Science. Waltz is currently the Emeritus Ford Professor of Political Science at the University of California, Berkeley, and an adjunct professor of political science at Columbia University. Books by Kenneth Waltz that express his ideas are *The Spread of Nuclear Weapons: A Debate* (with Scott Kagan; 1995), *Theory of International Politics* (1979), *Foreign Policy and Democratic Politics: The American and British Experience* (1967, 1992), and *Man, the State, and War: A Theoretical Analysis* (1959).

Martin Wolf (1946–)

Martin Wolf is a British financial journalist and proponent of economic globalization. He writes for the *Financial Times,* a premier business daily based in London. His columns argue that globalization is beneficial because it is the primary catalyst in raising the incomes of the world's poor. He is against socialism and skeptical of government intervention in free markets. Although he possesses such skepticism, he notes that economic globalization must be managed, to a limited extent, to diminish challenges caused by economic globalization.

Wolf earned a master of philosophy degree in economics at Oxford University in 1971. The same year he joined the World Bank, eventually becoming a senior economist in 1974. In 1981, he joined the Trade Policy Research Center, based in London, where he worked on trade liberalization and multilateral trade agreements. He joined the *Financial Times* in 1987, becoming associate editor in 1990 and chief financial commentator in 1996.

Since 1999, Wolf has been a forum fellow at the annual meeting of the World Economic Forum in Davos, Switzerland. In 2000 he was awarded the title commander of the British Empire. He is currently a special professor in the School of Economics at Nottingham and a visiting fellow at Nuffield College at the University of Oxford. He explains his views of the benefits of economic globalization in his book *Why Globalization Works* (2004).

6

Data and Documents

To help the reader develop a deeper understanding of globalization, this chapter provides important information in the form of data tables and documents. Both the table and document sections of the chapter have introductions explaining the significance of the material presented. As in previous chapters, the information is subject to differing interpretations depending on one's view of globalization.

Data Tables

The following section is a collection of data tables and facts related to globalization. The tables are accompanied by explanations of themes related to globalization, including technology, the global economy, the environment, and global security. Remember that data are important not only for what the numbers say but for what they omit—a central point in understanding the context for the tables.

The Global Population

Table 6.1 shows the trend of the rise of the global human population. For most of human history population numbers remained relatively steady. With advances in technology, however, human population has risen accordingly. Table 6.1 shows the projected rise in human population to the year 2050.

As Table 6.1 shows, the global population is projected to number nearly 10 billion people by 2050 with most of the increase

TABLE 6.1
Global Human Population by Decade (1950–2050).

Year	Population
1950	2,556,518,868
1960	3,040,617,096
1970	3,707,918,808
1980	4,447,081,447
1990	5,273,414,884
2000	6,071,710,896
2010	6,834,934,808
2020	7,603,411,218
2030	8,290,331,407
2040	8,891,757,483
2050	9,401,550,854

Source: Data derived from the U.S. Census Bureau, International Data Base. "Total Midyear Population of the World." Retrieved online at www.census.gov/ipc/www/idb/worldpop.html.

occurring in developing countries. Problems such as food security, conflict, environmental degradation, and lack of natural resources could result from this rise in human population. Addressing and planning for the increasing global population will be a central challenge for the globalization process. To address this future, the United Nations has identified Millennium Development Goals shown in Table 6.2.

The United Nations goals are crucial in addressing the central challenges to globalization and the rise of human population. To end current and future misery of billions of people, these goals will have to be achieved. If the developing countries are left to suffer the effects of these problems, the entire world will likely be affected, including the developed nations. The goals are related to fulfilling the United Nations Universal Declaration of Human Rights, which is provided later in the chapter.

Technology

The next tables display the uneven diffusion of the technology that spawned globalization. Table 6.3 shows the rise and spread of access to the Internet.

TABLE 6.2
United Nations Millennium Development Goals.

Eradicate extreme poverty and hunger

Achieve universal primary education

Promote gender equality and empower women

Reduce child mortality

Improve maternal health

Combat HIV/AIDS, malaria, and other diseases

Ensure environmental sustainability

Develop a global partnership for development

Source: United Nations. Retrieved October 10, 2007 at www.un.org/millenniumgoals/

TABLE 6.3
Internet Users by Region, Level of Development, and Income (per 1,000 People).

Region/Classification	2005	2000	1995	1990
Asia (excluding Middle East)	101.7	30.1	1.1	0
Central America and the Caribbean	135.8	39.8	0.9	0
Europe	343.1	147.0	11.8	0.6
Middle East and North Africa	—	21.3	—	0
North America	664.8	438.7	88.7	7.6
Oceania	532.0	267.2	—	3.7
South America	157.3	38.5	1.2	0
Sub-Saharan Africa	29.8	5.4	—	0
Developed Countries	438.6	222.8	29.9	2.1
Developing Countries	83.1	19.4	—	0
High-Income Countries	571.1	319.9	40.6	3.0
Low-Income Countries	43.9	3.5	—	0
Middle-Income Countries	111.2	24.7	0.7	0

Note: Reproduced with the permission of International Telecommunication Union (ITU).

Source: International Telecommunication Union (ITU). 2007. World Telecommunication Indicators 2006. Geneva, Switzerland: ITU. Available online at www.itu.int/ITU-D/ict/publications/world/world.html

As Table 6.3 shows, in 1990 very few people accessed the Internet. Use of the Internet is a relatively new phenomenon; however, as Internet use has risen, its availability to the privileged and the poor has been dramatically uneven. Most of the world's population is left out of the Internet revolution and access to information. This technology gap could pose problems for the future of globalization.

The Internet is not the only form of technology that has been diffused unevenly. The convenience of cellular phones has also been enjoyed largely by those in the developed world with high incomes.

The use of cellular phones is also relatively new. As Table 6.4 shows, nobody used cellular phones in 1980. Now a majority of the population in developed countries with high incomes has them. The data in Table 6.4 demonstrate that communication technology, a central factor in globalization, is not enjoyed evenly across the globe—another example of the unevenness and inequality that exists in the global system.

The Global Economy

The uneven spread of technology is associated with the uneven spread of investment. The next two tables indicate that developed countries invest in each other's economies more than in the developing world. Table 6.5 shows that developed countries, led by the United States, overwhelmingly account for the foreign direct investment (FDI) in other countries. Table 6.6 shows that not only do developed countries account for most FDI, but they are also the recipients of most FDI. The global economy, in terms of global investment, is largely shared among developed countries. The United States tops the lists in both tables, showing its central role in the global economy as the leading investor and also the leading recipient of foreign investment. These tables show that global investment is limited largely to developed countries, although Brazil and China have risen to the top 25 in both tables.

Table 6.7 relates the balance of payments of countries that have the largest positive and negative current accounts. A country's balance of payments is an account of the inflow and outflow

TABLE 6.4
Cellular Mobile Telephone Subscribers by Region, Level of Development, and Income (per 1,000 people).

Region/ classification	2005	2000	1995	1990	1985	1980
Asia (excluding Middle East)	226.7	62.4	6.7	.4	0	0
Central America and the Caribbean	376.3	112.4	7.3	.6	0	0
Europe	882.8	377.8	32.3	4.7	0.5	0
Middle East and North Africa	335.9	75.6	3.9	0.4	0	0
North America	696.4	378.7	123.1	21.3	1.3	0
Oceania	693.5	331.7	90.5	8.9	0	0
South America	458	127.6	8.5	0.1	0	0
Sub-Saharan Africa	123.4	17.8	1.0	0	0	0
Developed Countries	779.5	365.6	58.1	8.3	0.6	0
Developing Countries	224.7	50.2	3.4	0.2	0	0
High-Income Countries	849	512	84.3	12.3	1.0	0
Low-Income Countries	78	3.8	0.1	0	0	0
Middle-Income Countries	382.3	76.9	4.4	0.1	0	0

Note: Reproduced with the permission of International Telecommunication Union (ITU).

Source: International Telecommunication Union (ITU). 2007. World Telecommunication Indicators 2006. Geneva, Switzerland: ITU. Available online at www.itu.int/ITU-D/ict/publications/world/world.html

of money in countries, similar to an individual bank statement but for a nation. If you overdraw your checking account at the bank, your account will reflect that you are living beyond your means. You will have to either lessen your spending, tap into your savings account, or go into debt. Conversely, if you consume less than you earn, your checking and savings accounts will grow, offering the opportunity to invest. The same holds true for countries.

TABLE 6.5
Value of Foreign Direct Investments Held Abroad by Countries, 2006.

Rank	Country	Stock of direct foreign investment abroad (in USDs)
1	United States	$2,306,000,000,000
2	United Kingdom	$1,487,000,000,000
3	France	$1,005,000,000,000
4	Germany	$941,400,000,000
5	Hong Kong	$689,000,000,000
6	Netherlands	$652,300,000,000
7	Switzerland	$546,600,000,000
8	Spain	$509,200,000,000
9	Belgium	$485,100,000,000
10	Japan	$459,600,000,000
11	Canada	$458,100,000,000
12	Italy	$375,800,000,000
13	Australia	$226,800,000,000
14	Sweden	$226,400,000,000
15	Denmark	$150,100,000,000
16	Ireland	$125,200,000,000
17	Norway	$104,700,000,000
18	Brazil	$99,990,000,000
19	Finland	$90,830,000,000
20	Taiwan	$85,700,000,000
21	Russia	$77,200,000,000
22	Austria	$74,890,000,000
23	China	$67,400,000,000
24	Portugal	$54,850,000,000
25	South Africa	$43,320,000,000

Note: USDs indicates U.S. dollars.

Source: Central Intelligence Agency (CIA). *The World Factbook 2007.* Available online at www.cia.gov/library/publications/the-world-factbook/rankorder/2199rank.html.

TABLE 6.6
Value of Foreign Direct Investments Held within Countries, 2006.

Rank	Country	Stock of direct foreign investment (in USDs)
1	United States	$1,818,000,000,000
2	United Kingdom	$1,135,000,000,000
3	Hong Kong	$769,100,000,000
4	Germany	$763,900,000,000
5	China	$699,500,000,000
6	France	$697,400,000,000
7	Belgium	$633,500,000,000
8	Netherlands	$450,900,000,000
9	Spain	$439,400,000,000
10	Canada	$398,400,000,000
11	Italy	$294,800,000,000
12	Australia	$246,200,000,000
13	Mexico	$236,200,000,000
14	Switzerland	$232,500,000,000
15	Brazil	$214,300,000,000
16	Sweden	$199,600,000,000
17	Singapore	$189,700,000,000
18	Ireland	$179,000,000,000
19	Denmark	$138,400,000,000
20	South Korea	$118,000,000,000
21	Poland	$104,200,000,000
22	Hungary	$96,610,000,000
23	Russia	$90,720,000,000
24	Japan	$88,620,000,000
25	Portugal	$85,520,000,000

Note: USDs indicates U.S. dollars.

Source: Central Intelligence Agency (CIA). *The World Factbook 2007.* Available online at www.cia.gov/library /publications/the-world-factbook/rankorder/2198rank.html.

TABLE 6.7
Top 20 Positive Current Account Balances and Bottom 20
Negative Current Account Balances, 2006.

Rank	Country	Positive current account balances (in USDs)
1	China	$249,900,000,000
2	Japan	$170,500,000,000
3	Germany	$147,800,000,000
4	Saudi Arabia	$104,100,000,000
5	Russia	$94,470,000,000
6	Switzerland	$63,490,000,000
7	Netherlands	$57,520,000,000
8	Norway	$55,210,000,000
9	Kuwait	$51,000,000,000
10	Singapore	$41,290,000,000
11	United Arab Emirates	$35,160,000,000
12	Algeria	$29,040,000,000
13	Sweden	$27,500,000,000
14	Venezuela	$27,170,000,000
15	Malaysia	$25,560,000,000
16	Taiwan	$24,660,000,000
17	Canada	$20,790,000,000
18	Hong Kong	$20,590,000,000
19	Iran	$16,510,000,000
20	Nigeria	$14,780,000,000

continues

Table 6.7 shows that China and Japan have the largest current account surplus while the United States has the largest current account deficit. As noted in chapter 3, this is largely because the United States imports more goods and services than it exports. China and Japan reinvest some of this surplus in United States treasury bonds, making FDIs in the United States. The position of the United States—paying more for imports and receiving less from its foreign investments than other countries receive in kind—is indicative of its role in the global

TABLE 6.7 Continued
Top 20 Positive Current Account Balances and Bottom 20
Negative Current Account Balances, 2006.

Rank	Country	Negative current account balances (in USDs)
1	United States	−$811,500,000,000
2	Spain	−$106,400,000,000
3	United Kingdom	−$88,100,000,000
4	Italy	−$47,310,000,000
5	Australia	−$41,140,000,000
6	Turkey	−$31,760,000,000
7	Greece	−$29,710,000,000
8	France	−$28,320,000,000
9	Portugal	−$18,280,000,000
10	South Africa	−$16,280,000,000
11	Romania	−$12,840,000,000
12	India	−$10,360,000,000
13	New Zealand	−$9,373,000,000
14	Ireland	−$9,136,000,000
15	Poland	−$7,926,000,000
16	Pakistan	−$6,795,000,000
17	Hungary	−$6,211,000,000
18	Bulgaria	−$5,010,000,000
19	Czech Republic	−$4,585,000,000
20	Slovakia	−$4,579,000,000

Note: USDs indicates U.S. dollars.

Source: Central Intelligence Agency (CIA). *The World Factbook 2007.* Available online at www.cia.gov/library /publications/the-world-factbook/rankorder/2187rank.html.

economy as "consumer of last resort" for the world's economic surplus.

This role as consumer of last result has led to trade deficits. The United States has also operated with budget deficits in the era of globalization. These twin deficits have led to a large amount of external debt, or debt that is owed to creditors outside the United States. The country must find investors to pay for its deficits, and many of them are in foreign countries. The data in Table 6.7 show that the United States leads in owing foreign creditors, although other developed countries find themselves in the same situation.

Data are important for what they show and what they do not show. Table 6.8, which lists the top 25 nations with external debt, indicates that the United States does lead in foreign debt obligations, but its total public debt compared to its gross domestic product (GDP) is not large in comparison to other countries. The total public debt owed by the United States is 64.7 of its GDP (CIA 2007). In contrast, many countries have much larger public debt obligations. For example, Japan's public debt accounts for 177.6 percent of its GDP. Developing countries such as Egypt and Zimbabwe owe 113. 4 and 96.4 percent, respectively (CIA 2007). (Please refer to chapter 8 for the reference to the CIA *World Factbook*.)

Global Oil Imports and Exports

The import and export of oil are central to globalization. Oil is necessary to run the global economy and central to political diplomacy and conflict. The consumption of oil is a large factor in environmental problems and climate change. Tables 6.9 and 6.10 list the top 25 oil-importing and oil-exporting countries.

Table 6.9 shows that the United States leads in global oil imports by a large margin. It also shows that many developed countries are also reliant on imported oil; their energy-intensive economies cannot rely on domestic oil supplies for their needs. Going back to Table 6.7, many countries with positive current accounts are also leaders of global oil exports, as shown in Table 6.10. Note that many countries considered to represent major foreign policy challenges to the United States are also major oil exporters. These countries include Russia, Saudi Arabia, Iran, Venezuela, Iraq, Libya, and Kazakhstan. While oil makes the global economy work, it also causes many of the problems facing globalization. This leads us to data concerning climate change and air pollution, two critical problems of globalization.

TABLE 6.8
Top 25 Countries with External Debt, 2006.

Rank	Country	External debt (in USDs)
1	United States	$10,040,000,000,000
2	United Kingdom	$8,280,000,000,000
3	Germany	$3,904,000,000,000
4	France	$3,461,000,000,000
5	Italy	$1,957,000,000,000
6	Netherlands	$1,899,000,000,000
7	Japan	$1,547,000,000,000
8	Ireland	$1,392,000,000,000
9	Switzerland	$1,077,000,000,000
10	Belgium	$1,053,000,000,000
11	Spain	$996,700,000,000
12	Canada	$684,700,000,000
13	Australia	$628,100,000,000
14	Sweden	$598,200,000,000
15	Austria	$594,300,000,000
16	Denmark	$405,000,000,000
17	Portugal	$368,200,000,000
18	Norway	$350,300,000,000
19	China	$315,000,000,000
20	Russia	$282,300,000,000
21	Finland	$251,900,000,000
22	Turkey	$207,400,000,000
23	Brazil	$191,200,000,000
24	South Korea	$187,200,000,000
25	Mexico	$164,700,000,000
	World Total	**$43,420,000,000,000**

Note: USDs indicates U.S. dollars.

Source: Central Intelligence Agency (CIA). *The World Factbook 2007*. Available online at www.cia.gov/library /publications/the-world-factbook/rankorder/2079rank.html.

TABLE 6.9
Top 25 Oil-Importing Countries, 2006.

Rank	Country	Oil imports (barrels per day)
1	United States	13,150,000
2	Japan	5,425,000
3	China	3,181,000
4	Germany	2,953,000
5	South Korea	2,830,000
6	Netherlands	2,465,000
7	Italy	2,182,000
8	India	2,098,000
9	France	1,890,000
10	Spain	1,714,000
11	United Kingdom	1,654,000
12	Canada	1,185,000
13	Belgium	1,109,000
14	Turkey	724,400
15	Brazil	674,500
16	Australia	611,400
17	Sweden	580,600
18	Greece	550,400
19	Poland	480,300
20	Ukraine	469,600
21	Indonesia	424,000
22	South Africa	398,000
23	Belarus	378,200
24	Portugal	361,300
25	Philippines	353,700
	World Total	**63,180,000**

Source: Central Intelligence Agency (CIA). *The World Factbook 2007.* Available online at www.cia.gov/library /publications/the-world-factbook/rankorder/2175rank.html.

TABLE 6.10
Top 25 Oil-Exporting Countries, 2006.

Rank	Country	Oil exports (barrels per day)
1	Saudi Arabia	8,554,000
2	Russia	7,000,000
3	Norway	3,018,000
4	Iran	2,836,000
5	United Arab Emirates	2,540,000
6	Venezuela	2,293,000
7	Canada	2,274,000
8	Mexico	2,268,000
9	Kuwait	2,200,000
10	United Kingdom	1,956,000
11	Algeria	1,724,000
12	Netherlands	1,546,000
13	Iraq	1,500,000
14	Libya	1,326,000
15	United States	1,048,000
16	Kazakhstan	1,000,000
17	Oman	733,100
18	South Korea	644,100
19	Malaysia	611,200
20	Belgium	523,400
21	Italy	521,400
22	Germany	518,700
23	France	474,200
24	Indonesia	474,000
25	China	443,300
	World Total	**63,760,000**

Source: Central Intelligence Agency (CIA). *The World Factbook 2007.* Available online at www.cia.gov/library /publications/the-world-factbook/rankorder/2176rank.html.

TABLE 6.11
Global CO_2 Emissions by Region (in Metric Tons of CO_2 per Person).

	2003	2000	1990
World	4.1	3.9	4.0
Asia (excluding Middle East)	2.4	2.1	1.7
Central America and the Caribbean	2.9	2.8	2.7
Europe	8.5	8.1	10.1
Middle East and North Africa	4.1	3.9	3.0
North America	19.3	19.8	18.6
South America	2.0	2.2	1.8

Sources: International Energy Agency (IEA) Statistics Division. 2006. *CO_2 Emissions from Fuel Combustion.* 2006 edition. Paris: IEA. Available online at data.iea.org/ieastore/default.asp.
Population Division of the Department of Economic and Social Affairs of the United Nations Secretariat, 2005. *World Population Prospects: The 2004 Revision.* Dataset on CD-ROM. New York: United Nations. Available online at www.un.org/esa/population/publications/WPP2004/wpp2004.htm.

Climate Change and Air Pollution

Table 6.11 shows that the developed countries in Europe and North America emit much more CO_2 per capita than the rest of the world. A high level of economic development is accompanied by a high level of CO_2 emissions.

Table 6.12 presents facts related to climate change. It shows the increase of CO_2 emissions over the course of much of the Industrial Revolution. It also shows that the global mean temperature is on the rise. The data in Table 6.12 indicate that although China surpassed the United States in total CO_2 emissions, its emissions per capita are much less than those in the United States. The data also make clear that other forms of air pollution are on the rise in the era of globalization.

Global Security, Arms, and Conflict

Table 6.13 provides facts regarding globalization and security. Together, these data imply that globalization exists in a militarized yet insecure state.

TABLE 6.12
Facts on the Climate Change and Atmospheric Pollution.

Climate

In 1850 global carbon dioxide emissions were 197,866,300 metric tons a year. In 1950 the total was 6,038,585,100 metric tons a year. In 2002 carbon dioxide reached 24,756,694,100 metric tons a year (WRI 2005).

In 1880 the global mean (average) temperature was 56.75 degrees Fahrenheit. In 1980 it had risen to 57.25 degrees Fahrenheit. By 2005 the global mean temperature reached 58.33 degrees Fahrenheit (GISS 2006).

In 2003, world carbon dioxide emissions per capita averaged 4.1 metric tons. In the United States carbon dioxide emissions per capita were 19.5 metric tons, while China emissions per capita were 3.2 metric tons (IEA 2006).

Global carbon dioxide emissions per unit of GDP (in millions of constant 1995 USDs) have been decreasing. In 1960 the global carbon dioxide per unit of GDP was 1,222.2 metric tons. This number decreased to 814.4 metric tons by 1990. In 2002 the global carbon dioxide emissions per unit of GDP were 706 metric tons (WRI 2005).

Air Pollution

In 1990 global carbon monoxide emissions were 841,082,200 metric tons. This amount rose to 1,076,751, 700 metric tons in 2000 (RIVM/MNP 2005).

In 1990 global emissions of nitrogen oxides were 99,282,500 metric tons. This amount rose to 2000 126,609,900 in 2000 (RIVM/MNP 2005).

In 1990 global sulfur dioxide emissions were 154,280,300 metric tons. This amount rose to 150,338,500 metric tons in 2000 (RIVM/MNP 2005).

The total atmospheric concentration of fluorinated gases (CFC-11, CFC-12, CFC-113) that cause climate change and destroy stratospheric ozone was 648.07 parts per trillion in 1986. By 2006 this number had risen to 863.54 parts per trillion (CDIAC 2007).

Sources: Goddard Institute for Space Studies (GISS). 2006. *NASA GISS Surface Temperature Analysis (GISTEMP).* New York: GISS. Available online at data.giss.nasa.gov/gistemp/
International Energy Agency (IEA), Statistics Division. 2006. *CO₂ Emissions from Fuel Combustion.* Paris: IEA. Available online at data.iea.org/ieastore/default.asp
World Resources Institute (WRI). 2005. *Climate Analysis Indicators Tool (CAIT).* Version 3.0. Washington, DC: World Resources Institute, 2005. Available online at cait.wri.org
The Netherlands National Institute for Public Health and the Environment/The Netherlands Environmental Assessment Agency (RIVM/MNP) and the Netherlands Organization for Applied Scientific Research (TNO). 2005 and 2001. The Emission Database for Global Atmospheric Research (EDGAR) 3.2 *Fast Track 2000* and 3.2. *Precursors: CO (Carbon Monoxide): Extended Emissions 2000 and Aggregated Emissions 1990/1995.* The Netherlands: RIVM. Electronic database available online at www.mnp.nl/edgar/
Carbon Dioxide Information Analysis Center (CDIAC), Environmental Sciences Division, Oak Ridge National Laboratory. 2007. ALE / GAGE / AGAGE Network Data on Concentrations of Greenhouse and Ozone-depleting Gases. Available online at cdiac.ornl.gov/ftp/ale_gage_Agage/

Table 6.14 provides the 15 countries with the 15 largest military expenditures. With its central role in securing the global system, the United States spends the most on its military. It is not surprising that allies of the United States and developed countries make up most of this list. Note also that India, China, and Brazil, while rapidly developing economically, are spending

TABLE 6.13
Facts on Globalization and Warfare.

Between 2002 and 2006, the United States accounted for 30.2 percent of world exports in conventional weaponry. Russia accounted for 28.9 percent. Combined, these two nations states accounted for nearly 60 percent of global exports in conventional weaponry.

Between 2002 and 2006, the international transfer of conventional weaponry increased by 50 percent.

In 2005 the top 100-arms manufacturing companies produced $290 billion USDs' worth of weaponry.

In 2006 there were 17 major conflicts actively being fought around the globe, with Asia the region with the highest number.

2006 saw the highest number of peacekeeping personnel deployed to peacekeeping missions. There were 60 ongoing peacekeeping missions in 2006.

World military expenditures exceeded $1.2 trillion USDs in 2006.

In 2006 the United States spent $528.7 billion USDs on its military, accounting for 46 percent of the global total.

In 2007 nuclear armed nation states possessed an estimated 27,000 nuclear warheads. (This includes spare and reserve warheads.)

Source: Stockholm International Peace Research Institute (SIPRI). *SIPRI Yearbook 2007. Armaments, Disarmament, and International Security.* Retrieved on the Web October 12, 2007, at www.yearbook2007.sipri.org/mini /yb07mini.pdf/download.

TABLE 6.14
The 15 Countries with the Largest Military Expenditures.

Rank	Country	Expenditures (in billions of USDs)
1	United States	$528.7
2	United Kingdom	$59.2
3	France	$53.1
4	China	$49.5
5	Japan	$43.7
6	Germany	$37.0
7	Russia	$34.7
8	Italy	$29.9
9	Saudi Arabia	$29.0
10	India	$23.9
11	South Korea	$21.9
12	Australia	$13.8
13	Canada	$13.5
14	Brazil	$13.4
15	Spain	$12.3

Note: USDs indicates U.S. dollars.

Source: Central Intelligence Agency (CIA). *The World Factbook 2007.* Available online at www.cia.gov/library /publications/the-world-factbook/rankorder/2199rank.html.

TABLE 6.15
Nuclear Powers and Size of Deployed Nuclear Arsenal.

Country	Number of deployed nuclear warheads
United States	5,045
Russia	5,614
United Kingdom	160
France	348
China	145
India	50
Pakistan	60
Israel	Undeclared (estimate is less than 100)
North Korea	Undeclared but tested as of 2006
Total	**11,530**

Source: Stockholm International Peace Research Institute (SIPRI). *SIPRI Yearbook 2007.* Armaments, Disarmament, and International Security. Retrieved on the Web October 12, 2007, at www.yearbook2007.sipri.org/mini /yb07mini.pdf/download.

much on their security. It is interesting that Saudi Arabia, a relatively small country with regard to territory and population, spends $29 billion U.S. dollars (USDs) a year on its military. Saudi Arabia, the world's leading oil producer and exporter, is an ally of the United States and has an unstable domestic political situation. Political upheaval in Saudi Arabia could destabilize the Middle East and global oil markets quite easily.

Table 6.15 provides a list of deployed nuclear arsenals among the world's nuclear powers. The United States and Russia maintain the largest nuclear arsenals. These large arsenals are overkill; they could destroy human civilization many times over. In fact, the relatively small arsenals of other nuclear powers would be sufficient to destroy the global system if they were ever to be used.

The dangers of conflict and nuclear war in the era of globalization are worrying. One hope, as liberal institutionalists would agree, are international agreements concerning rules of war and arms control agreements. Table 6.16 provides a selected list of such agreements.

Now that this chapter has provided data tables relevant to the study of globalization, the focus turns to central documents related to the globalization process.

TABLE 6.16
A Selected List of Arms Control Agreements and International Human Rights Law.

Protocol for the Prohibition of the Use in War of Asphyxiating, Poisonous or Other Gases, and of Bacteriological Methods of Warfare (1925)

Convention on the Prevention and Punishment of the Crime of Genocide (1948)

Geneva Convention (IV) Relative to the Protection of Civilian Persons in Time of War (1949)

Treaty Banning Nuclear Weapon Tests in the Atmosphere, in Outer Space, and Under Water (1963)

Treaty for the Prohibition of Nuclear Weapons in Latin America and the Caribbean (1967)

Treaty on the Non-proliferation of Nuclear Weapons (1968)

Treaty on the Prohibition of the Emplacement of Nuclear Weapons and Other Weapons of Mass Destruction on the Seabed and the Ocean Floor and in the Subsoil Thereof (1971)

Convention on the Prohibition of the Development, Production and Stockpiling of Bacteriological (Biological) and Toxin Weapons and on Their Destruction (1972)

Treaty on the Limitation of Underground Nuclear Weapon Tests (1974)

Treaty on Underground Nuclear Explosions for Peaceful Purposes (1976)

Convention on the Prohibition of Military or Any Other Hostile Use of Environmental Modification Techniques (1977)

Protocol I Additional to the 1949 Geneva Conventions, and Relating to the Protection of Victims of International Armed Conflicts (1977)

Protocol II Additional to the 1949 Geneva Conventions, and Relating to the Protection of Victims of Non-International Armed Conflicts (1977)

Convention on the Physical Protection of Nuclear Material and Nuclear Facilities (1980)

Convention on Prohibitions or Restrictions on the Use of Certain Conventional Weapons Which May Be Deemed to Be Excessively Injurious or to Have Indiscriminate Effects (1981)

South Pacific Nuclear Free Zone Treaty (1985)

Treaty on the Elimination of Intermediate-Range and Shorter-Range Missiles (1987)

Treaty on Conventional Armed Forces in Europe (1990)

Treaty on the Reduction and Limitation of Strategic Offensive Arms (1991)

Treaty on Open Skies (1992)

Concluding Act of the Negotiation on Personnel Strength of Conventional Armed Forces in Europe (1992)

Convention on the Prohibition of the Development, Production, Stockpiling and Use of Chemical Weapons and on Their Destruction (1993)

Treaty on the Southeast Asia Nuclear Weapon-Free Zone (1995)

Agreement on Sub-Regional Arms Control (1996)

Inter-American Convention against the Illicit Manufacturing of and Trafficking in Firearms, Ammunition, Explosives, and Other Related Materials (1997)

Convention on the Prohibition of the Use, Stockpiling, Production and Transfer of Anti-Personnel Mines and on their Destruction (1997)

Inter-American Convention on Transparency in Conventional Weapons Acquisitions (1999)

Treaty on Strategic Offensive Reductions (SORT) (2002)

Source: Stockholm International Peace Research Institute (SIPRI). *SIPRI Yearbook 2007. Armaments, Disarmament, and International Security.* Accessed October 12, 2007, at www.yearbook2007.sipri.org/mini/yb07mini.pdf /download.

Selected Documents

This section provides reprints of important documents related to globalization. These documents provide examples of how countries integrate their economies, security interests, observation of human rights, and concerns in meeting the challenge of global environmental problems. Brief introductions are provided for each document, stating the intent and purpose of each.

The Maastricht Treaty: Treaty on European Union (1992)

The Treaty on European Union, or the Maastricht Treaty, formed the European Union. The following passages include its preamble and primary articles. These selected passages show the intent and basis for the common institutional structure of the European Union.

His Majesty the King of the Belgians,
Her Majesty the Queen of Denmark,
The President of the Federal Republic of Germany,
The President of the Hellenic Republic,
His Majesty the King of Spain,
The President of the French Republic,
The President of Ireland,
The President of the Italian Republic,
His Royal Highness the Grand Duke of Luxembourg,
Her Majesty the Queen of the Netherlands,
The President of the Portuguese Republic,
Her Majesty the Queen of the United Kingdom of Great Britain and Northern Ireland,

RESOLVED to mark a new stage in the process of European integration undertaken with the establishment of the European Communities,

RECALLING the historic importance of the ending of the division of the European continent and the need to create firm bases for the construction of the future Europe,

CONFIRMING their attachment to the principles of liberty, democracy and respect for human rights and fundamental freedoms and of the rule of law,

DESIRING to deepen the solidarity between their peoples while respecting their history, their culture and their traditions,

DESIRING to enhance further the democratic and efficient functioning of the institutions so as to enable them better to carry out, within a single institutional framework, the tasks entrusted to them,

RESOLVED to achieve the strengthening and the convergence of their economies and to establish an economic and monetary union including, in accordance with the provisions of this Treaty, a single and stable currency,

DETERMINED to promote economic and social progress for their peoples, within the context of the accomplishment of the internal market and of reinforced cohesion and environmental protection, and to implement policies ensuring that advances in economic integration are accompanied by parallel progress in other fields,

RESOLVED to establish a citizenship common to nationals of their countries,

RESOLVED to implement a common foreign and security policy including the eventual framing of a common defence policy, which might in time lead to a common defence, thereby reinforcing the European identity and its independence in order to promote peace, security and progress in Europe and in the world,

REAFFIRMING their objective to facilitate the free movement of persons, while ensuring the safety and security of their peoples, by including provisions on justice and home affairs in this Treaty,

RESOLVED to continue the process of creating an ever closer union among the peoples of Europe, in which decisions are taken as closely as possible to the citizen in accordance with the principle of subsidiarity,

IN VIEW of further steps to be taken in order to advance European integration,

HAVE DECIDED to establish a European Union and to this end have designated as their plenipotentiaries: [a list of national ministers of foreign affairs and finance is listed in the original document but omitted from this reprinting]

TITLE I
COMMON PROVISIONS
Article A

By this Treaty, the High Contracting Parties establish among themselves a European Union, hereinafter called 'the Union'.

This Treaty marks a new stage in the process of creating an ever closer union among the peoples of Europe, in which decisions are taken as closely as possible to the citizen.

The Union shall be founded on the European Communities, supplemented by the policies and forms of co-operation established by this Treaty. Its task shall be to organize, in a manner demonstrating consistency and solidarity, relations between the Member States and between their peoples.

Article B

The Union shall set itself the following objectives:

—to promote economic and social progress which is balanced and sustainable, in particular through the creation of an area without internal frontiers, through the strengthening of economic and social cohesion and through the establishment of economic and monetary union, ultimately including a single currency in accordance with the provisions of this Treaty;

—to assert its identity on the international scene, in particular through the implementation of a common foreign and security policy including the eventual framing of a common defence policy, which might in time lead to a common defence;

—to strengthen the protection of the rights and interests of the nationals of its Member States through the introduction of a citizenship of the Union;

—to develop close co-operation on justice and home affairs;

—to maintain in full the *acquis communautaire* and build on it with a view to considering, through the procedure referred to in Article N(2), to what extent the policies and forms of co-operation introduced by this Treaty may need to be revised with the aim of ensuring the effectiveness of the mechanisms and the institutions of the Community.

The objectives of the Union shall be achieved as provided in this Treaty and in accordance with the conditions and the timetable set out therein while respecting the principle of subsidiarity as defined in Article 3b of the Treaty establishing the European Community.

Article C

The Union shall be served by a single institutional framework which shall ensure the consistency and the continuity of the activities carried out in order to attain its objectives while respecting and building upon the *acquis communautaire.*

The Union shall in particular ensure the consistency of its external activities as a whole in the context of its external relations, security, economic and development policies.

The Council and the Commission shall be responsible for ensuring such consistency.

They shall ensure the implementation of these policies, each in accordance with its respective powers.

Article D

The European Council shall provide the Union with the necessary impetus for its development and shall define the general political guidelines thereof.

The European Council shall bring together the Heads of State or Government of the Member States and the President of the Commission. They shall be assisted by the Ministers for Foreign Affairs of the Member States and by a Member of the Commission.

The European Council shall meet at least twice a year, under the chairmanship of the Head of State or Government of the Member State which holds the Presidency of the Council.

The European Council shall submit to the European Parliament a report after each of its meetings and a yearly written report on the progress achieved by the Union.

Article E

The European Parliament, the Council, the Commission and the Court of Justice shall exercise their powers under the conditions and for the purposes provided for, on the one hand, by the provisions of the Treaties establishing the European Communities and of the subsequent Treaties and Acts modifying and supplementing them and, on the other hand, by the other provisions of this Treaty.

Article F

1. The Union shall respect the national identities of its Member States, whose systems of government are founded on the principles of democracy.

2. The Union shall respect fundamental rights, as guaranteed by the European Convention for the Protection of Human Rights and Fundamental Freedoms signed in Rome on 4 November 1950 and as they result from the constitutional traditions common to the Member States, as general principles of Community law.

3. The Union shall provide itself with the means necessary to attain its objectives and carry through its policies.

Note: 'Only European Community legislation printed in the paper edition of the Official Journal of the European Union is deemed authentic.'

Source: European Union. "Treaty on European Union." www.eurlex .europa.eu/en/treaties/dat/11992M/htm/11992M.html#0001000001

The North Atlantic Treaty (NATO 1949)

The North Atlantic Treaty created NATO in 1949. NATO created a security alliance between the United States and Western European nation-states.

The Parties to this Treaty reaffirm their faith in the purposes and principles of the Charter of the United Nations and their desire to live in peace with all peoples and all governments.

They are determined to safeguard the freedom, common heritage and civilisation of their peoples, founded on the principles of democracy, individual liberty and the rule of law. They seek to promote stability and well-being in the North Atlantic area.

They are resolved to unite their efforts for collective defence and for the preservation of peace and security. They therefore agree to this North Atlantic Treaty:

Article 1
The Parties undertake, as set forth in the Charter of the United Nations, to settle any international dispute in which they may be involved by peaceful means in such a manner that international peace and security and justice are not endangered, and to refrain in their international relations from the threat or use of force in any manner inconsistent with the purposes of the United Nations.

Article 2
The Parties will contribute toward the further development of peaceful and friendly international relations by strengthening their free institutions, by bringing about a better understanding of the principles upon which these institutions are founded, and by promoting conditions of stability and well-being. They will seek to eliminate conflict in their international economic policies and will encourage economic collaboration between any or all of them.

Article 3
In order more effectively to achieve the objectives of this Treaty, the Parties, separately and jointly, by means of continuous and effective self-help and mutual aid, will maintain and develop their individual and collective capacity to resist armed attack.

Article 4
The Parties will consult together whenever, in the opinion of any of them, the territorial integrity, political independence or security of any of the Parties is threatened.

Article 5
The Parties agree that an armed attack against one or more of them in Europe or North America shall be considered an attack against them all and consequently they agree that, if such an armed attack occurs, each of them, in exercise of the right of individual or collective self-defence recognised by Article 51 of the Charter of the United Nations, will assist the Party or Parties so attacked by taking forthwith, individually and in

concert with the other Parties, such action as it deems necessary, including the use of armed force, to restore and maintain the security of the North Atlantic area.

Any such armed attack and all measures taken as a result thereof shall immediately be reported to the Security Council. Such measures shall be terminated when the Security Council has taken the measures necessary to restore and maintain international peace and security.

Article 6
For the purpose of Article 5, an armed attack on one or more of the Parties is deemed to include an armed attack:

- on the territory of any of the Parties in Europe or North America, on the Algerian Departments of France, on the territory of or on the Islands under the jurisdiction of any of the Parties in the North Atlantic area north of the Tropic of Cancer;
- on the forces, vessels, or aircraft of any of the Parties, when in or over these territories or any other area in Europe in which occupation forces of any of the Parties were stationed on the date when the Treaty entered into force or the Mediterranean Sea or the North Atlantic area north of the Tropic of Cancer.

Article 7
This Treaty does not affect, and shall not be interpreted as affecting in any way the rights and obligations under the Charter of the Parties which are members of the United Nations, or the primary responsibility of the Security Council for the maintenance of international peace and security.

Article 8
Each Party declares that none of the international engagements now in force between it and any other of the Parties or any third State is in conflict with the provisions of this Treaty, and undertakes not to enter into any international engagement in conflict with this Treaty.

Article 9
The Parties hereby establish a Council, on which each of them shall be represented, to consider matters concerning the implementation of this Treaty. The Council shall be so organised as to be able to meet promptly at any time. The Council shall set up such subsidiary bodies as may be necessary; in particular it shall establish immediately a defence committee which shall recommend measures for the implementation of Articles 3 and 5.

Article 10

The Parties may, by unanimous agreement, invite any other European State in a position to further the principles of this Treaty and to contribute to the security of the North Atlantic area to accede to this Treaty. Any State so invited may become a Party to the Treaty by depositing its instrument of accession with the Government of the United States of America. The Government of the United States of America will inform each of the Parties of the deposit of each such instrument of accession.

Article 11

This Treaty shall be ratified and its provisions carried out by the Parties in accordance with their respective constitutional processes. The instruments of ratification shall be deposited as soon as possible with the Government of the United States of America, which will notify all the other signatories of each deposit. The Treaty shall enter into force between the States which have ratified it as soon as the ratifications of the majority of the signatories, including the ratifications of Belgium, Canada, France, Luxembourg, the Netherlands, the United Kingdom and the United States, have been deposited and shall come into effect with respect to other States on the date of the deposit of their ratifications.

Article 12

After the Treaty has been in force for ten years, or at any time thereafter, the Parties shall, if any of them so requests, consult together for the purpose of reviewing the Treaty, having regard for the factors then affecting peace and security in the North Atlantic area, including the development of universal as well as regional arrangements under the Charter of the United Nations for the maintenance of international peace and security.

Article 13

After the Treaty has been in force for twenty years, any Party may cease to be a Party one year after its notice of denunciation has been given to the Government of the United States of America, which will inform the Governments of the other Parties of the deposit of each notice of denunciation.

Article 14

This Treaty, of which the English and French texts are equally authentic, shall be deposited in the archives of the Government of the United States of America. Duly certified copies will be transmitted by that Government to the Governments of other signatories.

1. The definition of the territories to which Article 5 applies was revised by Article 2 of the Protocol to the North Atlantic Treaty on the accession of Greece and Turkey signed on 22 October 1951.
2. On January 16, 1963, the North Atlantic Council noted that insofar as the former Algerian Departments of France were concerned, the relevant clauses of this Treaty had become inapplicable as from July 3, 1962.
3. The Treaty came into force on 24 August 1949, after the deposition of the ratifications of all signatory states.

Source: North Atlantic Treaty Organization. "The North Atlantic Treaty," www.nato.int/docu/basictxt/treaty.htm

Charter of the United Nations (1945)

The Charter of the United Nations created the United Nations (UN). The UN was designed to allow nation-states to have an institutional forum in which to discuss international issues. The UN has been instrumental in many aspects of globalization.

Preamble

We the Peoples of the United Nations,

Determined to save succeeding generations from the scourge of war, which twice in our lifetime has brought untold sorrow to mankind, and to reaffirm faith in fundamental human rights, in the dignity and worth of the human person, in the equal rights of men and women and of nations large and small, and to establish conditions under which justice and respect for the obligations arising from treaties and other sources of international law can be maintained, and to promote social progress and better standards of life in larger freedom,

And for These Ends to practice tolerance and live together in peace with one another as good neighbours, and to unite our strength to maintain international peace and security, and to ensure, by the acceptance of principles and the institution of methods, that armed force shall not be used, save in the common interest, and to employ international machinery for the promotion of the economic and social advancement of all peoples,

Have Resolved to Combine Our Efforts to Accomplish These Aims

Accordingly, our respective Governments, through representatives assembled in the city of San Francisco, who have exhibited their full powers found to be in good and due form, have agreed to the present Charter of the United Nations and do hereby establish an international organization to be known as the United Nations.

CHAPTER I
PURPOSES AND PRINCIPLES
Article 1

The Purposes of the United Nations are:

1. To maintain international peace and security, and to that end: to take effective collective measures for the prevention and removal of threats to the peace, and for the suppression of acts of aggression or other breaches of the peace, and to bring about by peaceful means, and in conformity with the principles of justice and international law, adjustment or settlement of international disputes or situations which might lead to a breach of the peace;

2. To develop friendly relations among nations based on respect for the principle of equal rights and self-determination of peoples, and to take other appropriate measures to strengthen universal peace;

3. To achieve international co-operation in solving international problems of an economic, social, cultural, or humanitarian character, and in promoting and encouraging respect for human rights and for fundamental freedoms for all without distinction as to race, sex, language, or religion; and

4. To be a centre for harmonizing the actions of nations in the attainment of these common ends.

Article 2

The Organization and its Members, in pursuit of the Purposes stated in Article 1, shall act in accordance with the following Principles.

1. The Organization is based on the principle of the sovereign equality of all its Members.

2. All Members, in order to ensure to all of them the rights and benefits resulting from membership, shall fulfill in good faith the obligations assumed by them in accordance with the present Charter.

3. All Members shall settle their international disputes by peaceful means in such a manner that international peace and security, and justice, are not endangered.

4. All Members shall refrain in their international relations from the threat or use of force against the territorial integrity or political independence of any state, or in any other manner inconsistent with the Purposes of the United Nations.

5. All Members shall give the United Nations every assistance in any action it takes in accordance with the present Charter, and shall refrain from giving assistance to any state against which the United Nations is taking preventive or enforcement action.

6. The Organization shall ensure that states which are not Members of the United Nations act in accordance with these Principles so far as may be necessary for the maintenance of international peace and security.

7. Nothing contained in the present Charter shall authorize the United Nations to intervene in matters which are essentially within the domestic jurisdiction of any state or shall require the Members to submit such matters to settlement under the present Charter; but this principle shall not prejudice the application of enforcement measures under Chapter Vll.

CHAPTER II
MEMBERSHIP
Article 3
The original Members of the United Nations shall be the states which, having participated in the United Nations Conference on International Organization at San Francisco, or having previously signed the Declaration by United Nations of 1 January 1942, sign the present Charter and ratify it in accordance with Article 110.

Article 4
1. Membership in the United Nations is open to all other peace-loving states which accept the obligations contained in the present Charter and, in the judgment of the Organization, are able and willing to carry out these obligations.
2. The admission of any such state to membership in the United Nations will be effected by a decision of the General Assembly upon the recommendation of the Security Council.

Article 5
A Member of the United Nations against which preventive or enforcement action has been taken by the Security Council may be suspended from the exercise of the rights and privileges of membership by the General Assembly upon the recommendation of the Security Council. The exercise of these rights and privileges may be restored by the Security Council.

Article 6
A Member of the United Nations which has persistently violated the Principles contained in the present Charter may be expelled from the Organization by the General Assembly upon the recommendation of the Security Council.

CHAPTER III
ORGANS
Article 7
1. There are established as the principal organs of the United Nations:

—a General Assembly
—a Security Council

—an Economic and Social Council
—a Trusteeship Council
—an International Court of Justice
—and a Secretariat.

2. Such subsidiary organs as may be found necessary may be established in accordance with the present Charter.

Article 8
The United Nations shall place no restrictions on the eligibility of men and women to participate in any capacity and under conditions of equality in its principal and subsidiary organs.
Source: United Nations, "Charter of the United Nations," www.un.org/aboutun/charter/

The Universal Declaration of Human Rights (1948)

The UDHR was adopted in 1948. This text serves as a basis for global human rights, irrespective of nationality, race, creed, religion, or sex. This is an important document, granting human rights to everyone.

Preamble
Whereas recognition of the inherent dignity and of the equal and inalienable rights of all members of the human family is the foundation of freedom, justice and peace in the world,

Whereas disregard and contempt for human rights have resulted in barbarous acts which have outraged the conscience of mankind, and the advent of a world in which human beings shall enjoy freedom of speech and belief and freedom from fear and want has been proclaimed as the highest aspiration of the common people,

Whereas it is essential, if man is not to be compelled to have recourse, as a last resort, to rebellion against tyranny and oppression, that human rights should be protected by the rule of law,

Whereas it is essential to promote the development of friendly relations between nations,

Whereas the peoples of the United Nations have in the Charter reaffirmed their faith in fundamental human rights, in the dignity and worth of the human person and in the equal rights of men and women and have determined to promote social progress and better standards of life in larger freedom,

Whereas Member States have pledged themselves to achieve, in co-operation with the United Nations, the promotion of universal respect for and observance of human rights and fundamental freedoms,

Whereas a common understanding of these rights and freedoms is of the greatest importance for the full realization of this pledge,

Now, Therefore,

The General Assembly proclaims

This Universal Declaration of Human Rights as a common standard of achievement for all peoples and all nations, to the end that every individual and every organ of society, keeping this Declaration constantly in mind, shall strive by teaching and education to promote respect for these rights and freedoms and by progressive measures, national and international, to secure their universal and effective recognition and observance, both among the peoples of Member States themselves and among the peoples of territories under their jurisdiction.

Article 1

All human beings are born free and equal in dignity and rights. They are endowed with reason and conscience and should act towards one another in a spirit of brotherhood.

Article 2

Everyone is entitled to all the rights and freedoms set forth in this Declaration, without distinction of any kind, such as race, colour, sex, language, religion, political or other opinion, national or social origin, property, birth or other status. Furthermore, no distinction shall be made on the basis of the political, jurisdictional or international status of the country or territory to which a person belongs, whether it be independent, trust, non-self-governing or under any other limitation of sovereignty.

Article 3

Everyone has the right to life, liberty and security of person.

Article 4

No one shall be held in slavery or servitude; slavery and the slave trade shall be prohibited in all their forms.

Article 5

No one shall be subjected to torture or to cruel, inhuman or degrading treatment or punishment.

Article 6

Everyone has the right to recognition everywhere as a person before the law.

Article 7

All are equal before the law and are entitled without any discrimination to equal protection of the law. All are entitled to equal protection against any discrimination in violation of this Declaration and against any incitement to such discrimination.

Article 8

Everyone has the right to an effective remedy by the competent national tribunals for acts violating the fundamental rights granted him by the constitution or by law.

Article 9

No one shall be subjected to arbitrary arrest, detention or exile.

Article 10

Everyone is entitled in full equality to a fair and public hearing by an independent and impartial tribunal, in the determination of his rights and obligations and of any criminal charge against him.

Article 11

1. Everyone charged with a penal offence has the right to be presumed innocent until proved guilty according to law in a public trial at which he has had all the guarantees necessary for his defence.

2. No one shall be held guilty of any penal offence on account of any act or omission which did not constitute a penal offence, under national or international law, at the time when it was committed. Nor shall a heavier penalty be imposed than the one that was applicable at the time the penal offence was committed.

Article 12

No one shall be subjected to arbitrary interference with his privacy, family, home or correspondence, nor to attacks upon his honour and reputation. Everyone has the right to the protection of the law against such interference or attacks.

Article 13

1. Everyone has the right to freedom of movement and residence within the borders of each state.

2. Everyone has the right to leave any country, including his own, and to return to his country.

Article 14

1. Everyone has the right to seek and to enjoy in other countries asylum from persecution.

2. This right may not be invoked in the case of prosecutions genuinely arising from non-political crimes or from acts contrary to the purposes and principles of the United Nations.

Article 15

1. Everyone has the right to a nationality.

2. No one shall be arbitrarily deprived of his nationality nor denied the right to change his nationality.

Article 16

1. Men and women of full age, without any limitation due to race, nationality or religion, have the right to marry and to found a family. They are entitled to equal rights as to marriage, during marriage and at its dissolution.

2. Marriage shall be entered into only with the free and full consent of the intending spouses.

3. The family is the natural and fundamental group unit of society and is entitled to protection by society and the State.

Article 17

1. Everyone has the right to own property alone as well as in association with others.

2. No one shall be arbitrarily deprived of his property.

Article 18

Everyone has the right to freedom of thought, conscience and religion; this right includes freedom to change his religion or belief, and freedom, either alone or in community with others and in public or private, to manifest his religion or belief in teaching, practice, worship and observance.

Article 19

Everyone has the right to freedom of opinion and expression; this right includes freedom to hold opinions without interference and to seek, receive and impart information and ideas through any media and regardless of frontiers.

Article 20

1. Everyone has the right to freedom of peaceful assembly and association.

2. No one may be compelled to belong to an association.

Article 21

1. Everyone has the right to take part in the government of his country, directly or through freely chosen representatives.

2. Everyone has the right of equal access to public service in his country.

3. The will of the people shall be the basis of the authority of government; this will shall be expressed in periodic and genuine elections which shall be by universal and equal suffrage and shall be held by secret vote or by equivalent free voting procedures.

Article 22

Everyone, as a member of society, has the right to social security and is entitled to realization, through national effort and international co-operation and in accordance with the organization and resources of each State, of the economic, social and cultural rights indispensable for his dignity and the free development of his personality.

Article 23

1. Everyone has the right to work, to free choice of employment, to just and favourable conditions of work and to protection against unemployment.

2. Everyone, without any discrimination, has the right to equal pay for equal work.

3. Everyone who works has the right to just and favourable remuneration ensuring for himself and his family an existence worthy of human dignity, and supplemented, if necessary, by other means of social protection.

4. Everyone has the right to form and to join trade unions for the protection of his interests.

Article 24

Everyone has the right to rest and leisure, including reasonable limitation of working hours and periodic holidays with pay.

Article 25

1. Everyone has the right to a standard of living adequate for the health and well-being of himself and of his family, including food, clothing, housing and medical care and necessary social services, and the right to security in the event of unemployment, sickness, disability, widowhood, old age or other lack of livelihood in circumstances beyond his control.

2. Motherhood and childhood are entitled to special care and assistance. All children, whether born in or out of wedlock, shall enjoy the same social protection.

Article 26

1. Everyone has the right to education. Education shall be free, at least in the elementary and fundamental stages. Elementary education

shall be compulsory. Technical and professional education shall be made generally available and higher education shall be equally accessible to all on the basis of merit.

2. Education shall be directed to the full development of the human personality and to the strengthening of respect for human rights and fundamental freedoms. It shall promote understanding, tolerance and friendship among all nations, racial or religious groups, and shall further the activities of the United Nations for the maintenance of peace.

3. Parents have a prior right to choose the kind of education that shall be given to their children.

Article 27

1. Everyone has the right freely to participate in the cultural life of the community, to enjoy the arts and to share in scientific advancement and its benefits.

2. Everyone has the right to the protection of the moral and material interests resulting from any scientific, literary or artistic production of which he is the author.

Article 28

Everyone is entitled to a social and international order in which the rights and freedoms set forth in this Declaration can be fully realized.

Article 29

1. Everyone has duties to the community in which alone the free and full development of his personality is possible.

2. In the exercise of his rights and freedoms, everyone shall be subject only to such limitations as are determined by law solely for the purpose of securing due recognition and respect for the rights and freedoms of others and of meeting the just requirements of morality, public order and the general welfare in a democratic society.

3. These rights and freedoms may in no case be exercised contrary to the purposes and principles of the United Nations.

Article 30

Nothing in this Declaration may be interpreted as implying for any State, group or person any right to engage in any activity or to perform any act aimed at the destruction of any of the rights and freedoms set forth herein.

Source: United Nations. www.un.org/Overview/rights.html

Free Trade Agreements

General Agreement on Trade and Tariffs (1947)

The GATT was created at the Bretton Woods Conference. It is the first post–World War II free trade agreement, having been adopted in 1947. It serves as a model for subsequent free trade agreements. Below is the introduction to the GATT. This short section reveals the intent behind GATT negotiations.

The Governments of the Commonwealth of Australia, the Kingdom of Belgium, the United States of Brazil, Burma, Canada, Ceylon, the Republic of Chile, the Republic of China, the Republic of Cuba, the Czechoslovak Republic, the French Republic, India, Lebanon, the Grand-Duchy of Luxemburg, the Kingdom of the Netherlands, New Zealand, the Kingdom of Norway, Pakistan, Southern Rhodesia, Syria, the Union of South Africa, the United Kingdom of Great Britain and Northern Ireland, and the United States of America:

Recognizing that their relations in the field of trade and economic endeavour should be conducted with a view to raising standards of living, ensuring full employment and a large and steadily growing volume of real income and effective demand, developing the full use of the resources of the world and expanding the production and exchange of goods,

Being desirous of contributing to these objectives by entering into reciprocal and mutually advantageous arrangements directed to the substantial reduction of tariffs and other barriers to trade and to the elimination of discriminatory treatment in international commerce . . .

Source: World Trade Organization (WTO). www.wto.org/english/docs_e/legal_e/gatt47_01_e.htm

North American Free Trade Agreement (1994)

NAFTA is a regional free trade agreement creating a trading bloc among North American nation-states. It went into effect in 1994. NAFTA increased economic integration between Canada, the United States, and Mexico. Below are the Preamble and important articles of NAFTA that provide a basic understanding of important aspects of this agreement.

Preamble
The Government of Canada, the Government of the United Mexican States and the Government of the United States of America, resolved to:

STRENGTHEN the special bonds of friendship and cooperation among their nations;

CONTRIBUTE to the harmonious development and expansion of world trade and provide a catalyst to broader international cooperation;

CREATE an expanded and secure market for the goods and services produced in their territories;

REDUCE distortions to trade;

ESTABLISH clear and mutually advantageous rules governing their trade;

ENSURE a predictable commercial framework for business planning and investment;

BUILD on their respective rights and obligations under the General Agreement on Tariffs and Trade and other multilateral and bilateral instruments of cooperation;

ENHANCE the competitiveness of their firms in global markets.

Part One: General Part
Chapter One: Objectives
Article 101: Establishment of the Free Trade Area

The Parties to this Agreement, consistent with Article XXIV of the . . . *General Agreement on Tariffs and Trade,* hereby establish a free trade area.

Article 103: Relation to Other Agreements

1. The Parties affirm their existing rights and obligations with respect to each other under the *General Agreement on Tariffs and Trade* and other agreements to which such Parties are party.

2. In the event of any inconsistency between this Agreement and such other agreements, this Agreement shall prevail to the extent of the inconsistency, except as otherwise provided in this Agreement.

Article 104: Relation to Environmental and Conservation Agreements

1. In the event of any inconsistency between this Agreement and the specific trade obligations set out in:

a) the *Convention on International Trade in Endangered Species of Wild Fauna and Flora,* done at Washington, March 3, 1973, as amended June 22, 1979,

b) the *Montreal Protocol on Substances that Deplete the Ozone Layer,* done at Montreal, September 16, 1987, as amended June 29, 1990,

c) the *Basel Convention on the Control of Transboundary Movements of Hazardous Wastes and Their Disposal,* done at Basel, March 22, 1989, on its entry into force for Canada, Mexico and the United States, or

d) the agreements set out in Annex 104.1,

such obligations shall prevail to the extent of the inconsistency, provided that where a Party has a choice among equally effective and reasonably available means of complying with such obligations, the Party chooses the alternative that is the least inconsistent with the other provisions of this Agreement.

2. The Parties may agree in writing to modify Annex 104.1 to include any amendment to an agreement referred to in paragraph 1, and any other environmental or conservation agreement.

Article 105: Extent of Obligations

The Parties shall ensure that all necessary measures are taken in order to give effect to the provisions of this Agreement, including their observance, except as otherwise provided in this Agreement, by state and provincial governments.

Annex 104.1: Bilateral and Other Environmental and Conservation Agreements

1. *The Agreement Between the Government of Canada and the Government of the United States of America Concerning the Transboundary Movement of Hazardous Waste,* signed at Ottawa, October 28, 1986.

2. *The Agreement Between the United States of America and the United Mexican States on Cooperation for the Protection and Improvement of the Environment in the Border Area,* signed at La Paz, Baja California Sur, August 14, 1983.

Part Two: Trade in Goods

Chapter Three: National Treatment and Market Access for Goods

Section A: National Treatment

Article 301: National Treatment

1. Each Party shall accord national treatment to the goods of another Party in accordance with Article III of the *General Agreement on Tariffs and Trade* (GATT), including its interpretative notes, and to this end Article III of the GATT and its interpretative notes, or any equivalent provision of a successor agreement to which all Parties are party, are incorporated into and made part of this Agreement.

2. The provisions of paragraph 1 regarding national treatment shall mean, with respect to a state or province, treatment no less favorable than the most favorable treatment accorded by such state or province to any like, directly competitive or substitutable goods, as the case may be, of the Party of which it forms a part.

3. Paragraphs 1 and 2 do not apply to the measures set out in Annex 301. 3.

Section B: Tariffs

Article 302: Tariff Elimination

1. Except as otherwise provided in this Agreement, no Party may increase any existing customs duty, or adopt any customs duty, on an originating good.

2. Except as otherwise provided in this Agreement, each Party shall progressively eliminate its customs duties on originating goods in accordance with its Schedule to Annex 302. 2.

3. On the request of any Party, the Parties shall consult to consider accelerating the elimination of customs duties set out in their Schedules. An agreement between two or more Parties to accelerate the elimination of a customs duty on a good shall supersede any duty rate or staging category determined pursuant to their Schedules for such good when approved by each such Party in accordance with its applicable legal procedures.

4. Each Party may adopt or maintain import measures to allocate in-quota imports made pursuant to a tariff rate quota set out in Annex 302. 2, provided that such measures do not have trade restrictive effects on imports additional to those caused by the imposition of the tariff rate quota.

5. On written request of any Party, a Party applying or intending to apply measures pursuant to paragraph 4 shall consult to review the administration of those measures.

Source: Organization of American States (OAS). North American Free Trade Agreement (NAFTA). www.sice.oas.org/Trade/NAFTA/naftatce.asp

Agreement Establishing the World Trade Organization (WTO)

The WTO descended from and replaced the GATT. The WTO went into effect in 1995 with the end of the Uruguay Round of Negotiations. Below are the introduction and primary articles of the WTO. Chapter 7 of this book provides contact information for the WTO and a description of this international economic organization.

The *Parties* to this Agreement,

Recognizing that their relations in the field of trade and economic endeavour should be conducted with a view to raising standards of living, ensuring full employment and a large and steadily growing volume of real income and effective demand, and expanding the production of and trade in goods and services, while allowing for the optimal use of the world's resources in accordance with the objective of sustainable development, seeking both to protect and preserve the environment and to enhance the means for doing so in a manner consistent with their respective needs and concerns at different levels of economic development,

Recognizing further that there is need for positive efforts designed to ensure that developing countries, and especially the least developed among them, secure a share in the growth in international trade commensurate with the needs of their economic development,

Being desirous of contributing to these objectives by entering into reciprocal and mutually advantageous arrangements directed to the substantial reduction of tariffs and other barriers to trade and to the elimination of discriminatory treatment in international trade relations,

Resolved, therefore, to develop an integrated, more viable and durable multilateral trading system encompassing the General Agreement on Tariffs and Trade, the results of past trade liberalization efforts, and all of the results of the Uruguay Round of Multilateral Trade Negotiations,

Determined to preserve the basic principles and to further the objectives underlying this multilateral trading system,

Agree as follows:

Article I
Establishment of the Organization
The World Trade Organization (hereinafter referred to as "the WTO") is hereby established.

Article II
Scope of the WTO
1. The WTO shall provide the common institutional framework for the conduct of trade relations among its Members in matters related to the agreements and associated legal instruments included in the Annexes to this Agreement.

2. The agreements and associated legal instruments included in Annexes 1, 2 and 3 (hereinafter referred to as "Multilateral Trade Agreements") are integral parts of this Agreement, binding on all Members.

3. The agreements and associated legal instruments included in Annex 4 (hereinafter referred to as "Plurilateral Trade Agreements") are also part of this Agreement for those Members that have accepted them, and are binding on those Members. The Plurilateral Trade Agreements do not create either obligations or rights for Members that have not accepted them.

4. The General Agreement on Tariffs and Trade 1994 as specified in Annex 1A (hereinafter referred to as "GATT 1994") is legally distinct from the General Agreement on Tariffs and Trade, dated 30 October 1947, annexed to the Final Act Adopted at the Conclusion of the Second Session of the Preparatory Committee of the United Nations Conference on Trade and Employment, as subsequently rectified, amended or modified (hereinafter referred to as "GATT 1947").

Article III

Functions of the WTO

1. The WTO shall facilitate the implementation, administration and operation, and further the objectives, of this Agreement and of the Multilateral Trade Agreements, and shall also provide the framework for the implementation, administration and operation of the Plurilateral Trade Agreements.

2. The WTO shall provide the forum for negotiations among its Members concerning their multilateral trade relations in matters dealt with under the agreements in the Annexes to this Agreement. The WTO may also provide a forum for further negotiations among its Members concerning their multilateral trade relations, and a framework for the implementation of the results of such negotiations, as may be decided by the Ministerial Conference.

3. The WTO shall administer the Understanding on Rules and Procedures Governing the Settlement of Disputes (hereinafter referred to as the "Dispute Settlement Understanding" or "DSU") in Annex 2 to this Agreement.

4. The WTO shall administer the Trade Policy Review Mechanism (hereinafter referred to as the "TPRM") provided for in Annex 3 to this Agreement.

5. With a view to achieving greater coherence in global economic policy-making, the WTO shall cooperate, as appropriate, with the International Monetary Fund and with the International Bank for Reconstruction and Development and its affiliated agencies.

Article IV

Structure of the WTO

1. There shall be a Ministerial Conference composed of representatives of all the Members, which shall meet at least once every two years. The Ministerial Conference shall carry out the functions of the WTO and take actions necessary to this effect. The Ministerial Conference shall have the authority to take decisions on all matters under any of the Multilateral Trade Agreements, if so requested by a Member, in accordance with the specific requirements for decision-making in this Agreement and in the relevant Multilateral Trade Agreement.

2. There shall be a General Council composed of representatives of all the Members, which shall meet as appropriate. In the intervals between meetings of the Ministerial Conference, its functions shall be conducted by the General Council. The General Council shall also carry out the functions assigned to it by this Agreement. The General Council shall establish its rules of procedure and approve the rules of procedure for the Committees provided for in paragraph 7.

3. The General Council shall convene as appropriate to discharge the responsibilities of the Dispute Settlement Body provided for in the Dispute Settlement Understanding. The Dispute Settlement Body may have its own chairman and shall establish such rules of procedure as it deems necessary for the fulfilment of those responsibilities.

4. The General Council shall convene as appropriate to discharge the responsibilities of the Trade Policy Review Body provided for in the TPRM. The Trade Policy Review Body may have its own chairman and shall establish such rules of procedure as it deems necessary for the fulfilment of those responsibilities.

5. There shall be a Council for Trade in Goods, a Council for Trade in Services and a Council for Trade-Related Aspects of Intellectual Property Rights (hereinafter referred to as the "Council for TRIPS"), which shall operate under the general guidance of the General Council. The Council for Trade in Goods shall oversee the functioning of the Multilateral Trade Agreements in Annex 1A. The Council for Trade in Services shall oversee the functioning of the General Agreement on Trade in Services (hereinafter referred to as "GATS"). The Council for TRIPS shall oversee the functioning of the Agreement on Trade-Related Aspects of Intellectual Property Rights (hereinafter referred to as the "Agreement on TRIPS"). These Councils shall carry out the functions assigned to them by their respective agreements and by the General Council. They shall establish their respective rules of procedure subject to the approval of the General Council. Membership in these Councils shall be open to representatives of all Members. These Councils shall meet as necessary to carry out their functions.

6. The Council for Trade in Goods, the Council for Trade in Services and the Council for TRIPS shall establish subsidiary bodies as required. These subsidiary bodies shall establish their respective rules of procedure subject to the approval of their respective Councils.

7. The Ministerial Conference shall establish a Committee on Trade and Development, a Committee on Balance-of-Payments Restrictions and a Committee on Budget, Finance and Administration, which shall carry out the functions assigned to them by this Agreement and by the Multilateral Trade Agreements, and any additional functions assigned to them by the General Council, and may establish such additional Committees with such functions as it may deem appropriate. As part of its functions, the Committee on Trade and Development shall periodically review the special provisions in the Multilateral Trade Agreements in favour of the least-developed country Members and report to the General Council for appropriate action. Membership in these Committees shall be open to representatives of all Members.

8. The bodies provided for under the Plurilateral Trade Agreements shall carry out the functions assigned to them under those Agreements and shall operate within the institutional framework of the WTO. These bodies shall keep the General Council informed of their activities on a regular basis.

Source: World Trade Organization (WTO). "Legal Texts: Agreement Establishing the World Trade Organization." www.wto.org/english/docs_e/legal_e/legal_e.htm#wtoagreement

Global Environmental Documents

Agenda 21

Agenda 21 was adopted at the United Nations Conference on Environment and Development in 1992. This conference is commonly referred to as the "Rio Conference" or "The Earth Summit." Below are the Preamble and Chapter 2 of Agenda 21. These selections stress the interconnectedness of human society and the need for cooperation to solve collective problems. Agenda 21 is a good example of attempts to further human development under environmental sustainability.

Preamble

1. 1. Humanity stands at a defining moment in history. We are confronted with a perpetuation of disparities between and within nations, a worsening of poverty, hunger, ill health and illiteracy, and the continuing deterioration of the ecosystems on which we depend for our well-being. However, integration of environment and development concerns and greater attention to them will lead to the fulfillment of basic needs, improved living standards for all, better protected and managed ecosystems and a safer, more prosperous future. No nation can achieve this on its own; but together we can—in a global partnership for sustainable development.

1. 2. This global partnership must build on the premises of General Assembly resolution 44/228 of 22 December 1989, which was adopted when the nations of the world called for the United Nations Conference on Environment and Development, and on the acceptance of the need to take a balanced and integrated approach to environment and development questions.

1. 3. Agenda 21 addresses the pressing problems of today and also aims at preparing the world for the challenges of the next century. It reflects a global consensus and political commitment at the highest level on development and environment cooperation. Its successful implementation is first and foremost the responsibility of Governments.

National strategies, plans, policies and processes are crucial in achieving this. International cooperation should support and supplement such national efforts. In this context, the United Nations system has a key role to play. Other international, regional and subregional organizations are also called upon to contribute to this effort. The broadest public participation and the active involvement of the non-governmental organizations and other groups should also be encouraged.

1. 4.   The developmental and environmental objectives of Agenda 21 will require a substantial flow of new and additional financial resources to developing countries, in order to cover the incremental costs for the actions they have to undertake to deal with global environmental problems and to accelerate sustainable development. Financial resources are also required for strengthening the capacity of international institutions for the implementation of Agenda 21. An indicative order-of-magnitude assessment of costs is included in each of the programme areas. This assessment will need to be examined and refined by the relevant implementing agencies and organizations.

1. 5.   In the implementation of the relevant programme areas identified in Agenda 21, special attention should be given to the particular circumstances facing the economies in transition. It must also be recognized that these countries are facing unprecedented challenges in transforming their economies, in some cases in the midst of considerable social and political tension.

1. 6.   The programme areas that constitute Agenda 21 are described in terms of the basis for action, objectives, activities and means of implementation. Agenda 21 is a dynamic programme. It will be carried out by the various actors according to the different situations, capacities and priorities of countries and regions in full respect of all the principles contained in the Rio Declaration on Environment and Development. It could evolve over time in the light of changing needs and circumstances. This process marks the beginning of a new global partnership for sustainable development.

Chapter 2
International Cooperation to Accelerate Sustainable Development In Developing Countries and Related Domestic Policies

2. 1.   In order to meet the challenges of environment and development, States have decided to establish a new global partnership. This partnership commits all States to engage in a continuous and constructive dialogue, inspired by the need to achieve a more efficient and equitable world economy, keeping in view the increasing interdependence of the community of nations and that sustainable development should become a priority item on the agenda of the international community. It is recognized that, for the success of this new partnership, it is important to overcome confrontation and to foster a climate of genuine cooperation and solidarity. It is equally important to strengthen national and international policies and multinational cooperation to adapt to the new realities.

2. 2. Economic policies of individual countries and international economic relations both have great relevance to sustainable development. The reactivation and acceleration of development requires both a dynamic and a supportive international economic environment and determined policies at the national level. It will be frustrated in the absence of either of these requirements. A supportive external economic environment is crucial. The development process will not gather momentum if the global economy lacks dynamism and stability and is beset with uncertainties. Neither will it gather momentum if the developing countries are weighted down by external indebtedness, if development finance is inadequate, if barriers restrict access to markets and if commodity prices and the terms of trade of developing countries remain depressed. The record of the 1980s was essentially negative on each of these counts and needs to be reversed. The policies and measures needed to create an international environment that is strongly supportive of national development efforts are thus vital. International cooperation in this area should be designed to complement and support—not to diminish or subsume—sound domestic economic policies, in both developed and developing countries, if global progress towards sustainable development is to be achieved.

2. 3. The international economy should provide a supportive international climate for achieving environment and development goals by:

Programme Areas
a. Promoting Sustainable Development Through Trade
Basis for Action

2. 5. An open, equitable, secure, non-discriminatory and predictable multilateral trading system that is consistent with the goals of sustainable development and leads to the optimal distribution of global production in accordance with comparative advantage is of benefit to all trading partners. Moreover, improved market access for developing countries' exports in conjunction with sound macroeconomic and environmental policies would have a positive environmental impact and therefore make an important contribution towards sustainable development.

2. 6. Experience has shown that sustainable development requires a commitment to sound economic policies and management, an effective and predictable public administration, the integration of environmental concerns into decision-making and progress towards democratic government, in the light of country-specific conditions, which allows for full participation of all parties concerned. These attributes are essential for the fulfillment of the policy directions and objectives listed below.

2. 7. The commodity sector dominates the economies of many developing countries in terms of production, employment and export earnings. An important feature of the world commodity economy in the 1980s was the prevalence of very low and declining real prices for most commodities in international markets and a resulting substantial contraction in commodity export earnings for many producing countries. The ability of those countries to mobilize, through international trade, the resources needed to finance investments required for sustainable development may be impaired by this development and by tariff and non-tariff impediments, including tariff escalation, limiting their access to export markets. The removal of existing distortions in international trade is essential. In particular, the achievement of this objective requires that there be substantial and progressive reduction in the support and protection of agriculture—covering internal regimes, market access and export subsidies—as well as of industry and other sectors, in order to avoid inflicting large losses on the more efficient producers, especially in developing countries. Thus, in agriculture, industry and other sectors, there is scope for initiatives aimed at trade liberalization and at policies to make production more responsive to environment and development needs. Trade liberalization should therefore be pursued on a global basis across economic sectors so as to contribute to sustainable development.

2. 8. The international trading environment has been affected by a number of developments that have created new challenges and opportunities and have made multilateral economic cooperation of even greater importance. World trade has continued to grow faster than world output in recent years. However, the expansion of world trade has been unevenly spread, and only a limited number of developing countries have been capable of achieving appreciable growth in their exports. Protectionist pressures and unilateral policy actions continue to endanger the functioning of an open multilateral trading system, affecting particularly the export interests of developing countries. Economic integration processes have intensified in recent years and should impart dynamism to global trade and enhance the trade and development possibilities for developing countries. In recent years, a growing number of these countries have adopted courageous policy reforms involving ambitious autonomous trade liberalization, while far-reaching reforms and profound restructuring processes are taking place in Central and Eastern European countries, paving the way for their integration into the world economy and the international trading system. Increased attention is being devoted to enhancing the role of enterprises and promoting competitive markets through adoption of competitive policies. The GSP has proved to be a useful trade policy instrument, although its objectives will have to be fulfilled, and trade facilitation strategies relating to electronic data interchange (EDI) have been effective in improving the trading efficiency of the public and private sectors. The interactions between environment policies and trade issues are manifold and have not yet been fully assessed. An early, balanced, comprehensive and successful outcome of the Uruguay Round of multilateral trade negotiations would bring about further liberalization and expansion of world trade, enhance the trade and development possibilities of developing countries and provide greater security and predictability to the international trading system.

Source: United Nations Division for Sustainable Development. "Agenda 21" www.un.org/esa/sustdev/documents/agenda21/english/agenda21toc.htm

The Montreal Protocol on Substances That Deplete the Ozone Layer (1987)

The Montreal Protocol is an international environmental agreement intended to protect stratospheric ozone. This agreement is a good example of the possibility of achieving effective international environmental agreements. The Montreal Protocol and the problem of ozone depletion is discussed in chapter 2.

Preamble
The Parties to this Protocol,
Being Parties to the Vienna Convention for the Protection of the Ozone Layer,

Mindful of their obligation under that Convention to take appropriate measures to protect human health and the environment against adverse effects resulting or likely to result from human activities which modify or are likely to modify the ozone layer,

Recognizing that world-wide emissions of certain substances can significantly deplete and otherwise modify the ozone layer in a manner that is likely to result in adverse effects on human health and the environment,

Conscious of the potential climatic effects of emissions of these substances,

Aware that measures taken to protect the ozone layer from depletion should be based on relevant scientific knowledge, taking into account technical and economic considerations,

Determined to protect the ozone layer by taking precautionary measures to control equitably total global emissions of substances that deplete it, with the ultimate objective of their elimination on the basis of developments in scientific knowledge, taking into account technical and economic considerations and bearing in mind the developmental needs of developing countries,

Acknowledging that special provision is required to meet the needs of developing countries, including the provision of additional financial resources and access to relevant technologies, bearing in mind that the magnitude of funds necessary is predictable, and the funds can be expected to make a substantial difference in the world's ability to address the scientifically established problem of ozone depletion and its harmful effects,

Noting the precautionary measures for controlling emissions of certain chlorofluorocarbons that have already been taken at national and regional levels,

Considering the importance of promoting international co-operation in the research, development and transfer of alternative technologies relating to the control and reduction of emissions of substances that deplete the ozone layer, bearing in mind in particular the needs of developing countries,

Have Agreed to as Follows:

Source: United Nations Environment Programme (UNEP). ozone. unep.org/pdfs/Montreal-Protocol2000.pdf

United Nations Framework Convention on Climate Change (1992)

The UNFCCC set the framework for international cooperation in dealing with the threat of climate change. Below is the Preamble to the UNFCCC. It expresses the shared concern of the threat of climate change in the international community.

The Parties to this Convention,

Acknowledging that change in the Earth's climate and its adverse effects are a common concern of humankind,

Concerned that human activities have been substantially increasing the atmospheric concentrations of greenhouse gases, that these increases enhance the natural greenhouse effect, and that this will result on average in an additional warming of the Earth's surface and atmosphere and may adversely affect natural ecosystems and humankind,

Noting that the largest share of historical and current global emissions of greenhouse gases has originated in developed countries, that per capita emissions in developing countries are still relatively low and that the share of global emissions originating in developing countries will grow to meet their social and development needs,

Aware of the role and importance in terrestrial and marine ecosystems of sinks and reservoirs of greenhouse gases,

Noting that there are many uncertainties in predictions of climate change, particularly with regard to the timing, magnitude and regional patterns thereof,

Acknowledging that the global nature of climate change calls for the widest possible cooperation by all countries and their participation in an effective and appropriate international response, in accordance with their common but differentiated responsibilities and respective capabilities and their social and economic conditions,

Recalling the pertinent provisions of the Declaration of the United Nations Conference on the Human Environment, adopted at Stockholm on 16 June 1972,

Recalling also that States have, in accordance with the Charter of the United Nations and the principles of international law, the sovereign right to exploit their own resources pursuant to their own environmental and developmental policies, and the responsibility to ensure that activities within their jurisdiction or control do not cause damage to the environment of other States or of areas beyond the limits of national jurisdiction,

Reaffirming the principle of sovereignty of States in international cooperation to address climate change,

Recognizing that States should enact effective environmental legislation, that environmental standards, management objectives and priorities should reflect the environmental and developmental context to which they apply, and that standards applied by some countries may be inappropriate and of unwarranted economic and social cost to other countries, in particular developing countries,

Recalling the provisions of General Assembly resolution 44/228 of 22 December 1989 on the United Nations Conference on Environment and Development, and resolutions 43/53 of 6 December 1988, 44/207 of 22 December 1989, 45/212 of 21 December 1990 and 46/169 of 19 December 1991 on protection of global climate for present and future generations of mankind,

Recalling also the provisions of General Assembly resolution 44/206 of 22 December 1989 on the possible adverse effects of sea level rise on islands and coastal areas, particularly low-lying coastal areas and the pertinent provisions of General Assembly resolution 44/172 of 19 December 1989 on the implementation of the Plan of Action to Combat Desertification,

Recalling further the Vienna Convention for the Protection of the Ozone Layer, 1985, and the Montreal Protocol on Substances that Deplete the Ozone Layer, 1987, as adjusted and amended on 29 June 1990,

Noting the Ministerial Declaration of the Second World Climate Conference adopted on 7 November 1990,

Conscious of the valuable analytical work being conducted by many States on climate change and of the important contributions of the World Meteorological Organization, the United Nations Environment Programme and other organs, organizations and bodies of the United Nations system, as well as other international and intergovernmental bodies, to the exchange of results of scientific research and the coordination of research,

Recognizing that steps required to understand and address climate change will be environmentally, socially and economically most effective if they are based on relevant scientific, technical and economic considerations and continually re-evaluated in the light of new findings in these areas,

Recognizing that various actions to address climate change can be justified economically in their own right and can also help in solving other environmental problems,

Recognizing also the need for developed countries to take immediate action in a flexible manner on the basis of clear priorities, as a first step towards comprehensive response strategies at the global, national and, where agreed, regional levels that take into account all greenhouse gases, with due consideration of their relative contributions to the enhancement of the greenhouse effect,

Recognizing further that low-lying and other small island countries, countries with low-lying coastal, arid and semi-arid areas or areas liable to floods, drought and desertification, and developing countries with fragile mountainous ecosystems are particularly vulnerable to the adverse effects of climate change,

Recognizing the special difficulties of those countries, especially developing countries, whose economies are particularly dependent on fossil fuel production, use and exportation, as a consequence of action taken on limiting greenhouse gas emissions,

Affirming that responses to climate change should be coordinated with social and economic development in an integrated manner with a view to avoiding adverse impacts on the latter, taking into full account the legitimate priority needs of developing countries for the achievement of sustained economic growth and the eradication of poverty,

Recognizing that all countries, especially developing countries, need access to resources required to achieve sustainable social and economic development and that, in order for developing countries to progress towards that goal, their energy consumption will need to grow taking into account the possibilities for achieving greater energy efficiency and for controlling greenhouse gas emissions in general, including through the application of new technologies on terms which make such an application economically and socially beneficial,

Determined to protect the climate system for present and future generations,

. . .

Source: United Nations Framework Convention on Climate Change (UNFCCC). www.unfccc.int/resource/docs/convkp/conveng.pdf

Kyoto Protocol to the United Nations Framework Convention on Climate Change

The Kyoto Protocol set targets for reducing greenhouse gas emissions from developed nation-states. It went into effect in 2005. Below are the introduction and Article I of the Kyoto Protocol. Article II is particularly important for it makes clear that developed nation-states are to be held responsible for reducing greenhouse gas emissions.

The Parties to this Protocol,
Being Parties to the United Nations Framework Convention on Climate Change, hereinafter referred to as "the Convention,"
In pursuit of the ultimate objective of the Convention as stated in its Article 2,
Recalling the provisions of the Convention,
Being guided by Article 3 of the Convention,
Pursuant to the Berlin Mandate adopted by decision 1/CP.1 of the Conference of the Parties to the Convention at its first session,
Have agreed as follows:

Article 2
1. Each Party included in Annex I, in achieving its quantified emission limitation and reduction commitments under Article 3, in order to promote sustainable development, shall:

(a) Implement and/or further elaborate policies and measures in accordance with its national circumstances, such as:

(i) Enhancement of energy efficiency in relevant sectors of the national economy;

(ii) Protection and enhancement of sinks and reservoirs of greenhouse gases not controlled by the Montreal Protocol, taking into account its commitments under relevant international environmental agreements; promotion of sustainable forest management practices, afforestation and reforestation;

(iii) Promotion of sustainable forms of agriculture in light of climate change considerations;

(iv) Research on, and promotion, development and increased use of, new and renewable forms of energy, of carbon dioxide sequestration technologies and of advanced and innovative environmentally sound technologies;

(v) Progressive reduction or phasing out of market imperfections, fiscal incentives, tax and duty exemptions and subsidies in all greenhouse gas emitting sectors that run counter to the objective of the Convention and application of market instruments;

(vi) Encouragement of appropriate reforms in relevant sectors aimed at promoting policies and measures which limit or reduce emissions of greenhouse gases not controlled by the Montreal Protocol;

(vii) Measures to limit and/or reduce emissions of greenhouse gases not controlled by the Montreal Protocol in the transport sector;

(viii) Limitation and/or reduction of methane emissions through recovery and use in waste management, as well as in the production, transport and distribution of energy;

(b) Cooperate with other such Parties to enhance the individual and combined effectiveness of their policies and measures adopted under this Article, pursuant to Article 4, paragraph 2(e)(i), of the Convention. To this end, these Parties shall take steps to share their experience and exchange information on such policies and measures, including developing ways of improving their comparability, transparency and effectiveness. The Conference of the Parties serving as the meeting of the Parties to this Protocol shall, at its first session or as soon as practicable thereafter, consider ways to facilitate such cooperation, taking into account all relevant information.

2. The Parties included in Annex I shall pursue limitation or reduction of emissions of greenhouse gases not controlled by the Montreal Protocol from aviation and marine bunker fuels, working through the International Civil Aviation Organization and the International Maritime Organization, respectively.

3. The Parties included in Annex I shall strive to implement policies and measures under this Article in such a way as to minimize adverse effects, including the adverse effects of climate change, effects on international trade, and social, environmental and economic impacts on other Parties, especially developing country Parties and in particular those identified in Article 4, paragraphs 8 and 9, of the Convention, taking into account Article 3 of the Convention. The Conference of the Parties serving as the meeting of the Parties to this Protocol may take further action, as appropriate, to promote the implementation of the provisions of this paragraph.

4. The Conference of the Parties serving as the meeting of the Parties to this Protocol, if it decides that it would be beneficial to coordinate any of the policies and measures in paragraph 1(a) above, taking into account different national circumstances and potential effects, shall consider ways and means to elaborate the coordination of such policies and measures.

Source: United Nations. "Kyoto Protocol to the United Nations Framework Convention on Climate Change." www.unfccc.int/resource/docs/convkp/kpeng.html

7

Directory of Organizations

This chapter provides a selected list of organizations actively involved in the globalization process. These organizations are divided into those of the United States government, international governmental organizations, nongovernmental organizations, and university-based research institutions. As an academic subject, globalization is fairly new and quite contentious. Collectively, the following annotations provide clear examples of the different views held by each of the listed organizations regarding globalization. This directory of organizations shows that those working within the globalization process interpret its unfolding in dramatically different ways.

Finally, this chapter is designed to provide the reader with a starting point to identify important organizations related to globalization. Given the multitude of actors involved, the following is only a basic account of a much more complex organizational reality.

United States Government Agencies

Central Intelligence Agency (CIA)
Office of Public Affairs, Washington, DC 20505
Phone: (703) 482–0623
Fax: (703) 482–1739
E-mail: online contact form
Web site: www.cia.gov

The Central Intelligence Agency was formed in 1947 with President Harry S. Truman's signing of the National Security Act. The CIA is headed by the director of central intelligence (DCI). The DCI is a principal intelligence adviser to the president of the United States. In this role, the DCI is responsible for briefing the president on intelligence concerning national security. With the passing of the Intelligence Reform and Terrorism Prevention Act of 2004, the DCI now reports to the director of National Intelligence.

The function of the CIA is to collect data, evaluate intelligence, and coordinate the intelligence-gathering needs of other executive federal agencies and departments. The agency is not involved in domestic policing or intelligence gathering. The CIA publishes the *World Factbook,* a comprehensive reference work on vital statistics of foreign nation-states. These profiles include information on population, economic conditions, government leadership and structure, geography, climate, and many other demographic indicators.

Office of the United States Trade Representative (USTR)
600 17th Street, NW, Washington, DC 20508
Phone: (202) 395–7360
E-mail: contactustr@ustr.eop.gov
Web site: www.ustr.gov

Founded in 1962, the office of the United States Trade Representative is located within the Executive Office of the president of the United States. The office is composed of over 200 trade professionals, with foreign offices in Brussels, Belgium, and Geneva, Switzerland. The USTR coordinates foreign trade and investment policy of the United States. It is responsible for negotiations with foreign nation-states on bilateral, regional, and global trade agreements. The ambassador of USTR is the president's principal trade adviser. The USTR is central in negotiating resolutions to disagreements concerning international trade. For example, it represents the United States on matters brought before the World Trade Organization. The USTR is responsible for preparing reports concerning international trade for the president, Congress, and the public.

United States Department of Defense (DOD)
Pentagon
Washington, DC 20001
Web site: www.defenselink.mil

The Department of Defense considers itself the largest and most successful company in the United States as it plays an integral role in the U.S. economy. The DOD is responsible for designing and implementing the global military strategy of the United States. Its primary function is to fight wars and coordinate peace-keeping missions. Composed of three subdepartments—the United States Army, Navy (including the Marines), and Air Force—the DOD is also responsible for maintaining the U.S. National Guard and Army Reserve.

The interests of the United States encompass the entire globe under current DOD strategy. These global responsibilities are split into regional command centers. The head of the DOD is the secretary of defense. He advises the president, who is commander in chief of the U.S. military. Through the orders of the president, the secretary of Defense directs the United States military through the Joint Chiefs of Staff (JCS). The JCS trains, coordinates, equips, and deploys the U.S. military. The JCS also advise the secretary of defense and the National Security Council.

United States Department of State (USDS)
2201 C Street, NW, Washington, DC 20520
Phone: (202) 647–4000
Web site: www.state.gov

The U.S. Department of State was founded in 1789. It is responsible for conducting diplomatic relations for the United States and oversees U.S. foreign embassies and their ambassador corps. The USDS has determined globalization to be a principal factor in the design of its efforts. The diplomacy pursued by the USDS is performed to maintain the complex security interests of the United States. The State Department considers U.S. leadership essential in the era of globalization, stressing the importance of multilateral relationships with other nation-states. In the era of globalization, an increasingly integrated world requires wise diplomatic efforts to maintain cooperation with other nation-states.

International Governmental Organizations

Association of Southeast Asian Nations (ASEAN)
The ASEAN Secretariat
70A, Jalan Sisingamangaraja

Jakarta 12110
Indonesia
Phone: (6221) 7262991, 7243372
Fax: (6221) 7398234, 7243504
E-mail: public@aseansec.org
Web site: www.aseansec.org

The Association of Southeast Asian Nations was formed in Bangkok, Thailand, in 1967. The organization has 10 member nation-states that hold yearly summits to discuss mutual interests and concerns. It is a regional international government organization that has resulted in increased regional integration. A primary goal of ASEAN is to increase economic growth in Southeast Asia while addressing environmentally sustainable development. The countries of ASEAN cooperate on many issue areas, including crime, terrorism, immigration, and the international trade of illegal drugs. ASEAN values the promotion of regional cultural development and social progress. In order to promote regional peace and stability, it established the ASEAN Security Community. To increase economic integration, ASEAN created the ASEAN Free Trade Area in 1992. ASEAN hopes to have a fully integrated economic community by 2020. This would create a single regional market in Southeast Asia, allowing the free flow of goods and services.

Bank for International Settlements (BIS)
CH–4002
Basel, Switzerland
Phone: (+41 61) 280–8080
Fax: (+41 61) 280–9100
E-mail: email@bis.org
Web site: www.bis.org

The Bank for International Settlements is the oldest international financial organization, created on May 17, 1930, to oversee the payment of German reparations provided for by the Treaty of Versailles. The BIS is based in Basel, Switzerland, with offices in Hong Kong, China, and Mexico City, Mexico. The bank is considered the "central bank of central banks." The BIS provides a forum for financial coordination among the central banks of nation-states. Its primary focus is the stability of the global banking system. It collects data and conducts research concerning the global economy. The BIS provides assistance to International Monetary Fund stabilization programs employed to prevent global financial crises. Such crises have been frequent occurrences in the era of globalization.

European Union (EU)
Phone: 32–2–299-96-96
E-mail: online contact form
Web site: www.europa.eu

Although preceded by multiple treaties enhancing cooperation and integration, the European Union was created with the Treaty of the European Union, commonly referred to as the Maastricht Treaty, which was ratified in 1992. The goal of the EU is to integrate European nation-states into a single common market. Toward this end, the EU has created a common currency, the euro. The EU pursues a regional development policy, enhancing cooperation to address collective problems.

The EU is a federal arrangement representing 27 European nation-states (as of 2007) through common institutions. These institutions include the European Parliament, the Council of the European Union, the European Commission, the Court of Justice, the Court of Auditors, the European Economic and Social Committee, the Committee of Regions, the European Central Bank, and the European Commercial Bank. The central governance institutions of the EU are based in Brussels, Belgium; Strasbourg, France; and Luxembourg.

Global Environmental Facility (GEF)
GEF Secretariat
1818 H Street, NW, MSN G6–602
Washington, DC 20433
Phone: (202) 473–0508
Fax: (202) 522–3240/3245
E-mail: secretariat@thegef.org
Web site: www.gefweb.org

The Global Environmental Facility was founded in 1991 to help developing nation-states address global environmental problems. The GEF provides grants to developing nation-states so they can implement environmental policies. These grants are applied to six areas: biodiversity, climate change, international waters, land degradation, the ozone layer, and persistent organic pollutants. As of 2007 the GEF has provided over 1,300 grants to 130 developing nation-states, amounting to $6.2 billion United States dollars (USDs). GEF-funded projects are implemented by the United Nations Environment Programme, the United Nations Development Programme and the World Bank. The organization has 177 member nation-states that meet at "assemblies" every three to four years. It relies on existing environmental agreements for designing its strategies. GEF environmental programs are structured to include local communities, respecting local agency and interests in the cause of addressing environmental problems.

Intergovernmental Panel on Climate Change (IPCC)
c/o World Meteorological Organization
7bis Avenue de la Paix
C.P. 2300
CH–1211 Geneva 2, Switzerland
Phone: (+41) 22–730–8208
Fax: (+41) 22–730–8025
E-mail: IPCC-Sec@wmo.int
Web site: www.ipcc.ch

The Intergovernmental Panel on Climate Change was formed by United Nations Environment Programme and the World Meteorological Organization in 1988. The IPCC assesses the state of scientific understanding concerning climate change. It does not collect data or produce its own research but monitors current research in order to understand scientific knowledge concerning climate change. The panel's responsibilities are divided into three working groups. Working Group I assesses the basis of the physical science of climate change. Working Group II assesses the impact of climate change on Earth's biosphere. Working Group III focuses on policies devised to mitigate climate change.

Findings by the IPCC are reached by consensus. The three working groups assess knowledge on climate change on the basis of scientific peer review. During this process the three working groups consider the scientific work of hundreds of scientists. With its emphasis on scientific peer review, the IPCC can be considered a conservative institution in its assessment of the dangers of climate change. The IPCC has been instrumental in providing the scientific legitimacy necessary for policy makers to address climate change.

International Labour Organization (ILO)

4 route des Morillons CH–121,1 Genève 22 Switzerland
Phone: +41 (0) 22 799 6111
Fax: +41 (0) 22 798 8685
E-mail: ilo@ilo.org
Web site: www.ilo.org

The International Labour Organization works for the rights of labor on a global scale. Its basic values concerning labor rights are justice, equity, security, and dignity. The ILO was founded in 1919, becoming an agency of the United Nations in 1946. It brings together governments and leaders of business and labor to promote just labor policies. It also sets and monitors global labor standards. The ILO believes the defense of fair and just labor conditions is the way out of poverty for the world's 2 billion people that live on less than $2 United States dollars a day.

International Monetary Fund (IMF)

700 19th Street, NW
Washington, DC 20431
Phone: (202) 623–7000
Fax: (202) 623–4661
E-mail: publicaffairs@imf.org
Web site: www.imf.org

The International Monetary Fund is sometimes referred to as the "sister institution" to the World Bank. Created at the Bretton Woods Conference, the initial responsibility of the IMF was to create and maintain a stable global monetary system. It currently (2007) has a membership of 184 nation-states. As of July 2006, the IMF had $28 billion United States dollars in outstanding loans to 74 nation-states. The IMF offers economic advice and policy prescriptions to nation-states with troubled economies.

The initial goal of the IMF was to facilitate international trade by ensuring the stability of current account balances (exports-imports) of nation-states. Current account balances are determined by the amount of a nation-state's imports and exports. Balancing current accounts is important because nation-states suffer balance-of-payment problems when their imports exceed their exports. Countries that have a negative current account balance place more of their currency in the hands of foreigners than it receives in kind. This results in a depreciated or less valuable currency.

With the onset of the global financial instability that is characteristic of globalization, the IMF took on the role of lender of last resort to protect developing nation-states (and the financial institutions that lent to them) from bankruptcy. The IMF would "bail out" developing nation-states with structural adjustment loans if they agreed to submit their economic policies to structural adjustment programs (SAPs). SAPs required nation-states receiving assistance to (1) reduce government spending to reduce inflation; (2) restrain or cut wages within the nation-state; (3) liberalize imports, providing incentives for investment to provide for much needed foreign exchange; (4) remove burdensome restrictions on foreign investment within the nation-state; (5) devalue the currency to make its exports more competitive; and (6) allow state enterprises to be privatized.

North Atlantic Treaty Organization (NATO)
Blvd Leopold III, 1110 Brussels, Belgium
E-mail: natodoc@hq.nato.int
Web site: www.nato.int

The North Atlantic Treaty Organization was formed on April 4, 1949. The United States led in the formation of NATO to unify European powers, with the United States as a collective security regime. NATO enabled the United States to be the dominant military power responsible for protecting the global system. The organization was initially designed to balance global power between the United States and the Soviet Union. With the end of the Cold War, NATO has retained its importance as a security alliance providing for mutual security interests of Europe and the United States.

As of 2007, NATO had 26 member nation-states. Some new members are former Warsaw Pact members that were under the sphere of influence of the Soviet Union. Under the NATO security alliance, all members contribute forces that are deployed in crises requiring military action. For example, NATO is responsible for directing forces in Afghanistan, taking over for the United States in 2006. Article 5 of the NATO charter declares that any attack against a NATO nation-state would be considered an attack against all NATO nation-states. The terrorist attacks on 9/11 were considered by NATO to be an attack on the NATO security alliance.

Organization for Economic Cooperation and Development (OECD)
OECD Washington Center (North America)
2001 L Street, NW, Suite 650
Washington, DC 20036–4922
Phone: (202) 785–6323
Fax: (202) 785–0350
E-mail: washington.contact@oecd.org
Web site: www.oecdwash.org

The Organization for Economic Cooperation and Development was formed in 1961. Descended from the Organization for European Economic Co-operation, which administered the economic aid provided by the Marshall Plan, the OECD is headquartered in France, having 30 member nation-states. All members are European except Japan, Canada, and the United States. The OECD is an organization composed primarily of developed nation-states.

The OECD promotes democracy and stable market economies. In the era of globalization, the focus has expanded to developing nation-states to which the OECD offers economic advice on the basis of the benefits of free markets. The organization monitors and analyzes economic trends, forecasting the future of the global economy and collecting data and conducting economic research into issues of development in order to implement effective economic policy. The OECD is favorable to the expansion of international trade, a central dimension of globalization.

Shanghai Cooperation Organization (SCO)
No 41. Liangmaqiao Road
Chaoyang District
Beijing, China, 100600
Phone: 86–10–65329807/65329836
Fax: 86–10–65329808/65329237
E-mail: sco@sectsco.org
Web site: www.sectsco.org

The Shanghai Cooperation Organization was formed in Shanghai, China, in 2001. Members include the People's Republic of China, the Russian Federation, Kazakhstan, Tajikistan, Uzbekistan, and the Kyrgyz Republic. Membership of the SCO represents three fifths of the physical geography of the Eurasian continent. In population numbers the SCO represents 1.5 billion people, or a quarter of Earth's total. The organization was created to increase the cooperation and integration of member nation-states. Members consider themselves to have collective economic, security, cultural, and environmental interests. The SCO's central decision-making body is the Heads of Government Council (HGC). The HGC meets once a year to coordinate strategies to identify and meet common interests. The SCO has two permanent institutions: its Secretariat in Beijing, China, and its primary security institution in Tashkent, Uzbekistan. The SCO undertook joint military exercises in 2007 to enhance collective security and express its mutual commitment to the rest of the world.

United Nations (UN)
1st Avenue at 46th Street
New York, NY 10017
Web site: www.un.org

The United Nations was founded in 1945 following the end of World War II. The UN serves as an institutional forum to address concerns among nation-states within the global system. The organization is composed of the Security Council with five permanent members (United States, Britain, France, China, and Russia) and 10 temporary positions that transition every two years. These positions are chosen through elections in the General Assembly. Each of the five permanent members of the UN Security Council can veto resolutions passed by the General Assembly, giving permanent members power over the UN decision-making processes.

The UN General Assembly is composed of all 192 member nation-states of the organization. The General Assembly provides the forum in which all members have their concerns addressed. Resolutions are issued in the General Assembly to be voted on by member nation-states. These resolutions are not binding, however, for the UN has no official enforcement mechanism to execute international law. Resolutions have the best chance of altering a nation-state's behavior if the permanent members of the Security Council support the resolution. If a resolution is not supported by just one permanent member of the Security Council, it can be vetoed, ending its significance. Examples of this can be seen in the long tradition of the United States vetoing resolutions concerning Israel's occupation of the West

Bank and Gaza Strip. Another example is France's threat to veto a resolution proposed by the United States to approve the use of force against Iraq in 2003.

Along with the Security Council and General Assembly, the UN contains many institutions to address common problems and collective goods that characterize globalization. The UN collects data, conducts research, and publishes reports in many issue areas, including the global economy, the state of the global environment, international security, and human rights.

The World Bank Group (WB)
1818 H Street, NW, Washington, DC 20433
Phone: (202) 473–1000
Fax: (202) 477–6391
E-mail: online comment form
Web site: www.worldbank.org

The World Bank is also known as the International Bank for Reconstruction and Development (IBRD). It was created at the Bretton Woods Conference to provide a means for transferring reconstruction loans to war-ravaged Europe following World War II. The IBRD was central in rebuilding the economies of Europe. IBRD loans were directed toward rebuilding cities and repairing industrial infrastructure. Coupled with the Marshall Plan, IBRD loans provided for the importation of goods from the United States. This benefited the economies of both the United States and Europe. Under the stewardship of the United States, the European powers were able to rebuild their economies after World War II in a much shorter time than after any previous war.

Following European reconstruction, the IBRD, now commonly known as the WB, shifted its focus to the developing world. The emphasis of WB loans remained on building industrial infrastructure through large-scale development projects, as modern infrastructure creates markets for goods and services produced in advanced industrial nation-states. WB loans also focused on improving agricultural infrastructure through the green revolution, which introduced modern machinery, synthetic pesticides, and petroleum-based fertilizers to the developing world. Another target of WB loans is to provide public education in developing nation-states. WB loans also increase the integration of the natural resources and labor of developing nation-states into the global economy as its development policy is to integrate much of the world into a single global economic system.

Today the WB has 184 member nation-states. Its institutional structure contains two development agencies: the IBRD and the International Development Agency. The WB's stated goal is to reduce poverty and to improve the standard of living of those targeted by WB development loans. The bank generates funding for its loans through two sources. The first is provided from dues paid by member nation-states. The second is acquired through selling bonds on international financial markets. The WB provides loans below market interest rates to nation-states that have difficulty finding willing lenders from private financial sources.

World Trade Organization (WTO)
Centre William Rappard
Rue de Lausanne 154
CH–1211 Geneva 21
Switzerland
Phone: (41–22) 739 51 11
Fax: (41–22) 731 42 06
E-mail: enquiries@wto.org
Web site: www.wto.org

The World Trade Organization was formed in negotiations at the Uruguay Round of the General Agreement on Tariffs and Trade, which began in 1986 and went into effect on January 1, 1995. The WTO is based in Geneva, Switzerland, and has 151 member nation-states (as of 2007). The goal of the WTO is to harmonize trade rules and reduce barriers to free trade, such as quotas and tariffs. The WTO also provides rules protecting intellectual property rights in trade and services. These rules, called Trade-Related Aspects of Intellectual Property Rights, protect intellectual property such as music, books, medicines, and scientific innovations in areas such as biotechnology.

The WTO contains an enforceable dispute mechanism. This mechanism binds member nation-states to rules that limit the economic policy member nation-states can pursue. The WTO can monetarily sanction its members for pursuing economic policies it considers to be in noncompliance with WTO rules. A prerequisite for nation-states to join the organization is to have their economic and public policies subject to WTO review.

Research Centers and Nongovernmental Organizations

Amnesty International (AI)
International Secretariat
1 Easton Street
London
WC1X 0DW, United Kingdom
Phone: +44–20–74135500
Fax: +44–20–79561157
E-mail: online contact form
Web site: www.amnesty.org

Amnesty International is a global human rights organization founded in Britain by Peter Benenson in 1961. AI bases its concern for human rights on the United Nations Declaration of Human Rights (see chapter 6). AI is opposed to all physical and mental abuse and supports the rights of "prisoners of conscience." The organization defends the rights of all people to live with dignity, free from the threat of coercion or force. As an organization, it is nonideological. It does not support or condone countries' actions so long as human rights are defended and valued.

AI has 2.2 million members in over 150 nation-states (as of 2007). Its institutional structure is democratic. Major decisions directing AI are made by the International Council, which represents all national AI sections. The work of the organization focuses on women's rights, torture, political "disappearances," and extrajudicial executions; it also monitors the behavior of peacekeeping missions. AI was awarded the Nobel Peace Prize in 1977 for its defense of human rights across the globe.

The Brookings Institution
1775 Massachusetts Avenue, NW
Washington, DC 20036
Phone: (202)–797–6000
Fax: (202)–797–6004
E-mail: online contact form
Web site: www.brookings.edu

The Brookings Institution is one of most influential think tanks in the United States. It was founded by entrepreneur and philanthropist Robert S. Brookings in 1916 as the Institute for Government Research. The Institution produces influential policy analysis in the United States, employing experts from government, academia, nongovernmental organizations, and the private sector. Much of the research produced by the Brookings Institution focuses on issue areas of globalization, including international trade, development, security, and environmental problems. The Brookings Institution is nonpartisan but proglobalization, citing the benefits of free markets. It encourages the advancement and diffusion of science and technology to lessen unequal outcomes among globalization's winners and losers.

Carnegie Endowment for International Peace (CEIP)
1779 Massachusetts Avenue, NW
Washington, DC 20036–2103
Phone: (202) 483–7600
Fax: (202) 483–1840
E-mail: info@CarnegieEndowment.org
Web site: www.ceip.org

The Carnegie Endowment for International Peace was founded in 1910 with a $10 million endowment from the wealthy steel magnate Andrew Carnegie. The trustees, administrators, and researchers of the organization come from leaders of government, academia, and business. CEIP research focuses on the promotion of international law and dispute resolution. The organization promotes the liberal institutionalist emphasis of international cooperation in economics and governance. Jessica T. Mathews, a prominent international relations scholar, is its president (as of 2007). The CEIP focuses on the rapid change globalization has produced among diverse people across the globe. It believes the United States must remain a central actor in international affairs. Considering itself a global think tank, the CEIP has offices in Moscow, Beijing, Brussels, and Beirut. The organization publishes *Foreign Policy*, a leading academic journal of international relations. CEIP research also covers many issues of globalization, including the proliferation of nuclear weapons, the rise of China as a major world power, and the effect a resurgent Russian Federation will have on the global system.

Cato Institute
1000 Massachusetts Avenue, NW
Washington, DC 20001–5403
Phone: (202) 842–0200
Fax: (202) 842–3490
Web site: www.cato.org

The Cato Institute was founded by Edward H. Crane in 1977. It is named after the "Cato Letters," libertarian pamphlets that circulated in colonial America and helped inspire rebellion from Britain. The institute's research focuses on the view that limited government and free markets lead to peace and prosperity. Its publications are the *Cato Policy Report* and the *Cato Journal.* The organization is composed of scholars who are self-described "market liberals." The institute is skeptical of government intervention in social, economic, and environmental matters and of proposals supporting U.S. engagement in foreign wars. The Cato Institute is a good example of the libertarian political philosophy as it exists in the United States.

The Center for Economic and Policy Research (CEPR)
1611 Connecticut Avenue, NW, Suite 400
Washington, DC 20009
Phone: (202) 293–5380
Fax: (202) 588–1356
E-mail: cepr@cepr.net
Web site: www.cepr.net

The Center for Economic and Policy Research focuses its efforts on educating the public about economic matters that affect their lives. CEPR was founded in 1999 as an attempt to open up debate on issues concerning democratic values and economic practice. The center was founded by economists and currently has Nobel Prize recipients on its advisory board. A notable member, economist, and Nobel Prize recipient is Joseph Stiglitz; he is a former World Bank (WB) economist who has spoken out against WB and International Monetary Fund policy. The CEPR produces research on globalization related to international trade and the impact of international finance institutions on economic growth and global poverty. The center supports economic globalization but believes it must be reformed and managed to respect democratic values.

The Center for Research on Globalization (CRG)
PO Box 55019 11 Ouest Notre-Dame
Montreal, Quebec
H2Y 4A7 Canada
Phone: (514) 425–3814
Fax: (514) 425–6224
Web site: www.globalresearch.ca

The Center for Research on Globalization is composed of scholars, journalists, and writers who are critical of globalization. The
CGR views globalization as a process that maintains and extends
the United States empire. The center was established in 2001 by
Michel Chossudovsky, professor of economics at the University
of Ottawa. It maintains a popular Web site for critics of globalization in its current form. The CGR conducts research expressing
its negative vision of the globalization process. Topics it covers
are the global economy, the environment, biotechnology, militarization, energy policy and resources, and the ownership of mass
media. Some work produced by the CGR may be deemed controversial, but this organization is worthy of consideration in the
study of globalization.

Center for Strategic and International Studies (CSIS)
1800 K Street, NW
Washington, DC 20006
Phone: (202) 887–0200
Fax: (202) 775–3199
Web site: www.csis.org

The Center for Strategic and International Studies is an influential public policy research center in the United States. CSIS policy
research has affected many dimensions of public policy in the
United States since it was founded in 1962. The center conducts
strategic policy research intended to advance the global security
and economic interests of the United States. It has three high-pri-
ority focus areas: globalization, regional transformation, and U.S.
defense and security policy. The scope of CSIS research is global,
encompassing all inhabited continents. The goal of the CSIS is to
anticipate challenges to U.S. security in the era of globalization.
Its board of advisers and trustees is composed of leaders in business, finance, and academia, and former top policy makers in the
United States. In 2006, the CSIS partnered with the Iraq Study
Group, contributing to much of its research findings.

Corpwatch
1611 Telegraph Avenue #720
Oakland, CA 94612
Phone: (510) 271–8080
E-mail: online contact form
Web site: www.corpwatch.org

Corpwatch is a human rights organization founded in 1996 as the Transnational Resource and Action Center. A small organization composed of anti–corporate globalization activists, it conducts research into the activities of multinational corporations (MNCs) around the globe and offers a critical perspective on many aspects of globalization. Corpwatch documents fraud and corruption, environmental degradation, and human rights abuses. It is critical of U.S. MNCs that profit from the "global war on terror." Although a small organization, it publishes books and policy reports focusing on many issue areas of globalization.

Council on Foreign Relations (CFR)
The Harold Pratt House
58 East 68th Street
New York, NY 10065
Phone: (212) 434–9400
Fax: (212) 434–9800
Web site: www.cfr.org

The Council on Foreign Relations is a private group restricted to U.S. citizens. Founded in 1921, it has since worked closely with business leaders in the United States. To become a life member of the CFR, one must be nominated by a current member and supported by at least three other members. Many business, academic, and government leaders in the United States are CFR members. The CFR publishes the influential international relations journal *Foreign Affairs.* The organization works to inform citizens, business leaders, and policy makers in the United States about the global system. It coordinates regional meetings in the United States of leading business leaders and academics. These meetings are used as forums to discuss globalization.

Economic Policy Institute (EPI)
1333 H Street, NW
Suite 300, East Tower
Washington, DC 20005–4707

Phone: (202) 775–8810
Fax: (202) 775–0819
Web site: www.epinet.org

The Economic Policy Institute was founded in 1986 by economic policy experts from government and academia. EPI focuses on ensuring that economic prosperity is shared among the global population in a fair and just manner. It warns that globalization has caused instability in the global system by increasing inequality within and between nation-states and that the interests of working people should have a voice in economic policy decisions if global stability is to be achieved. EPI research focuses on the promotion of a strong labor movement and supports labor rights. EPI researchers focus on a wide range of economic indicators, evaluating how they affect the standard of living for workers. The institute's Web site offers many economic indicators and indices that are important in globalization research.

Global Exchange
2017 Mission Street, 2nd Floor
San Francisco, CA 94110
Phone: (415) 255–7296
Fax: (415) 255–7498
Web site: www.globalexchange.org

Global Exchange is an international human rights organization. Founded in 1988, it works to educate the public on matters concerning globalization. The Global Exchange has a critical view of the current globalization process. Its work is largely in the defense of the United Nations Declaration on Human Rights. Global Exchange attempts to create international links between activists around the globe. It undertakes campaigns that favor "fair trade" over "free trade" and support the rights of the poor over the rights of multinational corporations (MNCs). The Global Exchange maintains that the social, economic, and political impacts MNCs have on the global poor are negative and unjust. This organization conducts "reality tours," allowing citizens in industrial nation-states to see firsthand the plight of the poor in the developing world.

Global Policy Forum (GPF)
777 UN Plaza, Suite D

New York, NY 10017
Phone: (212) 557–3161
Fax: (212) 557–3165
E-mail: gpf@globalpolicy.org
Web site: www.globalpolicy.org

The Global Policy Forum monitors and acts as a policy consultant at the United Nations (UN). It promotes reform of the UN, stressing the need for defending state sovereignty. The forum's position is that the role and power of nongovernmental organizations (NGOs) in global affairs must increase to promote global justice. To achieve this end they collaborate with other NGOs. The GPF operates a comprehensive Web site citing the critical arguments against many aspects of globalization and covering a wide range of topics, including the global economy, politics, culture, and international law.

The forum's primary focus is on issues concerning international peace and justice. Founded in 1993, GPF works globally to mobilize citizens in an effort to increase democratic possibilities. GPF is critical of economic globalization, arguing that it is currently lacking in democratic values. The forum's view is that globalization is a projection of United States empire. The organization's research is designed to inform citizens of the global power of multinational corporations (MNCs). It promotes strengthening international law and building an environmentally sustainable global society. It collects data, conducts research, and publishes policy papers expressing the organization's critical view of MNCs and economic globalization.

Heritage Foundation
214 Massachusetts Avenue, NE
Washington DC 20002–4999
Phone: (202) 546–4400
Fax: (202) 546–8328
Web site: www.heritage.org

Founded in 1973, the Heritage Foundation is a politically conservative think tank made up of academic experts who produce research and commentary. The foundation supports a central role for the United States in globalization. It promotes limited government in economic matters but emphasizes the need for strong national defense, basing its views on the Reagan–Thatcher emphasis on economic deregulation as necessary for the realization of liberty and freedom. The Heritage Foundation is unapologetic concerning the duty of the United States to pursue its rightful security interests. These interests are global and include the need to defend global markets and maintain energy security based on the use of fossil fuels.

Human Rights Watch (HRW)
350 Fifth Avenue, 34th Floor
New York, NY 10118–3299
Phone: (212) 290–4700
Fax: (212) 736–1300
E-mail: hrwnyc@hrw.org
Web site: www.hrw.org

Human Rights Watch was formed in 1978 as Helsinki Watch. HRW evolved into a global human rights organization that has offices in major metropolitan cities across the globe including Chicago, San Francisco, Los Angeles, Washington, DC, London, Brussels, Geneva, Berlin, and Toronto. The organization investigates human rights abuses perpetrated by governments and subnational organizations. By documenting such abuses, HRW works to have those committing such acts brought to justice. HRW covers many issues related to globalization, including the treatment of prisoners, arms sales, the rights of children, cultural rights, migration, refugees, and women's rights. Its strategy is to promote human rights and limit abuse through public education campaigns. HRW funds a yearly "traveling film festival" which provides a venue for independent films that document human rights issues and abuses.

The Institute for Policy Studies (IPS)
1112 16th St. NW, Suite 600
Washington, DC 20036
Phone: (202) 234–9382
Fax: (202) 387–7915
E-mail: info@ips-dc.org
Web site: www.ips-dc.org

A self-described progressive organization focusing on peace, justice, nuclear disarmament, and environmental sustainability, the Institute for Policy Studies works on many issue areas pertaining to globalization. IPS research and programs focus on global justice. The organization promotes a "new internationalism" that considers the pursuit of peace to be the best security strategy. IPS is the parent organization of Foreign Policy in Focus (FPIF), which considers itself the foreign policy "think tank without walls." FPIF publishes foreign policy research from a wide collection of progressive scholars and activists and promotes a U.S. foreign policy based on the values of peace and justice.

IPS advocates alternative economic strategies that promote environmental sustainability. Its research and commentary are critical of the current globalization process. IPS works with many social movements, striving to activate and mobilize grassroots groups. It also publishes the online weekly *World Beat.*

Institute for Science and International Security (ISIS)
236 Massachusetts Avenue, NE, Suite 500
Washington, DC 20002
Phone: (202) 547–3633
Fax: (202) 547–3634
E-mail: isis@isis-online.org
Web site: www.isis-online.org

The Institute for Science and International Security was formed in 1993 with the central purpose of stopping nuclear proliferation. This scientist-based organization works to educate the public about nuclear issues, focusing on the reduction of existing nuclear arsenals. ISIS researchers try to create greater transparency in issues pertaining to nuclear technology. They publish their findings in major newspapers and academic journals. Currently, much of their work assesses the state of nuclear programs in nation-states such as Iran and North Korea. They also concentrate on the volatile relations between India and Pakistan, two nation-states that have developed nuclear weapons in recent years. An important research report produced by ISIS concerning the diffusion of nuclear technology is *Global Stocks of Nuclear Explosive Materials.*

International Committee of the Red Cross (ICRC)
19 avenue de la Paix CH 1202
Geneva, Switzerland
Phone: + 41 (22) 734 60 01

Fax: + 41 (22) 733 20 57
E-mail: online contact form
Web site: www.icrc.org

The International Committee of the Red Cross was founded in 1863 as a response to the need to defend the rights of victims of warfare. It is a politically neutral human rights organization. The ICRC has been central in promoting, framing, and developing international humanitarian law. It organized the international conferences that gave life to the Geneva Conventions concerning laws of warfare and was central in 1864 in promoting the ratification of the Geneva Convention for the Amelioration of the Condition of the Wounded in Armies in the Field. The ICRC has been a crucial actor in subsequent additions and amendments to international humanitarian law.

The committee has been opposed to the use of chemical weapons in warfare since World War I. It acts as an advocate for prisoners of war, monitoring their treatment as it applies to the Geneva Conventions. It also works to defend the rights of civilians, refugees, and combatants. The committee supplies relief material such as food, shelter, and medical aid to those who have been victimized by warfare. Its Web site offers a comprehensive history of the organization's activities. The ICRC has won the Nobel Peace Prize four times (1901, 1917, 1944, and 1963).

International Forum on Globalization (IFG)
1009 General Kennedy Avenue #2
San Francisco, CA 94129
Phone: (415) 561–7650
Fax: (415) 561–7651
E-mail ifg@ifg.org
Web site: www.ifg.org

The International Forum on Globalization is composed of activists and scholars critical of corporate-led economic globalization. It publishes books, hosts seminars, and holds press conferences on issues related to globalization. Formed in 1994, IFG maintains that the World Trade Organization, International Monetary Fund, and World Bank are restructuring the global economy away from democracy and environmental sustainability. The organization argues that economic globalization favors investors over workers and that the development model currently being pursued under economic globalization is geared to benefit investors who are represented by global governance institutions..

IFG promotes the rise of citizen movements against economic globalization, arguing that global governance institutions are losing legitimacy across the globe. The forum conducts programs explaining the effects of economic globalization on agriculture, development, and indigenous rights. It is also critical of the effect multinational corporation–owned media has on the global population. A particularly interesting program that warrants further attention is their "Global Project on Economic Transitions: The Triple Crisis—Climate Chaos; Peak Oil (the End of Cheap Energy); and Global Resource Depletion."

Oxfam International
Oxfam International Secretariat
266 Banbury Road, Oxford, Suite 20
OX2 7DL, UK
Phone: +44–1865–339–100
Fax: +44–1865–339–101
E-mail: information@oxfaminternational.org
Web site: www.oxfam.org

"Oxfam" is derived from "Oxford Committee for Famine Relief." Oxfam was originally founded in Britain during World War II (1942). At that time, Oxfam lobbied to ship food to Greece while that country was under an Allied naval blockade. Oxfam International was founded in 1995 to fight poverty and hunger on a global level. Its goal is to promote cooperation among the world's people to achieve greater global equity. Oxfam International is a confederated organization of 13 members operating in more than 100 nation-states. Its secretariat is in Britain, with advocacy offices in Washington, DC, New York, Brussels, and Geneva. Oxfam provides assistance in humanitarian disasters. It uses strategies based on the human right to organize people toward improving their livelihood. Oxfam produces research on poverty and hunger and operates campaigns to promote public health, addressing issues such as HIV prevention and public health education. Oxfam lobbies government leaders to support their cause, attempting to foster a greater sense of global citizenship.

Project for a New American Century (PNAC)
1150 17th Street, NW
Suite 510
Washington, DC 20036
Phone: (202) 293–4983
Fax: (202) 293–4572
E-mail: project@newamericancentury.org
Web site: www.newamericancentury.org

Project for a New American Century was founded in 1997 to promote the neoconservative strategic vision for U.S. global leadership. PNAC maintains that the United States must actively shape the world to fit its interests in the 21st century and promotes a strong emphasis on military power to achieve these ends. Given this emphasis, PNAC supports increased military spending in the United States. The organization believes such an increase is necessary to expand and modernize the United States military to meet current and future challenges.

PNAC's position is that the United States must act proactively to achieve its global interests, preempting potential challenges before they occur. It focuses on long-term strategic interests over short-term commercial interests. The organization's Web site contains a long list of policy papers and other writings supporting their views on many topics in such areas as defense and national security, North Atlantic Tready Organization/Europe, Iraq/Middle East, East Asia, Balkans/Caucasus, and global issues. PNAC has been very influential under the administration of George W. Bush. Original signers of its "Statement of Principles" include former and current Bush administration officials: Elliott Abrams, Dick Cheney, Zalmay Khalizad, I. Lewis "Scooter" Libby, Donald Rumsfeld, and Paul Wolfowitz.

Transnational Institute (TI)
PO Box 14656, 1001 LD
Amsterdam, The Netherlands
Phone: 31 20 662 66 08
Fax: 31 20 675 71 76
E-mail: tni@tni.org
Web site: www.tni.org

Founded in 1974, the Transnational Institute focuses on international cooperation to find solutions to militarism and international conflict. TI research centers on the poverty, injustice, and environmental degradation that result from globalization. To address these problems, the organization has undertaken a wide range of global programs including these: the Alternative Regionalisms Program to improve democratic participation and regional coalition building; the Drugs and Democracy Program, which focuses on alternative policies to combat drug addiction and the militarized strategies employed to alleviate the global drug trade; the New Politics Program, which examines social movements worldwide; the Environmental Justice Project, which looks at social justice in environmental matters; the Militarism and Globalization Project, which presents security alternatives, promoting the formation of new security structures based on humanist values; and the Water Justice Project based on the belief that water is a public good, not a commodity to be supplied by private interests for a profit.

The Trilateral Commission
1156 Fifteenth Street, NW
Washington, DC 20005
Phone: (202) 467–5410
Fax: (202) 467–5415
E-mail: contactus@trilateral.org
Web site: www.trilateral.org

The Trilateral Commission is a private organization founded in 1973 to increase cooperation and understanding among the three economic blocs centered in Europe, North America, and Asia. It focuses on global issues and effective global governance.

The Trilateral Commission emerged as a result of Japan and Europe's economic emergence relative to the United States. As Europe and Japan grew economically, the United States was displaced as the sole engine of the global economy. The rise of "trilateralism" increased economic interdependence, making coordination between the three economic blocs very important.

The intent of the commission, which is composed of about 350 global leaders from business, academia, media, nongovernmental organizations, and government, is to maintain the stability of the global system. The commission holds annual meetings to address challenges to the global system. Institutionally, the Trilateral Commission is split into three groups: the North American Group, the European Group, and the Asia-Pacific Group. The Commission is based in Washington, DC with offices in France and Japan.

World Resources Institute (WRI)
10 G Street, NE, Suite 800
Washington, DC 20002
Phone: (202) 729–7600
Fax: (202) 729–7610
Web site: www.wri.org

The World Resources Institute was formed in 1982 with a $15 million grant from the John D. and Catherine T. MacArthur Foundation. It is a think tank that focuses on finding practical ways to address global environmental problems. Specifically, WRI addresses climate change, deforestation, and desertification. The view of WRI is that we can improve human lives while also protecting the environment. It hopes to transform human society by providing ideas and policy solutions for global environmental problems. While focusing its research on environmental problems, the WRI is also concerned with natural resources, human population, and issues of economic development. WRI maintains the Earthtrends database, a comprehensive data source related to human demographics and the state of the natural environment. It also produces podcasts, multimedia, and PowerPoint presentations reflecting the state of the global environment.

World Security Institute (WSI)
1779 Massachusetts Avenue, NW
Washington, DC 20036
Phone: (202) 332–0900
Fax: (202) 462–4559
E-mail: info@worldsecurityinstitute.org
Web site: www.worldsecurityinstitute.org

The World Security Institute produces independent research and journalism on issues concerning global security. These issues include U.S. national security and defense policy, nuclear proliferation, space security, missile defense, small arms, and military transformation. WSI emphasizes the "soft power" theorized by Joseph Nye as critical to attaining global security. As an organization, WSI emphasizes being politically neutral and nonideological in research and analysis. Using numerous media technologies to disseminate its views on security matters around the globe, the WSI operates foreign-language news services, produces books and weekly online security reviews, and publishes the academic journals *The Defense Monitor, China Security, Cauca-*

sus Context, and *Arab Insight.* WSI also produces videos, documentaries, podcasts, and *WSI Brussels Policy Briefs.* WSI research informs policy makers around the globe.

Academic/University-Based Research Centers

The Centre for the Study of Global Governance (CsGG)
Houghton Street
London WC2A 2AE
United Kingdom
Phone: 020 7955 7583
E-mail: h.c.gallagher@lse.ac.uk (center manager)
Web site: www.lse.ac.uk/Depts/global/index.htm

The Centre for the Study of Global Governance was founded 1992 at the London School of Economics. Research at the CsGG is dedicated to issues pertaining to global governance, stressing the complex nature of globalization and noting its often contentious nature. It focuses on the need for an international legal framework to deal with problems associated with globalization. The CsGG produces research into globalization with the intent to "inquire," "inform," and "influence." By this the CsGG works to spread knowledge to the public to persuade government and nonstate actors to cooperate in addressing problems of globalization. A central focus of the CsGG is the rise of global civil society, maintaining that this is important for increasing international cooperation and institution building. David Held, an important scholar of globalization, is co-director of the CsGG.

Centre for the Study of Globalisation and Regionalisation (CSGR)
University of Warwick
Coventry CV4 7AL
United Kingdom
Phone: 44 (0) 24 7657 2533
Fax: 44 (0) 24 7657 2548
E-mail: csgr@warwick.ac.uk
Web site: www.warwick.ac.uk/fac/soc/csgr

The Centre for the Study of Globalisation and Regionalisation is a university-based research center that focuses on globalization. Founded in 1997 and operated by the University of Warwick in Britain, the CSGR researches globalization and regionalism with an interdisciplinary emphasis. Scholars from anthropology, business, economics, politics, and law focus on clarifying globalization. CSGR holds the view that globalization is a broad and ambiguous term that elicits much debate among the academic community. It has created a "globalization index" that measures multiple dimensions of globalization. The intent of the organization is to inform and promote effective global governance given potential problems and crises that arise with globalization.

Focus on the Global South (FOCUS)
Chulalongkorn University Social Research Institute (CUSRI)
Wisit Prachuabmoh Building, Bangkok–10330, Thailand
Phone: 66–2–2187363–65
Fax: 66–2–2559976
E-mail: admin@focusweb.org
Web site: www.focusweb.org

Focus on the Global South was founded in 1995. Its current director (as of 2007) is Walden Bello, a noted academic and antiglobalization activist. FOCUS is critical of the current form of globalization, maintaining that economic globalization dominated by multinational corporations (MNCs) and international financial institutions is unjust. The organization promotes democratic alternatives to what it argues are oppressive institutions of globalization.

FOCUS is explicitly critical of the World Trade Organization and contends that the focus of globalization must be altered from the needs of MNCs to the needs of communities. FOCUS promotes national sovereignty and defends land rights for the world's poor. In this it wishes to defend the global commons against privatization while working toward a demilitarization of globalization. FOCUS produces annual reports on trends of globalization and a wide range of research related to its concerns.

International Studies Association (ISA)
324 Social Sciences
University of Arizona
Tucson, Arizona 85721
Phone: (520) 621–7715
Fax: (520) 621–5780
E-mail: isa@u.arizona.edu
Web site: www.isanet.org

Founded in 1959, the International Studies Association is one of the most respected professional organizations in the academic field of international relations. The ISA is a member of the International Social Science Council and is involved with 57 other international studies organizations in more than 30 countries. It holds annual conventions taking place across the globe with global academic participation in 23 interdisciplinary sections. The ISA publishes the academic journals *International Studies Quarterly, International Studies Review, International Studies Perspectives, Foreign Policy Analysis,* and *International Political Sociology.*

Yale Center for the Study of Globalization
Betts House
393 Prospect Street
P.O. Box 208360
New Haven, CT 06520–8360
Phone: (203) 432–1900
Fax: (203) 432–1200
Web site: www.ycsg.yale.edu

The Yale Center for the Study of Globalization was formed in 2001 at Yale University to research globalization. This research center supports conferences, workshops, lectures, and research regarding challenges to globalization. The YCSG maintains that globalization has been an overall beneficial process but notes that many people have been excluded from its benefits. The director of the YCSG is former Mexican president Ernesto Zedillo (as of 2007). The YCSG publishes the online weekly *YaleGlobal Online.*

8

Resources

This chapter offers annotated references to print and non-print resources for the study of globalization. The first section includes major reference works followed by scholarly books and articles. The second section lists Web sites related to globalization, online data bases, videos, podcasts, and other Web-based multimedia. Many of the Web-based resources offer links to other related material. The authors of this book specifically chose Web-based resources that offer the best links to other resources to help the reader research globalization. The next section has videos focusing on globalization. These are useful in the classroom and help viewers acquire a basic understanding of different aspects of globalization. Finally, Web sites that offer podcasts and other multimedia related to globalization are listed, representing hundreds of audio and video resources.

Print Resources

Reference Works

Chan, Stephen, and Cerwyn Moore, eds. 2006. *Theories of International Relations*. Vols. 1–4. London: Sage Library of International Relations, Sage Publications. 1,551 pages.

This four-volume set covers four distinct schools of thought in the academic field of international relations. Volume I represents scholars from the "realist" school of thought. Realists argue that nation-states must rely on self-help within an anarchic global system. Volume II presents scholars from the pluralist or liberal tradition of international relations. These scholars argue that international relations integrate the world with common concerns, goals, and understanding, lessening the possibility of conflict. Volume III presents structuralist scholars from Marxist and other critical schools of international relations. These scholars argue that international relations are characterized by unequal political and economic power relations that form the global system. Volume IV is composed of works by "reflexive" scholars of international relations, or those who are generally skeptical of theories that claim to explain the essence of international relations. These scholars argue that dominant theories of international relations reify the global system itself, thus reproducing and legitimizing it through their chosen discourses. Many contributors to this four-volume set are discussed in this reference handbook.

Robertson, Roland, and Jan Aart Scholte, eds. 2007. *Encyclopedia of Globalization*, Vols. 1–4. New York: Routledge, Taylor and Francis Group. 1,804 pages.

This reference work is organized around central concepts related to globalization. The entries reflect many dimensions of globalization while also offering entries on globalization's central institutions and processes. These entries include arguments for and against the globalization process. This is a good work for advanced students of globalization given the broad scope of this multivolume reference work.

Vaidya, Ashish K., ed. 2006. *Globalization: Encyclopedia of Trade, Labor, and Politics*, Vols. 1–2. Santa Barbara, CA: ABC-CLIO. 968 pages.

This is a comprehensive reference work on globalization representing scholars from around the world. This reference work covers many aspects of globalization, including trade, investment, regionalism, labor, technology, and many other subjects. It contains a substantive bibliography on globalization, providing the reader with a strong foundation of the academic field. Given its comprehensive nature, this work is beneficial to those who wish to possess more than a basic knowledge of globalization.

Selected Books and Scholarly Articles

Arrighi, Giovanni. 2005. "Hegemony Unravelling: 1." *New Left Review* 32, March/April: 23–79.

Arrighi offers the critical argument that the United States cannot play or maintain a central role in the global imperial project. The unipolar stance proposed for the United States by the George W. Bush administration after the terror attacks of 9/11 is untenable given the state of the global system. Arrighi argues that the United States' projection of military power is intended to open markets for capitalists. The United States can no longer convince many other nation-states to willfully submit to its leadership; thus, it has been forced to employ coercion and violence. Arrighi notes that the "Coalition of the Willing" formed to invade Iraq was lacking major European powers (except the United Kingdom) and China. The United States will fail in its global endeavors because capitalism has displaced all other economic systems around the globe, offering no new markets to be exploited.

Coupled with this problem is the current public indebtedness of the United States and the likely unwillingness of other nation-states to endlessly support this debt. To Arrighi, economic globalization is racked with contradictions. These contradictions lead him to conclude that the current economic globalization project under United States leadership has failed. This failure will result in global economic collapse as the United States dollar (USD) loses its value, leading to a new global system, possibly dominated by China.

Bello, Walden. 1999. *Dark Victory. The United States and Global Poverty,* 2nd ed. London: Pluto Press. 162 pages.

Walden Bello argues that the transition from Keynesianism to neoliberal monetarist economic policies represents a global "rollback." By rollback, Bello means that previous gains made by developing nation-states and the working classes within advanced industrial nation-states are seen as a threat to the economically powerful. Neoliberal prescriptions focusing on minimalist government intervention represent an intentional recolonizing of the developing world and a rollback of high wages and benefits in the industrial world. To Bello, the recycling of petrodollars to developing nation-states was an intentional policy created by the "Baker Plan" (named after political power broker in the United States, James Baker) to bankrupt developing nation-states. Once developing nation-states were bankrupted, their economic policies could be controlled by those to whom they were indebted and dependent on for future economic and political stability.

Brawley, Mark R. 2003. *The Politics of Globalization: Gaining Perspective, Assessing Consequences.* **Ontario, Canada: Broadview Press. 223 pages.**

This book explores globalization as a contentious issue that has many different definitions and dimensions. The author provides multiple definitions and theoretical perspectives regarding globalization, then assesses evidence pertaining to the existence of the globalization process. Following this, Brawley addresses the impact of globalization on domestic politics, sovereignty, and cultural identity. This book offers a historical examination of globalization in the 19th century as well as the current era. The author concludes by suggesting potential future scenarios for globalization and assessing the role international institutions will play.

Broad, Robin. 2004. "The Washington Consensus Meets the Global Backlash: Shifting Debates and Policies." *Globalizations* **1, no. 2 (December): 129–154.**

This article discusses and analyzes the growing debate over the neoliberal view of economic globalization. The author provides evidence for the debate by discussing "elite" dissatisfaction with the neoliberal project as represented by powerful actors and institutions. The analysis of dissatisfaction is broken down into five categories: trade liberalization, deregulation, privatization, financial liberalization, and debt-crisis management.

Brown, Lester R. 2003. *Plan B. Rescuing a Planet under Stress and a Civilization in Trouble.* **New York: W.W. Norton. 285 pages.**

Liberal institutionalists argue that global environmental problems such as climate change offer an opportunity for the United States to exert a leadership role in the global system. Suggesting a program similar to Al Gore's environmental "Marshall Plan,"

Lester Brown of the World Watch Institute calls on the United States to take the lead in transforming the global economy into a sustainable framework to address global environmental problems. Brown believes the global economy is a "bubble" that is feeding off Earth's natural assets. This bubble, if not gradually deflated through effective policy, will eventually lead to a collapse of the global system, effectively ending globalization. Brown cites climate change, soil erosion, deteriorating rangelands, collapsing fisheries, and falling water tables as signs of human activities transgressing Earth's natural carrying capacity.

Brown calls for an economic and social "Plan B" for which the United States must take the lead with a "wartime mobilization" similar in scale to the planning of World War II. Brown's Plan B includes adopting realistic prices for limited and exhaustible natural resources. Plan B calls for limiting the global consumption of beef and pork, for which farmed fish and poultry would be substituted. Plan B would transform the global economy through an energy transition to hydrogen that would be complemented by alternative energy sources such as wind and solar power. Brown estimates that Plan B would cut global CO_2 emissions in half.

Brown's argument is similar to those of ecological economists. He argues that the global system is in trouble because humans are currently living unsustainably, relying on the depletion of Earth's nonrenewable natural resources. Brown believes in the benefits of markets but argues that markets must be honest in pricing the Earth's natural capital and ecological services (for example, in allowing forests to provide water filtration, in protecting soil from erosion, and extracting CO_2 from the air). Brown is optimistic that if the nation-states of the world were to act, the transition to Plan B could take place. He notes, however, that the world does not currently possess the necessary leadership to make the leap to Plan B, citing the United States' focus on security in the form of economic growth and military might as a reflection of this fact.

Brzezinski, Zbigniew. 2004. *The Choice, Global Domination or Global Leadership.* **New York: Basic Books. 242 pages.**

According to Brzezinski, globalization has universalized nation-state insecurity. The spread of technology in weaponry and scientific advancement has diffused organized violence to subnational actors. These subnational actors, such as terrorist organizations, now possess the ability to harm even the most powerful nation-states. Globalization, in this sense, has broken the connection between sovereignty and security. Brzezinski argues that the United States impacts the entire world yet is very protective of own sovereignty. This dual standard breeds resentment as it is seen as a dismissal of the rights of those living outside the United States. The United States is responsible in its role as stabilizer of the global system but does so as it experiences a relative decline in power. The challenge for the United States in the era of globalization will be to retain its hegemonic rule.

Brzezinski argues that the United States is a global "social pioneer," shaping and impacting humanity on a global basis. Were the United States to pull back from its global presence, chaos would assuredly ensue from the resultant power vacuum. Within globalization, the nation-state is still of central importance, but interdependence characterizes the true interests of nation-states. This interdependence makes cooperation on issues such as terrorism essential for global stability. Terrorism, according to Brzezinski, has a political dimension that cannot be dismissed. Any solution intended to lessen the threat of terrorism would have to address the political basis behind the motivations of terrorists. Brzezinski criticizes current U.S. policy for not recognizing the political dimension of terrorism. The United States's "war on terrorism" could lead to what political scientist Samuel Huntington calls the "clash of civilizations."

Given that the fundamental threat facing the United States is global anarchy, the country must reevaluate its global role. Brzezinski argues that resistance to globalization is rising with a global political awakening among its losers. This, coupled with a "revolution in military affairs," endangers the national security of the United States. In the end, globalization is an ideology supported by political and economic elites in the United States who argue that it represents the wave of the future. He argues that this overly optimistic view of globalization has its own antithesis, or countermovement. This movement may rise as a powerful global political movement. The population explosion in developing nation-states will unfold along with low economic growth, making global political instability a real possibility.

Chan, Steve, and James R. Scarritt, eds. 2002. *Coping with Globalization.* **London: Frank Cass. 244 pages.**

This book is a collection of essays focusing on quantitative and comparative studies of globalization. The editors explain that this edition differs from others in that it is interdisciplinary and is not limited by the ideology that often skews works on globalization. They note that to understand globalization, one must be aware of the complex interaction between economic, political, and social factors. The editors conclude that globalization is not a process with a definite trajectory but is dependent on the choices and decisions of political, social, and economic actors.

Chomsky, Noam. 2003. *Hegemony or Survival. America's Quest for Global Dominance.* **New York: Henry Holt. 278 pages.**

In his well-known critical style, Noam Chomsky argues that the United States' quest for power is a potentially terminal process for the human species. Chomsky claims that the George W. Bush administration has expanded on an imperial project that has been pursued by previous administrations. This expansion has come in the form of explicit unilateralism and preemption of threats that have yet to be realized, or exist. The United States has begun a retreat from multilateralism in favor of an aggressive pursuit of its global power interests. This book caused quite a stir in the General Assembly at the United Nations in 2006. Speaking before the General Assembly, Venezuelan president Hugo Chavez recommended it as essential reading to understand United States imperialism and the logic of economic globalization.

Clapp, Jennifer, and Peter Dauvergne. 2005. *Paths to a Green World: The Political Economy of the Global Environment.* **Cambridge, MA: MIT Press. 327 pages.**

This book concentrates on the political economy of the global environment and claims to be the first to do so. It focuses on contending visions of political economy designed toward ensuring environmental security. The authors address many dimensions of globalization, focusing on the ways they impact the global environment. These dimensions include global wealth and poverty, the rise of global environmentalism, international trade, and foreign investment. The book compares and contrasts these dimensions through the worldviews of market liberals, institutionalists, bioenvironmentalists, and social greens.

Conca, Ken. 2001. "Consumption and Environment in a Global Economy." *Global Environmental Politics* **1, no. 3 (August): 53–71.**

This article argues that the critique of modern consumption patterns has lost its importance in the environmentalist discourse. This loss is due to mainstream environmental nongovernmental organizations having evolved into groups that operate within the confines of corporate capitalism. The author claims that consumption patterns characteristic of economic globalization should be analyzed with the "sustainable middle" in mind. The sustainable middle represents the best possibility of a sustainable future, but this potential is eroding as economic globalization polarizes the rich from the poor on a global scale.

Dembinski, Paul H. 2003. *Economic and Financial Globalization. What the Numbers Say.* **Geneva, Switzerland: United Nations Institute for Training and Research), Observatoire de la Finance. 176 pages.**

This study assesses trends of economic and financial globalization. It comes with a CD-ROM that provides access to numerous data tables. Among the data collected are trends concerning the global population, the spread of telecommunications, and transport. This study assesses the global economy in terms of trade and finance, documenting numerous trends that affect and characterize economic globalization. The work is an intensive investigation into economic globalization, citing many problems that threaten to plague economic globalization in the future.

Eckes, Alfred E., Jr., and Thomas W. Zeiler. 2003. *Globalization and the American Century.* **Cambridge, UK: Cambridge University Press. 343 pages.**

In this book the authors trace the role of the United States in international affairs leading up to the current era of globalization. The authors argue that the support of the United States toward free markets, coupled with technological innovation, has led to the current era of globalization. The United States played a pivotal role in the 20th century by recreating the global economy disrupted by World War I, the Great Depression, and World War II. This book provides a good historical account of the global role the United States has played up to the end of the 20th century. The authors conclude that globalization led by the United States is not a given fact for the future. They cite global financial volatility as a potential factor that could disrupt globalization under United States hegemony.

Forsythe, David P., Patrice C. McMahon, and Andrew Wederman, eds. 2006. *American Foreign Policy in a Globalized World*. New York: Taylor and Francis Group. 350 pages.

This anthology examines United States foreign policy in the era of globalization. The contributors discuss the power of the United States as it embarks on its "war on terrorism." Much of the volume assesses the costs and benefits associated with maintaining the world's largest military. Two common themes are presented in this work: the United States military is overly burdened by the George W. Bush administration's foreign policy strategy, and United States hegemony requires approval from its allies. In this sense, preemption of perceived threats and unilateral military projection is unsustainable for it is economically costly and alienates important allies. Another point made in this work is that defining United States' power as military security is coming at the expense of the U.S. domestic economy. With the George W. Bush administration tax cuts, the United States can maintain its global military presence only through foreign investment. Both of these trends lessen the power of the United States because it lessens its global credibility.

Friedman, Thomas L. 2005. *The World Is Flat. A Brief History of the Twenty-First Century*. New York: Farrar, Straus and Giroux. 488 pages.

Friedman claims that globalization has entered its third phase (Globalization 3.0). This new phase of globalization is characterized by the leveling of the economic playing field among the world's nation-states. Globalization 3.0 will not be dominated by Westerners as previous phases had been. This new era will be a reflection of global diversity. Globalization 3.0, according to Friedman, has "flattened the world," allowing individuals to globalize their efforts through increased collaboration. Friedman argues that 10 factors have led to this flattening of the world.

Collectively, these factors have integrated the world through technology, making distant people virtual neighbors. This book supports economic globalization and is optimistic about the inevitability of its future.

Fukuyama, Francis. 2006. *America at the Crossroads. Democracy, Power, and the Neo-Conservative Legacy.* **New Haven, CT: Yale University Press. 226 pages.**

Fukuyama claims that it is too easy to interpret and explain the foreign policy of the George W. Bush administration on "neoconservatism." Neoconservatism, argues Fukuyama, is a diverse field of thought, not easily reducible to conspiratorial clichés. Fukuyama contends that neoconservatism has been an abused term in the United States, serving as a catch-all concept to explain the foreign policies of the George W. Bush administration. This book discusses different viewpoints concerning the appropriate role for the United States to pursue in the era of globalization. Fukuyama argues that the United States' "benevolent hegemony" is limited and this must be recognized in the era of globalization.

Gilpin, Robert. 2000. *The Challenge of Global Capitalism. The World Economy in the 21st Century.* **Princeton, NJ: Princeton University Press. 373 pages.**

Robert Gilpin, professor of political economy at Princeton University, argues that economic globalization is not an inevitable process. Global capitalism faces challenges that could alter its trajectory and form. Economic globalization ultimately relies on the political acceptance of the global population. Gilpin argues that the United States has played the role of global stabilizer since World War II but its ability to perform this role is now in jeopardy. Gilpin notes that the United States is no longer the unrivaled economic hegemon in the global system. Resistance to economic globalization, Gilpin argues, is on the rise. This resistance is a political challenge to those promoting economic globalization and must be addressed wisely by political leaders in the United States.

Greider, William. 1997. *One World Ready or Not. The Manic Logic of Global Capitalism.* **New York: Simon and Schuster. 528 pages.**

In his book *One World, Ready or Not,* Greider argues that economic globalization is guided by an international rentier regime operating under a "manic logic." This manic logic implies that the world's nation-states are governed by unforgiving imperatives of international capital markets. Greider, though not a Marxist, argues that global capitalism has revived the "Ghost of Marx" where deregulated finance and liberalized markets have once again set the interests of capital against those of labor. The manic logic governing global capitalism stands in stark contrast to Keynesianism, the New Deal of Franklin D. Roosevelt, and Lyndon B. Johnson's Great Society.

Technological advances, according to Greider, allow capital to migrate while workers remain geographically trapped. This results in dimming the economic prospects of workers, which in turn disrupts the political stability within nation-states. Global capitalism creates a pool of disenchanted people who will react against the imperatives of the manic logic. Greider believes the reaction of people left behind in economic globalization will cause global political instability. This political instability will take the form of either a return to socialism or a return to fascism.

Greider argues that global capitalism is on autopilot with no one at the controls. It has a logic of its own, and this logic will eventually succumb to the economic, political, and social contradictions it creates. Greider supports capitalism, citing its ability to allocate resources most efficiently. He is, however, against what he believes is neoliberal dogmatism, arguing that capitalism is limited in its ability to provide for social justice and stability. Greider calls for a democratic capitalism that diffuses ownership and is regulated by governments to provide for social justice. Greider's work reminds us that arguments put forth by Marxist scholars are still operational and did not end with the demise of the Soviet Union.

Hardt, Michael, and Antonio Negri. 2000. *Empire*. Cambridge, MA: Harvard University Press. 478 pages.

Hardt and Negri argue that globalization represents a new era of social relations. Empire, they argue, differs from past historical eras of imperialism because there are no longer any external boundaries for Empire to transcend. In the era of Empire, there is no center where power is concentrated. Empire exists beyond territory and time, encompassing the globe through complex networks.

Empire exists through the exploitation of bio-power. Bio-power flows horizontally through global society, controlling the lives of the global population in a manner of which many are unaware. It is, however, possible for the "multitude," or the diversity of the mutually oppressed, to resist Empire. This book is a good example of interpreting globalization through the lens of literary theory and the humanities.

Hartnett, Stephen John, and Laura Ann Stengrim. 2006. *Globalization and Empire. The U.S. Invasion of Iraq, Free Markets, and the Twilight of Democracy.* Tuscaloosa: University of Alabama Press. 387 pages.

This book takes a critical look at the rhetoric espoused by those who support globalization. These authors analyze the language and arguments put forth by these supporters, matching it with evidence that contradicts their claims. The authors also analyze the language and arguments put forth by the George W. Bush administration as it prosecutes the "war on terrorism." These authors find that the rhetoric of freedom and prosperity often hides explicit domination and injustice. According to the authors, many of the pro-globalization arguments that rest on the hegemony of the United States do not stand up to the scrutiny of rhetorical investigation.

Hay, Colin, and David Marsh, eds. 2000. *Demystifying Globalization.* New York: St. Martin's Press. 197 pages.

This book is a collection of essays that focuses on discourses of globalization and offers a critical assessment of the term. The volume intends to begin a "third wave" of globalization discourse by assessing the many processes that characterize the globalization process. The editors hope to demystify the term by critically assessing the many dimensions in which it is said to exist. The editors of this work stress that students of globalization need to examine their ideas about globalization, for it is ideas that inform actions and judgments about globalization.

Held, David, et al. 2005.. *Debating Globalization.* Cambridge, UK: Polity Press. 205 pages.

This book is a diverse collection of responses to the introductory chapter written by globalization scholar David Held. This debate provides a good example of scholars with different worldviews addressing each other's arguments about the nature of globalization. The debate offers examples of the neoliberal, liberal institutionalist, and critical view of globalization. Its 18 contributors offer broad yet succinct arguments in defense of their interpretation of globalization. David Held responds to the contributors in the final chapter. This book is a good primer on the debates scholars engage in when considering the complexities of globalization.

Held, David, Anthony McGrew, David Goldblatt, and Jonathan Perraton. 1999. *Global Transformations. Politics, Economics and Culture.* **Stanford, CA: Stanford University Press. 515 pages.**

Global Transformations is described by international relations theorist James Rosenau as "the definitive work on globalization"; its authors analyze the phenomenon of globalization not as something entirely new but as a process similar to phenomena of the past. This book assesses factors contributing to globalization by utilizing a spatio-temporal method that examines globalization's intensity, extensity, and velocity. The authors assess global markets, financial flows, corporate power networks, migration, diffusion of culture, environmental degradation, and the rise of the international arms dynamic. This book is considered by many scholars to be a crucial foundation in the study of globalization.

Hughes, Jane Elizabeth, and Scott B. MacDonald. 2004. *Carnival on Wall Street. Global Financial Markets in the 1990s.* **Hoboken, NJ: John Wiley. 258 pages.**

This book provides a comprehensive account of the rise of global finance in the 1990s. The authors explain the globalization of capital markets and the rise and importance of foreign exchange markets. International finance, characterized by crises and instability, grew explosively in the last few decades. The authors argue that the crises and instability caused by economic globalization have created an antiglobalization movement. They provide a good assessment of economic globalization's critics, noting their major points of contention. Although the book is supportive of economic globalization, the authors assert caution as to its future. This book critiques aspects of the global financial system and the role it plays in current problems associated with economic globalization.

Kelleher, Ann, and Laura Klein. 2006. *Global Perspectives. A Handbook for Understanding Global Issues,* **2nd ed. Upper Saddle River, NJ: Pearson, Prentice Hall. 226 pages.**

This handbook examines many dimensions of globalization through an interdisciplinary lens. It provides a history of globalization up to the current era and examines the current globalization process. The book offers an anthropological outlook on globalization, focusing on cultural diversity. It discusses a wide range of topics, including racism, issues of gender, patriotism, and tolerance. The authors examine the legacy of colonialism, explain theories of international relations, and address human relations to the environment. The book highlights its broad scope by providing case studies of global processes in action. It concludes with chapters focusing on issues of war and peace, focusing on the role of the United States in the global system.

Kennedy, Paul, Dirk Messner, and Franz Nuscheler, eds. 2002. *Global Trends and Global Governance.* **Sterling, VA: Pluto Press. 208 pages.**

This collection assesses major trends of globalization and their impacts on global governance. The authors collectively argue that an increase in population, disparity in income, and ecological limits threaten to destabilize the global system. Because the problems are global in nature, a system of global governance should be created to deal with future problems. It should be noted this volume stresses global governance, not a global government. Global governance involves cooperation and coordination among many global actors to achieve collective goods. National governments, nongovernmental organizations, and civil society all play a part in this conception of global governance. Globalization will require multiple networks within and among nation-states to address complex common pool problems.

Kwong, Jo. 2005. "Globalization's Effects on the Environment" *Society* **42, no. 2 (January/February): 21–28.**

This article assesses the impacts of economic globalization on environmental security. The author notes that disagreements on these impacts are based on different worldviews. He believes that globalization is simply an increase in the free movement of goods and services and human interaction, and he argues that many critical arguments toward economic globalization are too value laden and emotionally charged. The article identifies the central arguments of the economic globalization debate and argues that those supporting economic globalization are correct. Kwong holds the view that free markets combined with appropriate institutions that protect private property rights will lessen environmental degradation. This neoliberal argument states that the rule of law, private property, and free markets are sufficient to solve global environmental problems.

Lapping, Mark B. 2004. "Toward the Recovery of the Local in the Globalizing Food System: The Role of Alternative Agricultural and Food Models in the US." *Ethics, Place, and Environment* **7, no. 3 (October): 141–150.**

This article criticizes the economic globalization of agriculture, as it has been consolidated and is controlled by global agribusiness. Global agribusiness has furthered the internationalization of agricultural production and distribution, displacing subsistence farmers in the developing world. The author argues the need for local alternatives to global agribusiness. Two examples he supports are local farmers' markets and community-supported agricultural initiatives. Local production and consumption of food decrease energy use and increase the food security of local communities. Food security and the threat of starvation are very important issues to the majority of the world's population. This critical view argues that food self-sufficiency should take precedence over growing cash crops for export.

Mander, Jerry. 2001. "Economic Globalization and the Environment" *Tikkun* **16, no. 5 (September/October): 33–40.**

This article critiques the views held by proponents of economic globalization with regard to the environment. Mander argues that multinational corporations (MNCs) that control the global economy have little incentive to reinvest profits back into environmental protection. He argues that contrary to neoliberal claims, MNCs utilize profits to expand social exploitation and pursue economic growth strategies that cause environmental degradation. Mander offers the critical view that environmental side agreements attached to free trade agreements are insufficient in addressing environmental problems. Further, he argues that market-based pollution controls and technological fixes will also prove insufficient in solving global environmental degradation. He maintains that the global economic system itself is to blame for global environmental problems, something that students of globalization should not overlook.

National Intelligence Council. 2004. *Mapping the Global Future. Report of the National Intelligence Council's 2020 Project Based on Consultations with Nongovernmental Experts around the World.* **NIC 2004–13. Pittsburgh, PA: Government Printing Office. 104 pages.**

This report projects possible scenarios globalization may take in the future. It sets out noted contradictions of globalization based on social inequalities. These social inequalities are increasing with the increased expansion and integration of the global economy. This report also assesses the rise of potential challenges to the hegemony of the United States.

It imagines four potential scenarios for the future of globalization. The first is the "Davos World" where the rise of China and India give globalization a "non-Western face." This scenario will be characterized by continuing integration and economic growth but with ongoing social inequality. The Second Scenario is "Pax Americana" in which the global system remains secure through the stability provided by United States leadership. The third scenario is "A New Caliphate" in which religious radicalism and a rise in identity politics would emerge to challenge the global system. The last scenario is the "Cycle of Fear" in which illegal activities, such as illicit sales of weapons of mass destruction, destabilize the global system.

Nye, Joseph S. 2002. *The Paradox of American Power.* **New York: Oxford University Press. 222 pages.**

This book discusses the use of power by the United States in the era of globalization. Nye argues that although military power is central, it is not sufficient to maintain U.S. power. He explains his theory of "soft power," stressing its importance in the decisions of U.S. policy makers. Nye assesses the potential for rivals to challenge U.S. hegemony within the global system. He argues that the United States is the dominant nation-state within the global system, but it must cooperate with others. In the era of globalization, the power of the United States is reliant upon its complex interdependence with other nation-states.

Nye, Joseph, and John D. Donahue. 2000. *Governance in a Globalizing World.* **Washington, DC: Brookings Institution Press. 386 pages.**

This collection of articles represents an interdisciplinary approach to the study of globalization and global governance. The editors collected a variety of outlooks from many academic fields to address the multidimensional nature of globalization. This book is divided into three sections. The first section focuses on the economic, cultural, and military dimensions of globalization. The second section focuses on how globalization affects governance within nation-states. The third section analyzes how governance within nation-states affects globalization. The book operates under the liberal institutionalist theme that globalization must be managed to retain stability of the global system. The editors differentiate between globalization as a verb and globalism as a noun—that is, as an active process and as something that can be said to exist, possessing a structural form. For globalism to exist, networked relationships must be multicontinental in scope. The editors agree with globalization scholar David Held that the era of globalization is characterized by an increase in magnitude, complexity, and speed in the formation of global networks.

Paehlke, Robert. 2001. "Environment, Equity and Globalization: Beyond Resistance." *Global Environmental Politics* **1, no. 1 (February): 1–10.**

This article argues that globalization is a complex phenomenon with both positive and negative aspects. Paehlke is optimistic about the possibility that negative trends of globalization can be redirected. This redirection is possible through growing public resistance to the neoliberal strategy that dominates the current globalization process. Those who disapprove of globalization should keep in mind, however, the likely possibility that the global system will retain its stability. Globalization will probably continue in its current form into the near future.

Paehlke supports the potential to "de-materialize" economic activity made available through advances in technology. De-materializing the economy, he argues, will lessen the impact the global economy has on the global environment. He supports local initiatives toward environmental sustainability but argues that global institutions must ultimately provide for global environmental sustainability. This article represents a liberal institutionalist or middle-ground approach to global environmental problems.

Petras, James, and Henry Veltmeyer. 2001. *Globalization Unmasked: Imperialism in the 21st century.* **Halifax, Nova Scotia, Canada: Zed Books. 184 pages.**

This book argues that the concept "globalization" too often implies its inevitability under its current form. Petras and Veltmeyer explore the ideological dimensions of neoliberal globalization discourse and reintroduce imperialism as a central concept in analyzing the globalization process. The concept of "free markets" is replaced by the "imperial project," where the intent of global economic institutions is to create a world free of restraints on global capital. The authors argue that the emphasis of economic globalization on exports hinders developing nation-states because the national economic product is shifted to investors and away from workers. Globalization is the result of nation-state policy and internal economic interests, not a natural phenomenon arising for the good of humanity. In this view, globalization benefits the powerful classes within nation-states while hurting the prospects of the poor. To these authors, globalization is an ideological buzzword applied to the centuries-old process of imperialism.

Robinson, William I. 2004. *A Theory of Global Capitalism. Production, Class, and State in a Transnational World.* **Baltimore, MD: Johns Hopkins University Press. 200 pages.**

Globalization, to William Robinson, is the result of the historical evolution of capitalism. He argues that globalization represents a new historical epoch that has created a transnational capitalist class and quasi-global nation-state. Capitalism, argues Robinson, has spread into new dimensions of social life, making commodities of the world's communities and families. The global economy is fully integrated into one economic system, providing the material basis for a global culture and society. Robinson argues that globalization suffers from problems that will cause future social instability. However, this theory stresses that globalization will likely continue in the future. What form globalization will take is yet uncertain.

Using recent international financial crises as evidence, Robinson contends that global economic processes and decisions are better explained by examining capitalist interest in the form of a multinational elite class. To Robinson, economic globalization includes the globalization of social relations determined by the globalization of productive forces. This means that the ruling class of one nation-state has more interest in maintaining the power of their counterparts in other nation-states than investing in the welfare of citizens in their own nation-state.

Singh, Kavaljit. 1999. *The Globalization of Finance. A Citizen's Guide.* **New York: Zed Books. 191 pages.**

This book describes the rise of the globalization of finance. It provides an in-depth description of the many financial instruments used in globalization. The book consists of case studies, including the Mexican debt crisis and the East Asian financial collapse. The author argues that the global financial system is unstable and that investment capital must be regulated and restricted to cool the destabilizing effects of "hot money flows." One such tool recommended is the Tobin Tax, which would place a high penalty on speculative capital movements to deter investors from gambling in the global economic casino of financial capitalism.

Smil, Vaclav. 1993. *Global Ecology. Environmental Change and Social Flexibility.* **New York: Routledge. 240 pages.**

This book assesses the environmental challenges humanity faces on a global dimension and offers alternative possibilities to meet these challenges in the future. The author offers these alternatives while also claiming a non-normative stance. In his analysis he examines the extent of global environmental degradation along with the necessary ecological requirements for human existence. The author concludes his examination by arguing that rationality and creative thinking offer the best possibilities for solving the contradictions between the global economy and global environmental problems.

Speth, James Gustave, ed. 2003. *Worlds Apart. Globalization and the Environment.* **Yale School of Forestry and Environmental Studies. Washington, DC: Island Press. 180 pages.**

Worlds Apart is a collection of essays that seeks to clarify the impact globalization has on the environment. Collectively, these essays offer an interdisciplinary approach to this question while providing a voice to contesting worldviews on globalization. By focusing on the impact of globalization on the environment from differing perspectives, these essays provide the reader with an excellent overview of the diverse outlooks pertaining to issues of globalization and the environment.

The editor offers an introductory chapter explaining that even though globalization is a contested concept, most academics agree that it focuses on the compression of human interaction. This compression takes place in space and time, where advances in communications, transportation, and economic production have made the Earth a much smaller place. In this book, the focus is primarily on the economic and environmental dimensions of globalization. This focus assesses economic globalization's impact on the environment, and the potential for sustainable development and democracy in an increasingly globalized world.

Although there is general agreement that the forces of globalization have compressed the world, the impact of future economic globalization on the environment is a hotly contested issue. The neoliberal worldview cites economic globalization's ability to transfer environmentally friendly technology to developing nation-states. Neoliberals also cite trends showing the increase in public demand for a clean environment as incomes rise. Liberal institutionalists agree with these sentiments, but argue the need for global management to protect the global environment. They also argue that economic globalization must be managed to ensure that the demands of populations displaced by economic globalization are not ignored. Critics of economic globalization cite the destructive nature of capitalist free trade on the environment. They also argue that economic globalization represents the injustice of neocolonialism, where global economic institutions represent the interests of multinational capitalist interests over local sovereignty and democracy.

Tabb, William K. 2004. *Economic Governance in the Age of Globalization.* New York: Columbia University Press. 520 pages.

This book examines globalization as a "verb and a noun," that is, as an active process and as something that can be said to exist, possessing a structural form. The author explains the contested worldviews that color globalization debates. Tabb utilizes a critical approach, outlining the institutions and processes of the global political economy provided through post–World War II economic planning. He discusses and analyzes the rise of international economic interdependency and its evolution into economic globalization. The author argues that the global political economy is evolving toward rentier-dominated monopoly capitalism. Under this global economic system, the interests of investment capital are now in conflict with environment health and social welfare.

Nonprint Resources

Internet Resources

Facing the Future: People and the Planet
Web site: www.facingthefuture.org/

Facing the Future is an online resource for teachers of middle and high school students. It offers a downloadable curriculum on globalization. This curriculum has been offered to over 800,000 students across the world; it is currently being used by teachers and students in 49 states in the United States and 41 foreign nation-states. In 2004, over 8,000 teachers used the Facing the Future curriculum—in many academic subjects and in both public and private schools. The curriculum consists of crossword puzzles, trivia, discussions on environmental sustainability, and games related to many issues of globalization. This Web site is a useful resource for teachers who are creating lesson plans geared toward the study of globalization.

The Global Transformations Web site
Web site: www.polity.co.uk/global

This Web site is built around the book *Global Transformations* by David Held et al. as well as other books on globalization written by these authors. The Web site explains the theoretical and methodological basis for their work, including many indicators used to assess the globalization process. There are also essays and interviews on globalization, with many external links useful to the study of globalization.

The Globalist
Web site: www.theglobalist.com

The Globalist is an online daily magazine that has been covering many issues of globalization since 2000. It offers materials for syndication in major newspapers across the world. It also offers its *Global Connections for High School Students* online to increase their understanding of globalization. *The Globalist* is a useful resource for articles and research pertaining to globalization. It should be noted, however, that many features of this Web site do require fees for use.

Globalization 101
Web site: www.Globalization101.org

Globalization 101 is a Web-based project undertaken by the Carnegie Endowment for International Peace. It is designed as a primer for new students of globalization. Globalization 101 offers issue briefs covering many dimensions of globalization. This Web site also offers audio and video clips of experts talking about controversies of globalization. Designed as a resource for teachers, it has lesson plans for students inquiring about the complexities of globalization. This Web site also hosts many links to other Web sites that focus on globalization.

The Globalization Web site
Web site: www.sociology.emory.edu/globalization

The Globalization Web site is run out of the Department of Sociology at Emory University. It offers information on organizations operating globally, including multinational corporations, nongovernmental organizations, and intergovernmental organizations. This Web site explains multiple theories of globalization and provides a comprehensive glossary of terms related to globalization. It also contains a good list of print and nonprint resources. The Globalization Web site offers a brief synopsis of major debates of globalization. It is a good online reference for learning the basics of globalization.

YaleGlobal Online
Web site: www.yaleglobal.yale.edu/

YaleGlobal Online is an online publication of the Yale Center for the Study of Globalization (see chapter 7). This Web site offers articles and research on many aspects of globalization, including the economy, environment, gender, health, labor, politics, culture, science, security, and terrorism. It provides regional categories in addressing these issues and offers a definition and history of globalization. The Web site also reprints academic papers on globalization and offers excerpts from important books. *YaleGlobal Online* has video clips from globalization scholars and journalists, including Martin Wolf and Thomas Friedman (see chapter 7). It offers other multimedia, including flash and slide show presentations.

Online Databases

Central Intelligence Agency: *World Factbook 2007*
Web site: www.cia.gov/library/publications/the-world-
factbook/

The *World Factbook 2007* offers "country profiles" that consist of many important facts about nation-states around the globe. The country profiles offer a historical background and data on the nation-state's geography, people, government, economy, communications, transportation, military, and transnational issues. The CIA offers the *World Factbook 2007* online but also publishes this data set in print. Previous yearly editions of the *World Factbook* are offered for download. The online version also offers rank ordering of nation-states and many indicators related to globalization.

Earth Trends
Web site: www.earthtrends.wri.org

Earth Trends is an online database offered by the World Resources Institute. It is a collection of data derived from many sources, including the World Bank, International Monetary Fund, Organization for Cooperation and Development, United Nations, and International Telecommunications Union. This is a comprehensive yet user-friendly database focusing on hundreds of aspects related to globalization. Primary areas covered by *Earth Trends* include (1) coastal and marine ecosystems; (2) water resources and fresh water ecosystems; (3) climate and atmosphere; (4) population health and human well-being; (5) economics, business, and the environment; (6) energy and resources; (7) biodiversity and protected areas; (8) agriculture and food; (9) forests, grasslands, and drylands, and (10) environmental governance and institutions.

Globalis: An Interactive World Map
Web site: globalis.gvu.unu.edu/

Globalis offers an online map that can be used to show the impact of many variables affecting the world's nation-states. It is offered online by Global Virtual University, a consortium of universities operating under the United Nations University. Globalis allows the researcher to investigate trends of globalization by nation-state and continent. Its database covers many dimensions of global trends, including a map indicating the "Ecological Footprint" of nation-states around the globe. Globalis offers projected future trends in its "Human Impact 2050" map. This database is unique in that it provides visual descriptions relating the data to the student and researcher. The visual descriptions communicate differences among the world's people in terms of "themes" reflecting particular dimensions of globalization. Globalis is a useful teaching resource for online lesson plans on globalization.

International Monetary Fund: Data and Statistics
Web site: www.imf.org/external/data.htm

The International Monetary Fund collects data on economic globalization in the areas of trade, finance, debt, commodity prices, international currency reserves, and indicators of financial soundness. It also produces manuals, guides, and policy reports related to issues concerning economic globalization. The International Monetary Fund Web site offers the *World Economic Outlook Databases*, which include data on gross domestic product, inflation, payments balances, exports, imports, external debt, capital flows, commodity prices, and many other indicators related to economic globalization.

Organization for Economic Cooperation and Development:
 OECD *Factbook 2007*
Web site: oberon.sourceoecd.org/vl=1045713/cl=34/nw=1/
 rpsv/factbook/

The *OECD Factbook 2007* is available through the OECD's "statistical portal" on their Web site. It offers a wide range of data on member nation-states (see chapter 7). This data collection includes up-to-date indicators on population, macroeconomic trends, economic globalization, energy, labor markets, migration, quality of life, education, the environment, and science and technology. Although this dataset is fully acquired only through subscription, the Web site does offer many data tables, charts, and graphs that are useful to the student of globalization.

United Nations Statistics Division
Web site: unstats.un.org/unsd/default.htm
Online Data Sets:
Millennium Development Goals 2007: www.devinfo.info/
    mdginfo2007/
UN Common Data Base: unstats.un.org/unsd/cdb/cdb_help/
    cdb_quick_start.asp

The United Nations Statistics Division collects a wide range of data concerning many dimensions of globalization. The Division publishes the *Statistical Yearbook* and the *World Statistics Pocketbook.* It also collects data to help track the success of the Millennium Development Goals project. This data set is offered by the United Nations as *MDG 2007.* Another data set offered by the United Nations Statistics Division that is useful for researching globalization is the *United Nations Common Data Base.* This database is user friendly, offering simple access to important data. The United Nations conducts a wide range of research programs and collects an enormous amount of data on many topics. It is recommended that the student take the time to discover the research and data the United Nations has to offer.

World Bank Data and Research: *World Development Indicators*
Web site: www.worldbank.org

The World Bank (WB) Web site offers access to WB data and research papers. This includes the WB *World Development Indicators,* a comprehensive data set pertaining to global development. The *World Development Indicators* is available as a paperback publication for $75 U.S. dollars (USDs). It includes 80 tables and also categorizes data according to region, level of development, and global totals. The *World Development Indicators* is available as a CD-ROM for individual users at the price of $275 USDs. The CD-ROM version provides indicators spanning 45 years from 1960 to 2005. It contains over 1,000 tables related to development indicators of nation-states.

Videos

**Another World Is Possible: Impressions of the 2002 World
  Social Forum**
Produced by Moving Images/ Bullfrog Films
Directors: Mark Dworkin and Melissa Young
Format: VHS/DVD
Release Date: 2002
Run Time: 24 minutes

This short film introduces the activities and spirit of the World
Social Forum (WSF). The WSF represents a loose confederation
of many organizations that are critical of the current globalization process. This film documents the second WSF meeting in
2001 at Porto Alegre, Brazil. The WSF meets yearly; its most recent meeting was in Nairobi, Kenya, in 2007.

The second WSF meeting was composed of 50,000 anticorporate globalization activists from 131 nation-states. The WSF
considers itself a global social movement working toward a
moral world based on social, economic, and environmental justice. Issues that WSF activists work on include the globalization
of corporate-dominated agriculture, biopiracy, and genetically
modified organisms. The WSF explicitly supports human rights
in all social, political, and economic matters. This video features
anticorporate globalization activists Naomi Klein, Kevin Dana-
her, and Vandana Shiva. The producer of this film, Bullfrog
Films, creates many videos that take a critical slant on issues of
globalization.

Commanding Heights: The Battle for the World Economy
Produced by WGBH Boston
Directors: William Cran and Greg Barker
Format: DVD. Closed-captioned
Number of discs: 3
DVD Release Date: July 30, 2002
Run Time: 360 minutes

This six-part series examines the rise of the global economy and
the theories that inform its logic. It is based on a book of the same
name written by Daniel Yergin and Doug Stanislaw. The series
begins by examining the social chaos produced by World War I,
the Great Depression, and World War II. It introduces the ideas
of the economists John Maynard Keynes and Fredrick Von

Hayek. While noting that these economists were friends, the series explains how they disagreed in the theories they designed to
achieve a stable democratic society. Keynes believed government
intervention in economic matters was crucial. Hayek believed it
was the problem that led to totalitarianism.

Keynes won out during the first four decades after World
War II. The capitalist world believed in economic management
through public policy. Much of the developing world, including the Soviet Union, India, and China developed through central planning, with heavy industry owned by the state. The
series documents the economic problems developed and developing nation-states faced with sluggish growth, leading to a
decline of many forms of economic planning. Economic problems led to a transition in economic theory across many parts
of the globe. This transition replaced Keynes with Hayek as the
favored economic theorist to follow. This transition is exempli-
fied by the economic policies of United States president
Ronald Reagan and United Kingdom prime minister Margaret
Thatcher in the 1980s.

This series documents the transition, showing that it did not
go smoothly. The rise of neoliberalism (as supported by followers
of Hayek) was matched with social instability and financial crises.
The final part of the series focuses on global financial crises, including the Japanese deflation of the 1990s and the crises in Mexico, East Asia, and Russia. The series ends by addressing the
debate on economic globalization and offering alternatives to the
neoliberal model of globalization.

Guns, Germs, and Steel
Produced by National Geographic Video
Director: Tim Lambert
Number of Discs: 2
DVD Release Date: July 12, 2005
Run Time: 165 minutes

This three-part series by National Geographic is based on Jared
Diamond's book by the same name. It offers a unique interpretation of globalization as a process that has been unfolding since
before human civilization itself. It seeks to uncover the roots of
power that have shaped human history. This series focuses on
Diamond's research into how Europeans came to dominate the
world through their conquests. Diamond argues that human

inequality and the advantages possessed by Europeans were ultimately due to the luck of living within prime geographic and climatic conditions.

These factors provided an advantage in the human transition from hunter-gatherer societies to those based on agriculture and the domestication of animals. This transition led to food surpluses, freeing people to specialize their labor away from the acquisition of food. Given that the crops and animals best suited for human use were geographically situated, geography served as a crucial factor in beginning the rise of modern civilization.

Part II focuses on the global conquest by European powers. Diamond uses Spanish conquistador Pizarro's conquest of the Incan Empire as an example of the powerful utility of steel weaponry. He also shows how the Spanish unwittingly caused lethal pandemics, such as smallpox, in the New World. Lethal pandemics were caused through the introduction of germs that indigenous peoples had no natural defenses to combat. Europeans were resistant to these infectious diseases for they had evolved from the livestock they had domesticated. The luck of possessing this immunity played an important part in the success of European conquest and expansion.

Finally, the European advantage of using steel and guns as weaponry in their expansion is a primary reason for their success. Part III documents the European conquest of Africa and the ruthless use of modern weaponry to displace indigenous peoples. In Africa, however, the advantages of guns, germs, and steel that Europeans held over others failed miserably. In tropical Africa, European crops would not grow, the colonizers' tools were ill adapted to the environment, their animals would die, and they would perish from infectious diseases such as malaria. As a result, early European attempts to colonize much of Africa failed. It was not until Belgium under King Leopold ruthlessly enslaved the Congo in the late 19th century that Africans had to abandon their complex civilizations.

An Inconvenient Truth
Produced by Paramount Studios
Director: Davis Guggenheim
Format: DVD
Number of discs: 1
DVD Release Date: November 21, 2006
Run Time: 96 minutes

This documentary follows former United States vice president Al Gore as he recounts his multidecade effort to heighten public awareness of climate change. The film includes an overview of climate science as well as an explanation of the multidimensional nature of climate change. It focuses on rising sea levels, the melting of the polar ice caps, loss of biodiversity, and the potential catastrophic impacts climate change may have on global humanity. As a documentary, this film provides a good overview of climate change in easy-to-understand terms. Much of the film features Al Gore's climate change presentation for which he has become well known for in recent years. This film won the Academy Award for Best Documentary in 2006.

The New Rulers of the World
Produced by Carlton International Media Ltd.
Produced, written, and presented by John Pilger
Director: Alan Lowery
DVD Release Date: 2002
Run Time: 53 Minutes

This documentary is critical of economic globalization. Journalist John Pilger travels to Indonesia to provide a case study of the impact multinational corporations have on the poor. He goes undercover to expose harsh working conditions for people who are paid extremely low wages (less than $2 U.S. dollars a day). Pilger visits shantytowns in Indonesia, citing the dire conditions under which these workers live. He argues that multinational corporations allied with international financial institutions have created a global production network characterized by exploitation and oppression.

This documentary provides interviews with those who support economic globalization and those who are critical of it. These interviews include representatives from the World Bank, the International Monetary Fund, and critics who are opposed to economic globalization under the "Washington Consensus" strategy. Pilger ends the documentary calling for a cancellation of the debt owed by developing nation-states. He also supports dismantling the World Bank, the International Monetary Fund, and the World Trade Organization and replacing them with democratically accountable institutions. To sum up his arguments, Pilger makes note of the United States Space Command's "Vision for 2020" report. This report, he argues, shows that the

United States is aware that economic globalization is creating "haves" and "have nots" that will destabilize the globalization process. A primary future responsibility of the United States military, according to the report, will be to quell global resistance that challenges the commercial interests of the United States.

Nova: World in the Balance: The Population Paradox
WGBH Boston
Produced by Linda Harrar
Director: Alan Ritsko
Format: DVD. Closed-captioned
Number of Discs: 1
DVD Release Date: June 29, 2004
Run Time: 120 minutes

This two-part series by Nova focuses on problems concerning the future growth of the human population. The primary question this series explores is the impact population growth will have on Earth's environment, food production, and climate change. It is estimated that Earth's human population will increase to 9–11 billion people by 2050. The Earth's biosphere will be imperiled as billions more people inhabit the planet, the majority of them rightfully demanding an improvement in their standard of living.

The first video assesses population trends of India, Japan, the United States, and sub-Saharan Africa. India faces a population boom coupled with limited natural resources and economic capacity. Japan is facing a rapidly declining population due to a culture based on the virtue of work and career. The United States population will grow to 400 million people, due in part to increases in immigration. Sub-Saharan Africa has the highest rate of population growth, even with the deaths caused by HIV infection and AIDS.

The second part of this series discusses the rapid rise of China and the challenges it faces. China faces water shortages for agriculture as its supplies are increasingly diverted to industrial production. Most of China's population are rural farmers, thus they may face future food and economic insecurity. China is experiencing rapid economic growth, but it also has the challenge of transitioning its rural agricultural population to modern industry-based lifestyles. China also faces the challenge of increasing the standard of living of its people while protecting their natural environment. China serves as an example of a nation-state whose choices toward development will greatly impact many dimensions of future globalization.

Podcasts

Conceptual Foundations of International Politics
Columbia Center for New Media Teaching and Learning
School of International and Public Affairs: Columbia University
Web site: ccnmtl.columbia.edu/podcasting/podcasts/courses/
    conceptual_foundations.html

These podcasts offered by Columbia University's School of International and Public Affairs feature lectures on many important aspects of globalization. This nine-part series offers central concepts, theories, and methods for understanding the academic field of international relations. Issues covered in these podcasts include human rights, international institutions, nation-state formation, nationalism and ethnic conflict, contested views of United States hegemony, United States foreign policy, political realism, and theories of public policy. These lectures provide the student with a basic foundation in the field of international relations, an academic field central to the study of globalization. These podcasts are offered in mp3 audio format from the Web site but are also available as videos.

Conversations with History
University of California Television
Institute of International Studies: University of California,
    Berkeley.
Web site: www.globetrotter.berkeley.edu/conversations/

This is a Web-based series of video interviews produced at the University of California at Berkeley. The host, Harry Kreisler, speaks to many important scientists, scholars, government leaders, and activists in many academic fields. The series consists of over 380 interviews. Many are centrally related to the subject of globalization and international relations. Interviews of Kenneth Waltz, John Mearsheimer, Stephen Walt, Noam Chomsky, Michael Hardt, and Kenneth Boulding are but a few examples of the discussions of issues pertaining to globalization. This is a highly informative resource for the study of globalization and many other academic subjects. These interviews are also informative for those beginning or investigating potential academic careers. Kreisler includes biographical questions, inquiring of guests how they got started and what it takes to succeed in their various disciplines. *Conversations with History* is funded by the United States Library of Congress and the National Science Foundation.

WGBH Forum Network
WGBH, Boston, and the Lowell Institute
Web site: www.forum.wgbh.org/wgbh/

This extensive collection of video podcasts is offered by WGBH in Boston in association with many universities and other organizations. These video podcasts cover a wide range of topics, including many associated with globalization. Topics related to globalization include business and economics, the environment, history, politics, society, culture, and technology. The podcasts are lectures given by scholars and journalists, including Niall Ferguson, Jagdish Bhagwati, Amartya Sen, Paul Krugman, Joseph Stiglitz, Lester Brown, James Gustave Speth, Noam Chomsky, and Kevin Phillips. This is a major resource of free, online lectures that will benefit not only students of globalization but those of other academic subjects as well.

Glossary

asymmetrical warfare   The strategy and tactics used by combatants whose ability to use force is much less than that of their adversaries.

balance of payments   An accounting of the payments and receipts of one country's economic transactions with other countries.

biosphere   The totality of all organic life and the physical environment upon which it relies for its existence.

capital flight   The process whereby investors remove their investment capital from the economy of a country they believe is experiencing economic instability.

clash of civilizations   The thesis that globalization will lead major civilizations (i.e., Islam and the West) to come into conflict due to incompatible differences in norms and values.

climate change   The theory that human activity is affecting the Earth's climate by releasing greenhouse gases into the atmosphere.

colonialism   The economic and political administration of a territory by foreigners to profit from the human and natural capital of that territory.

comparative advantage   The economic theory that countries should specialize in what they do best and trade their specialty with others who do the same.

complex interdependency   The state of affairs in which actors impact and are impacted by others, resulting in mutual concern for each other's actions and needs.

critical worldview   The view that globalization is largely a product of long-standing injustice, imperialism, and colonialism.

cultural homogenization   The process of decreasing cultural diversity and replacing it with cultural standardization and uniformity.

cultural hybridization   The fusion of traditional culture with modern consumer culture exported by developed countries, especially the United States.

cultural imperialism   The efforts of dominant cultures to control information and communication in an attempt to subvert diverse cultural norms and traditions.

empire   The ability of a hegemonic power to control lesser powers in a near-universal manner without serious challenge.

financial contagion   The spread of financial problems from one country to others due to investor panic and herd mentality.

free trade   The economic theory that markets are self-sufficient in the long term in providing benefits and should not be regulated by government.

global system   The collection of norms, beliefs, behaviors, and institutions that affect the economic, political, and social governance of human societies across the world.

globalization   The increased interaction and interdependence among the world's people measured in terms of intensity, extensity, velocity, and impact.

greenhouse gases (GHGs)   Gases including carbon dioxide (CO_2), methane, chlorofluorocarbons (CFCs), nitrous oxide, ozone, and water vapor, which are known to trap the Sun's energy within the Earth's atmosphere.

hegemony   The ability of a powerful nation-state to dominate and control the actions of other nation-states through co-optation, coercion, or force.

human rights   The totality of civil rights and liberties that humans are universally afforded irrespective of personal characteristics such as age, race, class, gender, and sexual orientation.

ideology   A set of principles and ideas that guide an individual or group's interpretation of reality.

imperialism   The intentional domination of one nation-state over another to control the economic and political resources of the dominated nation-state.

industrialization   The economic transition from agricultural society based on human and animal labor to urban society based on the products of machines and high energy use.

institutionalist worldview   The view that globalization can be an overall beneficial process if it is properly managed with appropriate public policy.

international anarchy   The reality that no global authority exists to control the behavior of nation states.

international governmental organization (IGO)   An organization composed of nation-states that work to address common issues and solve collective problems.

international nongovernmental organization (INGO)   A voluntary association of individuals and groups that work toward their collective interests on an international basis.

international regime   A set of shared values, principles, norms, and rules that can affect the behavior of those who hold the same values and beliefs.

less-developed countries   Countries with a low level of industrialization where much of the population suffers from poverty, lack of education, and lack of economic opportunity.

liberalism   The set of theories that the individual should be free from external coercion to the greatest extent possible so he or she can freely apply reason to complex issues.

mercantilism   The economic theory that government should support and protect private economic interests in order to maintain and expand the power of the nation-state.

most favored nation status   A principle of free trade whereby countries treat the foreign investment and business of another country as they treat domestic investors and enterprise.

mutually assured destruction (MAD)   The condition under which armed nuclear countries cannot strike each other because the result would be the destruction of both.

nation-state   A recognized political entity possessing sovereign authority over a population within determined geographical borders commonly referred to as country.

neocolonialism   The domination of a country or region through economic means rather than direct military threat or force.

neoliberal worldview   The view that globalization should be pursued and determined through free markets.

petrodollars   Dollars (U.S. dollars, or USDs) that are accumulated by oil-producing countries and then recycled into the international financial system.

realism   The theory of international relations that contends war is always possible, for nation-states will always pursue the maintenance and expansion of their power, often at the detriment of others.

realpolitik   The political pursuit of power based on material interests and practical policy rather than idealistic goals or ethical principles.

rentiers   Those who live exclusively off income produced by their investments and property rather than through their labor.

security dilemma   The situation in which building one's defenses for security purposes results in others feeling less secure.

sovereignty   The possession of legal authority over a defined territory and population.

Spaceship Earth   The idea that the Earth is a closed and limited system whose inhabitants must learn to live within the limits set by the biosphere.

supply side economics   The economic theory that economic growth is most likely when incentives such as low taxes and deregulated markets are provided to producers.

sustainable development   To meet the needs of current generations without jeopardizing the ability of future generations to do the same.

terrorism   The strategy of committing violent acts against civilian populations to achieve political and ideological ends.

theory   A set of propositions or principles logically ordered that seek to explain natural and social phenomena.

tragedy of the commons   The idea that individual acts of rational self-interest can lead to the collective harm of everyone.

unitary executive   the political theory that a strong executive must be unencumbered by outside authority so it can rightfully pursue and execute the power of the nation-state.

Index

Note: "t." indicates table.

About the Authors

Justin Ervin is a Ph.D. candidate in political science at Northern Arizona University in Flagstaff. Ervin's academic interests focus on international relations, international political economy, security, and environmental politics.

Zachary A. Smith is Regents' Professor of Political Science at Northern Arizona University in Flagstaff. Smith is the author or editor of 20 books and many scholarly articles focusing on environmental policy and other public policy topics.